In God's Shadow

In God's Shadow

Politics in the
Hebrew Bible

MICHAEL WALZER

Yale

UNIVERSITY PRESS

New Haven and London

"Biblical Politics: Where Were the Elders?" *Hebraic Political Studies* 3, no. 3 (Summer 2008): 225–238. Reprinted by permission of Shalem Press.

Exilpolitik in der Hebräischen Bibel (The Politics of Exile in the Hebrew Bible) (Tübingen: Mohr Siebeck, 2001). Reprinted by permission of Mohr Siebeck Tübingen.

"The Idea of Holy War in Ancient Israel," *The Journal of Religious Ethics* 20, no. 2 (Fall 1992): 215–228. Reprinted with permission.

"The Legal Codes of Ancient Israel," *Yale Journal of Law & the Humanities* 4, no. 2 (1992): 335–349. Reprinted by permission of the *Yale Journal of Law & the Humanities*.

"Prophecy and International Politics," *Hebraic Political Studies* 4, no. 4 (Fall 2009): 319–328. Reprinted by permission of Shalem Press.

Yale University Press books may be purchased in quantity for educational, business, or promotional use. For information, please e-mail sales.press@yale.edu (U.S. office) or sales@yaleup.co.uk (U.K. office).

Designed by Sonia Shannon.
Set in Bulmer type by Integrated Publishing Solutions, Grand Rapids, Michigan.
Printed in the United States of America.

Library of Congress Cataloging-in-Publication Data

Walzer, Michael.
In God's shadow : politics in the Hebrew Bible / Michael Walzer.
p. cm.
Includes bibliographical references (p.   ) and index.
ISBN 978-0-300-18044-2 (alk. paper)
1. Politics in the Bible.   2. Bible. O.T.—Criticism, interpretation, etc.   I. Title.
BS1199.P6W35 2012
221.8′32—dc23
2011044471

A catalogue record for this book is available from the British Library.

This paper meets the requirements of ANSI/NISO Z39.48–1992 (Permanence of Paper).

10   9   8   7   6   5   4   3   2   1

For Joseph, Katya, Jules, and Stefan
and for their children and grandchildren

l'dor v'dor

CONTENTS

Preface   ix

Acknowledgments   xix

1. The Covenants   1

2. The Legal Codes   16

3. Conquest and Holy War   34

4. The Rule of Kings   50

5. Prophets and Their Audience   72

6. Prophecy and International Politics   89

7. Exile   109

8. The Priestly Kingdom   126

9. The Politics of Wisdom   144

10. Messianism   169

11. Where Were the Elders?   185

12. Politics in the Shadow   199

Notes   213

Index   227

PREFACE

My aim in this book is to examine the ideas about politics, the understandings of government and law, that are expressed in the Hebrew
Bible. What did the biblical writers think about political life? I won't
pretend to answer this question as a biblical scholar; I don't know the
ancient languages; I have only a schoolboy's knowledge of biblical Hebrew and a layman's understanding of the history and archaeology of
the ancient world. I will be writing as an ordinary reader of the biblical
text as it has come down to us, in its various English translations.

More accurately, I will be writing as a political theorist, reading the
Bible in much the same way as I read John Locke, or *The Federalist Papers*, or Rousseau, or Hegel—and asking the same kinds of questions.
How is political society conceived? How should political power be
used? How is authority described, defended, and challenged? When is
it right to go to war? What is the implicit or explicit understanding of
hierarchy? What are the obligations/duties/tasks of ordinary citizens or
subjects? How is political space delineated? How is time understood,
the past used, the future imagined? And, of course, a last question, exactly as I would ask it if I were reading any political text: What can we
learn from this book, these writers?

Given the way the Bible is often studied in the academy, and the way
it figures in religious and political discourse, I need to be very clear

about what I am not trying to do in this book. First, I am not trying to figure out what really happened in the centuries during which the Bible was written. Among historians of those years, the biblical text is commonly read as a series of clues to a reality that lies somewhere behind the text. I assume that there was such a reality. In principle, the question What happened? has a right answer. But I don't know the answer, and I am not looking for it. I am interested only in what the biblical writers thought had happened and what they thought about what they thought had happened. I am interested in the history they told or retold or, perhaps, imagined.

Second, I am not trying to find biblical proof-texts or precedents for my own politics. I won't be suggesting that the biblical writers were good social democrats, or that they anticipated modern liberalism, or that they believed in human rights, or just war, or humanitarian intervention, or anything else that I have defended in my own voice in other books. I won't read the Bible as if it were a mirror in which to see myself. Though much of the Bible is familiar to me, and though, like many readers, I have been reading it all my life, I will do my best to recognize and acknowledge its otherness.

Third, I will not be trying to construct a pretty picture or an apologetic account of biblical politics. There are many beautiful passages, many laws that I admire, many stories that resonate across the centuries. But there are also ugly passages, laws that I would happily break (and do break), and stories that seem incomprehensible. I want to describe the politics of the biblical writers in the same way that Oliver Cromwell told the state portraitist he wanted to be painted: "Warts and all." I will avoid the homiletic style, which writers on the Bible fall into almost naturally. Interpretation is necessary, obviously, but overinterpretation, though easy, is always a mistake, and especially so when it has a preacherly purpose. I could read the story of the Tower of Babel, for example, as an anti-imperialist argument or as a defense of cultural pluralism. But that is the stuff of sermons.

Fourth, I won't be writing about the influence of biblical ideas on Western political thought—not in the Middle Ages, not in the early modern period (when biblical texts were most often studied and cited), not among religious fundamentalists today. My book *Exodus and Revolution* is a study of the uses of a biblical story (the liberation from Egyptian bondage, the march to the Promised Land) in many countries over many years.[1] But my purpose here is different. I want to figure out what the ideas of the biblical writers were in their own time and place. That is hard enough, given the texts that we have. Influence is even harder to recognize; the influence of the texts isn't the same as their use and citation. As Shakespeare wrote, "The devil can cite Scripture for his purpose." But the devil presumably isn't influenced by Scripture.

If I am not trying to figure out what really happened, and not looking to confirm my own political views, and not writing as an apologist, and not claiming that biblical politics is powerfully present in our own political thought, what is the purpose of a book like this? Why is it useful to ask the questions that a political theorist asks of *this* text? The Bible is, above all, a religious book—an account of the origins and development of a radically new religion, a strong and exclusivist monotheism. This new religion is carried by a people who, like other peoples, have leaders and laws, who experience bitter internal conflicts and wars with other nations, who disagree about authority and policy, who listen to public criticism of their government and society. What makes the literature of ancient Israel especially interesting, and worthy of close study, is that all this takes place in the shadow of an omnipotent God. So a special set of questions arises in the case of this book. How much room for politics can there be when God is the ultimate ruler? How much room is there for prudential decision-making in a nation that lives under divine command and divine protection? Does religious absolutism make for zealotry and holy war or for accommodation and peace? I don't know if I can answer these questions; in any case, I am sure that they have no single answer—there are many different voices in the Hebrew Bible. My aim is to figure out as best I can what those voices are saying.

The Bible is, above all, a religious book, but it is also a political book. Its histories give us a fascinating account of what is today called regime change—the tyranny of Pharaoh gives way to the leadership of Moses and Joshua; which is followed by the intermittent rule of the Judges, also called the rule of God; which is rejected by the elders and the people, who demand to be ruled by kings; who are overthrown centuries later by conquering armies of Assyrians and Babylonians and replaced by foreign emperors and their priestly collaborators. All this is described in some detail, so you can find in the Bible all the material necessary for a comparative politics. More than this, the biblical books include legal codes, rules for warfare, ideas about justice and obligation, social criticism, visions of the good society, accounts of exile and dispossession. Until the very end of the biblical period, Israelite religion is emphatically this-worldly; it is enacted in history, and the enactments are readily available for analysis and commentary.

But there is no political theory in the Bible. Political theory is a Greek invention. Nor is there a clear conception of an autonomous or distinct political realm, nor of an activity called politics, nor of a status resembling Greek citizenship. And there is no systematic effort to think about this realm, this activity, or this status, or to make conceptual maps, or to work out comparisons with other realms, activities, and statuses. Biblical Israel is a religious culture, whose texts are legal, historical, prophetic, liturgical, sapiential, and eschatological—never explicitly political. The biblical writers are engaged with politics, but they are in an important sense, as I will argue again and again in this book, not very interested in politics. Or, better, a few of the writers are interested, some are indifferent, and some are actively hostile. There is a strong anti-political tendency in the biblical texts, which follows from the idea that God is a "man of war" (Exodus 15:3) and a supreme king—so what is there for human beings to do? Antipolitics makes its first appearance in the exodus story, which describes a liberation with no acknowledged and autonomous human agents, and it is reiterated, centuries later, in the prophetic writings.

Still, antipolitics is a kind of politics, and writers who are uninterested in politics nonetheless have a lot to say that is politically interesting. Moreover, the biblical writers are obviously interested, and explicitly so, in law and justice—which are for us, if not for them, highly politicized subjects. Hence my program in this book: to look at the biblical writings, more or less chronologically, as they deal with the different covenants, the three legal codes, the successive regimes, the wars of Israelite judges and kings, and the experience of imperial conquest and to describe the arguments, or at least the recognizable arguments, that the writers make about legitimacy, hierarchy, and social justice. I will view all these arguments not so much in historical context, although I will have to make some assumptions about the history, as in the context of the texts. Just as the Bible is a book of books, a story of stories, so it is also a political writing of political writings, and each piece has to be placed among the others and compared with them. As I have already suggested, I will be asking what characteristic forms politics and thinking about politics take in a religious culture, where every regime and every law has, or is said to have, divine connections and where no regime or legal code has practical or acknowledged autonomy. What is the place in this culture of kings and priests, of judicial courts and royal courts, of mercenaries and magistrates, of meetings at city gates and in temple courtyards, of prophets who speak "smoothly" (Isaiah 30:10) and prophets who speak critically?

I will need to insist, again and again, that there isn't a single version of the good political life, and there isn't a preferred regime. Many, perhaps most, of the biblical writers were monarchists, but the texts also contain sharp critiques of monarchy. Compared to the kingship of God, human kingship seems idolatrous—a creation by human beings, to which we ascribe powers that belong only to the true Sovereign. But the rule of the true Sovereign is not, properly speaking, political, whereas human kingship is a political regime, and insofar as the biblical writers think politically, they do so from the vantage point of the king, as Allan Silver argues in *The Jewish Political Tradition*.[2] Republics and democracies make no appearance in the biblical texts (though commentators have found them there); the last biblical regime, after the returning Babylonian exiles fail to restore the royal Davidic line, is a priestly oligarchy. Given the different rulers—judges, kings, and priests—and the arguments over kingship, there can't be anything like an authoritative political constitution in the Hebrew Bible. The book of Deuteronomy (rather, one piece of it: 16:18–18:22) may have been written in the hope that it would serve as a constitutional text, but it is never given that status in the Deuteronomic histories or the Chronicles, and the specific form of limited monarchy described in Deuteronomy doesn't seem to have been a regulative idea for the prophets.

In seventeenth-century Europe, there were many scholarly efforts to construct a Hebrew constitution, and there were many different constructions.[3] Certainly the material is there, in the several legal codes and in a history extending over eight or nine hundred years, out of which a defense of absolute monarchy can be put together, or a defense of limited monarchy, or theocracy, or republican government, or a "primitive democracy" of elders, or a temple regime of priests. The real question, however, is why the biblical writers themselves had so little interest in undertaking such constructions.

My intention is to read the Bible as it is, but it quickly becomes apparent to any reader that some assumptions about the different pieces of the text and the order of their composition are necessary. The scholarly literature about these questions is vast, and the disagreements among distinguished and immensely learned scholars are breathtaking. The documentary thesis, which broke the Bible down into seven or eight pieces—the J and E documents in the Torah, the priestly writings, the work of the Deuteronomists and the historians who followed them, the wisdom literature, the prophetic writings, and the rewritten histories of the Chroniclers—has been revised or perhaps displaced by a large number of subdocumentary theses. All the pieces have pieces; the Bible today is a bizarre jigsaw puzzle that can be put together in many different ways—though, so far, every scholarly resolution of the puzzle leaves some of the pieces disconnected and unexplained. I admire much of this literature, recognize its erudition, and have tried to learn from it. But reading the Bible in pieces makes political understanding, and every other kind of understanding, very difficult. Clearly, that's not the way its writers and editors wanted it to be read. The final group of editors, whoever they were, intended to compose a unified work. We have to try to read it that way. At the same time, we can't deny that the composition shows its stitches, and we can't avoid recognizing the different pieces—or at least some of them.

So my way of reading the Bible is a compromise in which I try to attend simultaneously to the ancient editors who put the whole thing together and to the modern scholars who have taken it apart and then struggled to put it together again. But since the scholars have produced such different accounts of the pieces of the text and its most plausible reconstructions, it is impossible to attend to all of them. Nor can I make anything more than educated guesses about which of them have things right. I have chosen the scholars who seemed most helpful for my project—who turn out, mostly, to be the scholars of my own generation (and their students), with whom I grew up and who were my first guides to the texts. I have also regularly consulted the early rabbinic readers of the Bible, in the midrashic and talmudic literature, and also the later commentaries of Rashi and Nahmanides. The midrashic readings are sometimes wonderfully outlandish (though hardly more so than those of modern biblical critics) and sometimes pointed and insightful.

The books of the Hebrew Bible are arranged differently from the same books in the Christian Old Testament. The arrangements reflect different religious sensibilities: Christians make of the Bible a grand story that extends from creation to redemption; the Jewish version reflects an unfinished engagement with history. My account of biblical politics assumes the unfinished engagement; I take the Chroniclers' history as the last part of the story, and the priestly temple-state as the last of the biblical regimes. The establishment of the Jewish canon was a long process, not finished until the work of the rabbis of Yavneh, around 100 CE.[4] But the actual writing was pretty much complete (except possibly for the book of Daniel) some three hundred years earlier. For my purposes here, the period after 200 BCE is postbiblical. The political history of Israel up to that point is my subject—though, again, not what really happened but what the biblical writers report and how they report it.

I won't be reading the text as the word of God but as the word of its writers. We don't know who the writers were, except for the literary prophets and Ezra and Nehemiah, who are presumably the authors of (at least some parts of) the books that bear their names.[5] We also don't know when the writers wrote, or when the texts were edited, or to what extent they were revised when they were edited. Rabbinic commentators insist that the text, as the word of God, has no temporal sequence. All the words were delivered simultaneously; earlier and later (even within the Bible's own historical account) are irrelevant categories; any verse can explain any other. But I shall assume some sequence, following as best I can the biblical scholars who seem to me best—as when I read the discussion of kingship in Deuteronomy 17 as a commentary on the argument about kingship in First Samuel and the story of Solomon's rule in First Kings. Michael Fishbane has written a brilliant account of inner-biblical exegesis, and I have tried to follow him and scholars like him, particularly with regard to legal readings and revisions.[6]

But it should be clear that when I ascribe political views to this or that biblical writer or set of writers, I am not actually identifying authors and editors. In a sense, the texts themselves are my "subjects"—although

I am not a postmodern reader. I always imagine actual authors, subjects in the strong sense, with ideas and commitments of their own, which I am trying to understand.

In the end, there are no authoritative understandings of the Bible. The sheer multitude of religious readings, preacherly appropriations, and scholarly analyses is overwhelming. It is possible to criticize and discard many of these, but it simply can't be the case that they are all reducible to a single correct account. All of us who write about this text are joining an argument that has been going on for several thousand years and that has no end in view. The prophet Zechariah says that in the days to come, "there shall be one Lord and his name one" (14:9). But even then, I am certain that the Lord's word will not be one; religious believers, as well as skeptics and unbelievers, will disagree about the meaning of the biblical text and the political views of its writers.

When I quote the Bible, I use the King James version most of the time, simply because of its beautiful English—the English of Shakespeare and Donne. But I have checked all the passages against more recent scholarly translations, especially the 1988 Jewish Publication Society's *Tanakh: The Holy Scriptures*, which is particularly admirable for the number of verses that it footnotes with the phrase "Meaning of Heb. uncertain."[7] I use this translation occasionally, when it seems more accurate or when it is more comprehensible to modern readers, and indicate these uses with the initials NJPS. All other quotations are from King James, though I have given up the all-capital LORD, romanized the scattered italics, and ignored the one verse/one paragraph rule of the seventeenth-century editors. I have also consulted Robert Alter's lovely annotated translation of the Torah, which discusses many of the uncertainties of the first five books.[8] Great scholars can make educated guesses about the meaning of the text; ordinary readers must get by with less educated guesses. Reading the Bible is a complex and speculative business, but it isn't a business for which we need an invitation; we are all readers if we want to be.

ACKNOWLEDGMENTS

I first studied the Hebrew Bible with Rabbi Hayim Goren Perelmuter, a superb teacher, in Johnstown, Pennsylvania, in the late 1940s. I have studied it more recently, and continue to study it, together with the members of the "traditional/egalitarian" minyan at Princeton University's Center for Jewish Life. Our weekly discussions helped me decide to finish this book, which has been many years in the making. It began with a course on biblical politics at the New School for Social Research in New York in 1990. I prepared the final version while holding fellowships at the Tikvah Center at New York University Law School and at Hebrew University's Institute for Advanced Studies in Jerusalem.

I owe a special debt to Moshe Greenberg, who read biblical texts with me in Jerusalem long ago (when I was working on *Exodus and Revolution*) and encouraged me to write about the Bible from the perspective of a political theorist. Moshe was a great scholar and a wonderfully sweet and gentle man, whose encouragement was a kind of license—I don't think that I could have written this book without it. David Hartman gave me an intellectual home in Jerusalem and provided an example of textual engagement and Jewish commitment that has inspired much of my work over the past decades, not only on this book but also—along with colleagues from the Shalom Hartman Institute—on *The Jewish Political Tradition*. Menachem Lorberbaum, Moshe Halbertal, Noam Zohar,

xix

Haim Shapira, Ariel Furstenberg, Yitzhak Benbaji, and Yuval Jobani read some of these chapters and provided heartening support and useful criticism. I learned a great deal from discussions with Bernard Levinson and Allan Silver during their years at the Institute for Advanced Study in Princeton—and with Allan also at meetings in Jerusalem. Gary Anderson was my colleague at the Tikvah Center and introduced me to some recent Christian readings of the biblical texts. I am intellectually indebted to Robert Alter, Michael Fishbane, and Israel Knohl, whose books taught me how to read the Bible. And I took courage from Daniel Elazar and Aaron Wildavsky, Bible-reading political scientists: I walk in their footsteps even though I have taken a different path. None of these people are responsible for the presumptuousness of this book or for its mistakes. Judith Walzer read all the chapters and listened to most of the lectures in which I tried out my arguments (to some of them more than once); she is my most demanding critic, but I can't blame her for my mistakes either.

I gave three of these chapters (4, 5, and 11) as the Samuel and Althea Stroum Lectures at the University of Washington—and benefited from lively discussions with students and faculty members there. The chapter on biblical wisdom was a lecture first at the Shalom Hartman Institute in Jerusalem and then at the University of Toronto. I experimented with the chapter on prophecy and international politics at the Tavistock Institute in London. The chapter on the legal codes was the first Robert Cover Lecture at Yale Law School and was then published in *The Yale Journal of Law and the Humanities*—whose readers' comments generated the first of many revisions. An earlier version of the chapter on holy war appeared, years ago, in *The Journal of Religious Ethics*, together with a response from John Howard Yoder. The chapter on exile was originally a lecture given when I was awarded the Leopold Lucas Prize at the University of Tübingen; it was published as *Exilpolitik in der Hebräischen Bibel* by Mohr Siebeck in 2001. Chapters 6 and 11, on the prophets and the elders, were published more recently in the new journal *Hebraic Political Studies.* I am grateful to all the editors, publishers, and organizers of lectures who have given me the chance to write and talk about the Hebrew Bible.

I have been a professor (and now a professor emeritus) at the Institute for Advanced Study in Princeton for over thirty years. It is hard to imagine a better place to work or better colleagues than I have had there, or a more competent and helpful staff. I am particularly grateful to Amelia Dyckman, Linda Garat, and Nancy Cotterman, whose expert secretarial assistance made the writing of this book much easier than it would otherwise have been.

Yale University Press provided its now familiar and always excellent help. William Frucht's gentle prodding moved the book along more quickly than I would have moved it, and Mary Pasti's skillful copyediting made it a better book.

In God's Shadow

ONE

The Covenants

Israel was founded twice, once as a family, a kin group, once as a nation, a political and religious community—and both times the founding instrument was a covenant. The first covenant was with Abraham (it is twice described, in Genesis 15 and 17), and it involves a promise and a prophecy about his "seed." Abraham will be "a father of many nations" (17:5), but of one nation in particular, his direct descendants, who will one day inherit the land of Canaan. This is a covenant of the flesh, as everlasting as the succession of generations, and it is sealed by circumcision. The covenant, or at least the seal of the covenant, is extended to strangers but only to strangers—slaves or servants—who live within the household of Abraham and his heirs: "he that is born in the house or bought with money" (17:12). Essentially, God's promise is familial, a birthright passed from one generation to the next.[1]

The second covenant is with the people of Israel at Sinai—not, it should be stressed, with Moses and his descendants. Moses serves as an intermediary. He runs up and down the mountain, carrying messages, but so far as the covenant is concerned, he is merely one of the people. He shares with the others in the general promise; nothing is said of his "seed"—and, later on, we hear virtually nothing of his offspring.[2] The covenant at Sinai is a covenant of the law, and it is passed on with words, not knives. "And these words, which I command thee this day, shall be in thine heart: And thou shalt teach them diligently unto thy children" (Deuteronomy 6:6–7). Later on, the prophets accuse their fellow Israelites of having "uncircumcised hearts," which means that they have been faithless to the (second) covenant; they have not lived in accordance with the law. This covenant is not marked in their flesh; it is as uncertain in its effects as words are, even words diligently taught.

Although the Deuteronomists write that God's words are to be taught "unto thy children," the words can be taught to anyone. God himself speaks not only to the descendants of Abraham but also to the "mixed multitude" that came out of Egypt with them (Exodus 12:38), and when the covenant is reaffirmed in Deuteronomy 29, the strangers in the camp, as well as the men, women, and children of Israel, join in the affirmation. The household is still the primary unit of this covenantal community, and the strangers in Deuteronomy are "hewers of wood and drawers of water," analogous to Abraham's servants, though far more numerous and with households of their own. Now the covenant brings together a large number of families, of known and unknown lineage.

Many centuries later, the rabbis blamed the "mixed multitude" for all of Israel's rebellions against God and Moses in the wilderness years— the ten "murmurings." The accusation suggests a strong commitment to the kinship model: the seed of Abraham could not have sinned so badly and so frequently. By contrast, the biblical writers blame the Israelites themselves for the murmurings; the only exception is Numbers 11:4: "The riff-raff [*asafsoof*] in their midst felt a gluttonous craving" (NJPS).[3] Rashi tells us that "this is the mixed multitude that had gathered themselves unto them when they left Egypt," and the King James translation of Numbers 11:4 follows him ("And the mixt multitude that was among

In God's Shadow

them fell a lusting"). In any case, the group is never mentioned again. The writers seem to assume that the mixed multitude was absorbed, though whether into the nation or the family, by covenant or by intermarriage, is unclear.

These two covenants reflect the biblical understanding of what is, after all, a common feature of political and religious communities: people can be born into them, as most of their members have been, but people can also come in, join up, through some process of adherence (naturalization or conversion). There is a permanent, built-in tension between the birth model and the adherence model.[4] The first favors a politics of nativism and exclusion (as in the books of Ezra and Nehemiah), the second a politics of openness and welcome, proselytism and expansion (and even forced conversion, as in Hasmonean times, though adherence is supposed to be voluntary). Intermarriage tests the relative strength of the two covenants. Abraham, nearing death, makes his eldest and presumably most trustworthy servant swear "that thou shalt not take a wife unto my son of the daughters of the Canaanites, among whom I dwell: But thou shalt go unto my country and to my kindred" (Genesis 24:3-4). Nehemiah exacts a similar promise from fifth-century Judeans: "that we would not give our daughters unto the people of the land, nor take their daughters for our sons" (10:30). By contrast, the book of Ruth (which may have been written in opposition to the policies of Ezra and Nehemiah and which certainly reflects a different sensibility) tells a story not only of intermarriage but also of voluntary adherence: "thy people shall be my people, and thy God my God" (1:16). Ruth might have added, thy law my law, for her life as an Israelite woman was largely determined by the marriage laws.

In principle, the covenant of law is open to anyone prepared to accept its burdens; hence it isn't entirely implausible to say that there is no chosen people, only people who choose. But it would be wrong to claim that the second covenant supersedes the first. Throughout biblical history, the doctrine of adherence is shadowed, and sometimes overshadowed, by the doctrine of kinship, the law by the flesh, choice by chosenness. The ever-renewed hope that God will not abandon a people whose members regularly violate his law rests on the kinship and chosenness model. In the long debate over proselytism, which seems to begin during the Babylonian exile and which continued for many centuries, the advocates of adherence won out in the end, though the victory was something less than decisive: a deep suspicion of converts survived among the members of the covenantal community. Israel's elites prided themselves on their genealogy (until the rabbis, who divided on this issue). The priestly covenant with Aaron and the royal covenant with David are both modeled on God's promise to Abraham: they are covenants of flesh, seed, and generational succession.

The polemical thrust of the book of Ruth is manifest when its heroine, born a Moabite woman, is given a proud place in the lineage of King David. The Deuteronomists, by contrast, stress the necessary kinship of kings: "One from among thy brethren shalt thou set king over thee: thou mayest not set a stranger over thee, which is not thy brother" (17:15). This verse has been compared to the American constitutional rule that presidents must be born, not naturalized, citizens—evidence that the tension of the two covenants is secular as well as religious, modern as well as ancient. I am not sure, however, that the Deuteronomists would have accepted the son, or even the great-grandson, of a "naturalized" Moabite as a legitimate king of Israel. As for priests, their legitimacy depended, according to Leviticus, on direct descent from Aaron. Those who could not prove their descent were disqualified—as in the case of some exiles returning from Babylonia in 538 BCE: "These sought their register among those that were reckoned by genealogy, but they were not found: therefore were they, as polluted, put from the priesthood" (Ezra 2:62).

The covenant at Sinai, following upon the liberation from Egyptian bondage, was the most important of Israel's covenants, and the biblical writers seem to have had no doubt that it depended on consent, not blood. The laws were binding only because they had been accepted by the people. Rabbinic writers are especially clear on this point, even suggesting in a famous midrash (commentary) that God had offered his covenant to other nations—there is no suggestion of this in the biblical text—who had refused it. Another midrash describes Moses standing before the people, book in hand: "Moses read aloud to the people all of the Torah [the Pentateuch], that they might know exactly what they were taking upon themselves." The crucial conditions of what is today called consent theory are here recognized.[5] Before consent is effective, there must be full knowledge and the possibility of refusal.

But is it really possible to say no to an omnipotent God? A more skeptical and ironic rabbinic story suggests the difficulty. Now God is said to have lifted up the mountain, held it over the heads of the assembled Israelites, and told them: "If you accept the Torah, it is well; otherwise you will find your grave under this mountain." One of the rabbis, a good consent theorist, says of the telling of this story that it is "a great protest against the Torah." Indeed, it makes the Torah into nonbinding law, grounded on force alone, not on commitment.[6] The book of Exodus has nothing to say about these theoretical issues. But it does insist upon the consent of the people and so provides a platform, as it were, for later speculation.

The story is told twice, suggesting that different traditions have been stitched together, but the crucial words appear in each telling: on this question of popular consent, the traditions do not differ. In Exodus 19, Moses delivers a very brief divine message, and then "all the people answered together, and said, All that the Lord hath spoken we will do." In Exodus 24, after a long recital of covenantal obligations, the response is repeated: "All that the Lord hath said will we do, and be obedient." The agreement is wholesale; all the people accept all the laws. There is no record of any debate among the Israelites: this is not a negotiated covenant. I will suggest in the next chapter that the substance of the laws must have been debated, if not on the spot, then over the years, for we have three different legal codes, all said to have been revealed by God at Sinai. They seem in fact to represent successive or competing understandings of what God meant to reveal or of what his revelation could have meant. We have to imagine priests, prophets, and scribes arguing among themselves; otherwise, since God does not change his mind or his laws, the written record makes no sense. And the editors who compiled the last version of the written record must somehow have recognized and accepted this legal pluralism (the term is anachronistic; I will qualify it later).

The founding myth, though it insists upon consent, has no room for argument. The covenantal partners are not equals. Making an agreement with God is nothing like striking a bargain. What is it like? A number of scholars have argued for the close resemblance of the Sinai covenant to ancient Near Eastern suzerainty treaties between kings and their vassals.[7] The resemblances are indeed so close as to make it fairly certain that the biblical writers knew and used the treaty model. God was Israel's king; Israel was God's vassal or servant nation. And the motives that made for covenantal agreement were perhaps similar to the motives that led to the acceptance of secular suzerainty: some combination of gratitude, prudence, and necessity. But there are also important differences between treaties and covenants; the model was not only used but transformed.

Treaties are international in scope, imposed by more powerful rulers upon less powerful rulers, stipulating only the foreign policy obligations of the two—sometimes only the obligations of the one, the less powerful ruler, who promises never to seek another suzerain. Israel makes a similar promise—namely, to worship no other gods. But its covenant is essentially domestic in character: the people commit themselves to live in a certain way. There is, as I have already said, no special agreement with the leader of the people; nor is the agreement limited to what leaders do. Its stipulations, greatly detailed, reach to the daily life of each individual. In a sense, as one of the rabbinic commentators argues, there isn't a single covenant but 600,000 between God and the Israelites at Sinai. Each act of consent is also an act of adherence, an agreement to be part of the covenantal community. And that is why the biblical covenant, modeled on the ancient treaty, serves in turn as a model for the modern (sixteenth- and seventeenth-century) social contract.[8]

The emphasis on individual adherence implies another motive for the covenant, one that plays no part in suzerainty treaties—that is, belief in *this* God and admiration for his laws. In Deuteronomy, which can be read as one long covenant document, Moses urges admiration as well as gratitude upon the people:

> For this is your wisdom and your understanding in the sight of the nations, which shall hear all these statutes, and say, Surely this great nation is a wise and understanding people . . . And what nation is there . . . that hath statutes and judgments so righteous as all this law, which I set before you this day? (4:6, 8)

The law describes the best way to live, not merely because it is commanded by a divine and omnipotent king but because it is recognizable to human beings—to all human beings, not only to those who have had the historical experience of the Israelites—as a wise and righteous law. The recognition of righteousness is not a product of the law, the text seems to say, but something prior to it, a matter of intuition or common knowledge. There are many hard questions here, in which the biblical writers, even the Deuteronomists, can't be said to take an interest. In any case, they clearly believe that the people have a reason to accept the law—it is a good law, and therefore they ought to accept it. But they are obligated by its provisions only if they do.

One of these provisions, as we have seen, requires members of the covenantal community to teach the law to their children. Are the children obligated to follow the teaching—or is their consent also necessary before the obligation takes hold? With this question, the biblical writers were clearly engaged, though it is difficult to tease out of their texts any coherent doctrinal response. The tension of kinship and consent is much in evidence here. In Deuteronomy's historical prologue, Moses tells the people that "the Lord our God made a covenant with us in Horeb [Sinai]. The Lord made not this covenant with our fathers, but with us, even us, who are all of us here alive this day" (5:2–3).

This statement is not historically accurate. The adults who stood at Sinai were all of them dead (except for Joshua and Caleb) by the time of Moses' oration; the people addressed here were children at Sinai or were not yet born. The first-person-plural pronoun is, so to speak, a genealogical collective. It designates the heirs of the generation that stood at Sinai. The benefits of liberation have been passed on, but have the obligations of the covenant also been passed on? The answer to this question is unclear. In one sense, no, for the whole purpose of Moses' oration is to persuade the people "alive this day" to covenant again, to reaffirm Israel's commitment, and it appears that the affirmation is, in principle, as free this second time as it was the first time. "I have set before you," says Moses, "life and death, blessing and cursing: therefore choose life" (Deuteronomy 30:19).

In another sense, however, the choice does seem to have consequences that reach beyond the actual men and women who make it. And here, too, the text is explicit:

> Neither with you only do I make this covenant and this oath; But
> with him that standeth here . . . this day before the Lord our God,
> and also with him that is not here with us this day. (29:14–15)

The author of this passage is not arguing that everyone in the world is caught up in the covenant. Only Israelites who are "not here"—which is to say, the future generations of Israel—are treated as if they are here at the covenanting. For them, it would seem, the covenant and all its obligations are indeed inherited; the genealogical collective, the plural "you" or "us" who stood at Sinai, reappears in each generation and determines the necessary response whenever the ancient agreement is renewed.

But if the covenant is inherited, why is it necessary for Israel to covenant again and again? Some scholars claim to have found traces in the text of an annual ceremony in which the covenant is not so much renewed as the original covenanting is reenacted in a ritual that assumes the underlying continuity of the legal and moral bond whose history it calls to mind and reinstates in popular consciousness.[9] But the actual occasions of re-covenanting don't appear to be ceremonial; at least they are not merely ceremonial. Much more is at stake than getting the ritual right. In Joshua 24, at the putative end of the conquest of Canaan, as the tribes are about to disperse, the renewal of the covenant has an obvious political purpose. And Joshua, who demands renewal, seems to anticipate opposition:

> And if it seem evil unto you to serve the Lord, choose you this
> day whom ye will serve; whether the gods which your fathers
> served that were on the other side of the [river], or the gods of
> the Amorites, in whose land ye dwell: but as for me and my
> house, we will serve the Lord. (24:15)

Here again, as in Exodus and Deuteronomy, a real choice is involved, or so the writer wants us to believe, perhaps because he shares with us the sense that without choice, there is no obligation.

The two other great renewals occur in the time of King Josiah's reformation, when the "book of the law" was found in the temple, and in the time of Ezra's reformation, after the return from Babylonia, when another "book of the law" was presented to the popular assembly. Josiah gathered "all the people, both small and great: and he read in their ears all the words of the book." He then expounded the obligations entailed by their agreement: "to walk after the Lord, and to keep his commandments . . . with all their heart and all their soul." "And all the people stood to the covenant" (2 Kings 23:2–3). No arguments—

unanimity again—but the occasion is clearly not ceremonial. The book had to be accepted because it was about to be enforced—indeed, rigorously enforced, at considerable cost to some members of the community.

The case is the same with Ezra's covenant, where we know that the agreement had a particular political purpose, which encountered strong opposition. In Nehemiah 8, 9, and 10, two very different events seem to be run together: first, the reading of the "book of the law" to "all the people . . . men and women," with the Levites in attendance to explain exactly what it all meant—"so they read in the book . . . distinctly, and gave the sense, and caused them to understand the reading" (8:8)—and, second, a more narrow, perhaps even sectarian, covenanting, in which only some of the people joined, their names duly appended. What really happened on this occasion I cannot explain; the scholarly controversies are fascinating but probably not relevant to the issues at hand. More clearly here than anywhere else, however, the centrality and seriousness of the covenant in Israelite thinking are made plain. The people understand the terms of the agreement; rejection is possible (and probably actual on the part of at least some of them); and acceptance has immediate political consequences.

It seems to follow from all this that the leaders of Israel need the agreement of the people at critical moments: when radically new policies are contemplated or when religious reform is thought to be necessary. But was Israel itself constituted and reconstituted by these agreements? Did people who refused to agree drop out of the community? Did young adults become full members only when they heard the "book of the law" read, and understood the reading, and accepted the commandments? The answer to this last question is that we have no record of any such acceptances (on, say, the sixteenth-century Anabaptist model) until the age of proselytism and conversion, which is largely post-biblical. The people who periodically assembled to hear the reading of the book were already Israelites, bound in the genealogical collective. As with other historical nations, kinship and covenant, descent and consent, are simultaneously at work. What is striking in the Bible is the intense awareness of both: this covenant, which requires our consent before it becomes obligatory, is also the "covenant of our fathers," to which we have already consented and which is already obligatory.

To what does the covenant oblige its subjects? After the people say, "We will do," what is to be done? Each individual who joins himself or herself in that "we" is bound to obey God's law. It is probably a good thing that they agree early on, in Exodus 19, before they have seen the full extent of the law, the sheer number of commandments. In any case they are bound to observance, obedience, religious faithfulness. That this bond is consistently understood, over many centuries, in covenantal terms is attested by the standard prophetic image of unfaithfulness, which describes Israel as an adulterous woman and God as a betrayed lover and husband. God is not often a father figure in the prophetic writings (he appears more frequently as the God *of our fathers*), and Israel is not a child but a consenting adult.[10] Its individual members are also, each of them, consenting adults, bound to do what they have promised to do.

But all that they have promised is their own obedience and faithfulness. Nothing in the biblical texts seems to reach beyond that; there is no demand on individuals that they act politically to ensure general obedience and faithfulness or to help create a holy or a just community. The question doesn't arise; the political activity of ordinary people is not a biblical subject; nor is there any explicit recognition of political space, an agora or forum, where people congregate to argue about and decide on the policies of the community. "The gates of the city" are the biblical equivalent of public space, but it is legal, not political, business that is transacted there, according to our texts. In Deuteronomy 16 and 17, the people are addressed collectively and commanded (or permitted) to appoint a king and also to appoint judges ("Judges and officers shalt thou make thee in all thy gates . . . throughout thy tribes" [16:18]), but there is no subsequent account of them assembling to make such appointments.

Because of the covenants, the people exist as a collective, but they don't appear to act collectively.[11]

There are communal officials and semi-officials whose responsibilities extend beyond obedience to God's law, reaching to legal judgments about what the law is, to policy decisions, and to what we call social criticism. These people are born to their offices, like priests and latter-day kings (first kings, the founders of dynasties, are chosen by God through his prophets), or they are appointed—we don't know how or by whom—like judges. Prophets are divinely "called" and commonly tell us the story of their calling; if self-appointed, they are false prophets. Citizens in the Greek sense, who understand that they ought to take an interest in politics and defend the common good, make no appearance. The elders of Israel, who might be said to represent the citizenry, make many appearances, but they have no doctrinal presence (see Chapter 11); little is said about their role or their authority—in sharp contrast to kings, priests, prophets, and judges, about whom the text has much to say.

Whether the responsibility of individual Israelites extends beyond obedience is a question never asked, so far as I can tell, in the biblical period. Later on, rabbinic commentators on Exodus 19 worried about it and disagreed among themselves. I have already mentioned the rabbi who claimed that there were 600,000 covenants at Sinai, with each Israelite making a pledge to God. Another rabbi said that there were 600,000 × 600,000 covenants, with each Israelite pledging to every other Israelite to live in accordance with God's law. "What is the issue between them? Rabbi Mesharsheya said, The issue between them is that of personal responsibility and responsibility for others."[12] I don't think that the biblical writers had any sense that ordinary Israelites were responsible for one another's behavior. They were responsible, as we shall see, for one another's well-being; the covenant required them to attend to the needs of the most vulnerable members of the community. But they were not politically responsible: no biblical writer argues that those wealthy and powerful Israelites who, according to the prophet Amos, "afflict the just . . . take a bribe, and . . . turn aside the poor in the gate from their right" (5:12) ought to have been criticized by other Israelites (in addition to the prophets) or challenged by a party or movement of angry citizens. There is no trace in the Bible of this kind of unauthorized criticism or challenge—unless we take the prophets themselves to be unauthorized and self-appointed, despite the stories they tell.

Prophecy, in its critical mode, is hard to imagine without the covenant, for the prophets don't invent obligations for the people; they remind the people of the obligations they already have and know that they have.[13] And it is worth noting that the prophets don't come uniformly from the upper reaches of Israelite society but from all social strata. Here again the covenant may have played an enabling role, making it possible for someone like Amos, "an herdsman and a gatherer of sycomore fruit" (7:14), to confront priests and kings. Amos would have been included even in the least inclusive of the covenant accounts, that of Joshua 24, where only the male heads of Israel's households are brought together. The Deuteronomic list of assembled Israelites includes almost everyone (unmarried women don't appear); Josiah's covenant, as I have already indicated, is made with "both small and great," and Ezra reads the law to a congregation "of men and women." But, except for the prophets, these people are never described in an active role; neither in large numbers nor in small did they seize the opportunity to denounce violations of covenantal law. Perhaps this testifies to the strength of the social hierarchy. At the same time, however, prophetic denunciation testifies to the hierarchy's vulnerability.

The people ought to have taken an interest in covenant violations— so we might think—since they were repeatedly held responsible for them. God's punishments are almost always collective in character. I will discuss the question of collective responsibility in detail in Chapter 7. Here it is enough to say that military defeat, conquest, and exile are as inclusive in their effects as the covenants are. The covenant binds everyone, and everyone suffers in the divine punishments. Sometimes punishment is dynastic rather than national, as in the case of Solomon's and Jereboam's heirs; more rarely it is individual, as in the case of Jezebel. But the disasters foretold by the prophets are most often general disasters, even though the sins the prophets denounce are, overwhelmingly, the sins of the wealthy and the powerful. I suppose there is nothing unusual in this: surely many nations have suffered because of the wickedness of their elites. If anything is different about Israel, it is that the avoidance of wickedness isn't an obligation of leaders alone but of the whole nation. The moral law, because of the repeated covenanting, is in principle, though not yet in practice, radically democratized.

"Avoidance of wickedness" is exactly the right phrase here (but see my discussion of this issue in Chapter 9), because it helps us understand what happened to the practice of covenanting in the centuries after the Babylonian exile. The clearest examples are post-biblical, dating from the last centuries of the common era; the Qum'ran sect suggests the new form of covenanted community. But Nehemiah 9 and 10 may represent an early case of the same thing: the covenanting there seems to involve a subset of the whole nation—"they that had separated themselves from the people of the lands unto the law of God" (10:28)—which takes itself to represent the nation. There is too much scholarly dispute about this incident for anything to be said with certainty: we don't know who was included in the "people of the lands" or who the separatists were (even though we have at least some their names).[14] But the verb "separated" seems to point, as I hinted earlier, to a sectarian grouping whose members are more concerned to reform their own lives than the common life of the people among whom they live—and the author of the text seems to be sympathetic to their concern. This is the hallmark of sectarianism in both religion and politics. Using the instrument of the covenant, later sectaries take on special obligations for the sake of purity and righteousness, both of which are rigorously defined; and they leave the others, whoever the others are, to wallow in corruption. They constitute themselves as a "remnant" and hope one day to replace the fallen community to which they once belonged.

In the political history of the West, sectarianism is most often a response to the failure of political practice. In Israel's history, sectarianism seems to arise in the absence of any actual practice of politics—but also in the aftermath of two dramatic political disappointments: first, the inability of the returning exiles to reestablish Davidic kingship and, second, centuries later, the transformation of the Hasmonean rebels, after their military victory, into Hellenistic priest-kings. The second of these is especially interesting because the rebellion began with a stirring reaffirmation of the national covenant. Thus Mattathias at Modin: "All who are zealous for the sake of the Torah, who uphold the covenant, march out after me!" (1 Maccabees 2:27). The words are deliberately reminiscent of Moses' rallying cry at the time of the golden calf incident: "Who is on the Lord's side? let him come unto me!" (Exodus 32:26). More than a thousand years pass between Moses and Mattathias, and in all that time there are no comparable calls to political mobilization (none of Israel's prophets ever sought to organize a popular following). When the Hasmoneans did not meet the expectations they raised, pious Israelites were faced with a classic choice between what Albert Hirschman has called "voice" and "exit," political protest and separation.[15] In the absence of a popular tradition of protest, separation was the more likely option; and the covenantal commitment to live in a certain way was readily adapted to sectarian purposes. But so was the idea of chosenness: originally applied to the genealogical collective, the nation as family, it seems to have worked equally well for the separatist "remnant." Had not the Pharisees, whose name probably derives from the verb "to separate," retained a strong sense of national connection, Israel might well have disintegrated into a multitude of warring sects. Whether it was kinship or covenantal faith that finally sustained the unity of the nation is a question I cannot answer here. The biblical writers understood Israel to have been founded on the two together.

The Legal Codes

The Bible contains many laws, but also and more importantly it contains legal codes: three different ones. The many laws are easy to understand, and it is equally easy to understand the popular wish that the yoke of the covenant be less onerous. An old folktale claims that on the day after the Sinai revelation, the Israelites rose early and marched at double speed away from the mountain so they wouldn't be given any more laws.[1] A quick getaway did them no good. Historically, the laws kept piling up—not, however in the form of explicit additions and revisions to the covenant code, Exodus 20–23, but in the form of two new codes: the priestly code of Leviticus and the Deuteronomic code. Each of these is described as if it, too, had been delivered at Sinai, yet little effort is made, early or late—not even when the books of the Bible were canonized—to bring Leviticus and Deuteronomy into harmony with Exodus. The three codes are significantly different in the range of social activities they cover, the style in which they are written, and the substantive rules they establish. Yet all of them are divinely com-

16

manded by the same God. There hasn't been a succession of gods, each with his own law, as in other countries of the ancient Near East, where a succession of kings promulgated new and divergent legal codes, the most recent one replacing the one before. How can divergence be explained when a single divine lawgiver rules eternally?

The documentary thesis provides a historical explanation that, as I have already said, I assume to be right, at least in its most general form. The codes represent three different traditions, oral or written, dating from different periods, transmitted by different groups, brought together at some late date by unknown editors. I will draw upon this thesis in the course of my own argument, but it does not answer what is surely the hard and interesting question: Why were the different traditions *brought together*, set side by side, rather than serially replaced or rewritten and harmonized? How can we explain the survival of all three?

From a theological point of view, the three codes are literally inexplicable—and that is why the differences among them are never acknowledged in the text. No human lawmaking is recognized; hence there are no stipulated procedures for adding to the divinely revealed law or for revising it, let alone for replacing it. The rule of Deuteronomy 4:2—"Ye shall not add unto the word which I command you, neither shall ye diminish aught from it, that ye may keep the commandments of the Lord"—applies also, in principle, to the covenant code of Exodus and ought to have precluded the writing of Deuteronomy itself. Yet the writing went on, and—as Michael Fishbane has demonstrated in his study of "inner-biblical legal exegesis"—argument, interpretation, and revision, in law courts and scribal schools, accompanied the writing.[2] With the publication of the first code, a process began of adding and subtracting. In a sense, this was an entirely normal process of adaptation to social change. But since it is an unacknowledged process, it can't have an acknowledged outcome. The adding and subtracting is surreptitious, and the result is a divine word inconsistent with itself.

It may well be, as some scholars think, that Deuteronomy was intended by its authors to replace earlier formulations of God's law—that it was a self-conscious attempt to provide a new and alternative text.[3] In the event, the authors provided a text that doesn't supplant but rather coexists with the earlier versions. The case is the same here as in the historical writings: the authors of Chronicles probably meant to replace the books of Samuel and Kings with their own expurgated history, heavily emphasizing the temple cult and the role of the priesthood. They must have hoped for readers who would find only their account available. But what they got, from the beginning, were readers like us, for whom Chronicles is simply *another* account, oddly different from Samuel and Kings but coexisting with them and laying claim to the same authority. The written history of God's people, like the codifications of God's law, can't be supplanted. Each version pretends to be the only one, even though the quickest reading of the Bible as a whole exposes the pretense.

The failure of every attempt at replacement and the piling up of different versions of law and history give the Bible its special character. It is as if God presides over and therefore validates the different versions and also, necessarily, the disagreements they reflect. The disagreements can't be openly recognized, but they also can't be written out of the text.[4] They make further exegesis imperative, since legal decisions and political and religious policies have to be justified in textual terms; and new exegesis gives rise in turn to new disagreements. And again, because the new disagreements can't be acknowledged, they can't be resolved.

The biblical text camouflages, as Fishbane writes, the "dependence of the divine word upon its human transmission and interpretation."[5] The camouflage conceals the divergence of interpretations, and it also conceals the identity, the proper names, and the social location of the rival interpreters. Though we know the names of all the high priests and some of the royal scribes, the authors of the priestly code and of Deuteronomy are necessarily anonymous; officially, they do not exist. And because the interpreters can't be identified, they can't be ranked; it isn't possible to establish the authority of some of them over others. So far as the text is concerned, the only author is God himself (or Moses, writing at his instruction). But behind this God, covered by his authority, speaking in his name, are a host of human authors, who make the law by reading, commenting on, and applying it. Priests, judges, scribes, and prophets: only the last of these tell us who they are and announce what sometimes sounds like a new divine word; the others (the prophets, too, almost all of the time) read and revise the old words. No one has a monopoly on the production of new legal versions. Or, better, God's monopoly works against the consolidation of interpretive power in Israelite society and serves to legitimize the plurality of interpreters. These are the secret legislators of Israel. Had there been no doctrine of the divine word, their work would probably have been normalized, and some political or religious group would have seized control, establishing a monopoly on legal interpretation. But there could be no normalization so long as denial and anonymity (except for the prophets) were religiously required.

Eventually, centuries after the last biblical texts were written, the rabbis managed to establish something like an interpretive monopoly (though the Karaites resisted it). But they could do this only by insisting that the law was now a human possession, no longer God's to give. Citing a line from Deuteronomy, they declared that the law "is not in heaven" (30:12)—that is, its meaning had to be determined here on earth, by a majority of this or that rabbinic court (BT Baba Metzia 59b). What the Deuteronomic authors meant by this line, however, was very different. They meant that the law was easy to know, readily available not for interpretation but for obedience. One had only to study their text. They did not give the law an earthly location in order to justify their own legislative activity, for they did not, could not, acknowledge that activity. And therefore they could not prevent other people from doing what they had done—so long as the doing was secret.

The three codes (and many scattered examples of independently announced law and legal exegesis) are therefore all equally valid and simultaneously in force. The earliest is the covenant code of Exodus, which was probably, in one form or another, the law of the tribal confederation and the early monarchy.[6] Like the other codes, this one is far from a complete set of laws, and scholars have as yet found no principles of inclusion or arrangement. Leviticus is mostly new law, though its central section, the Holiness Code of chapters 19–25, goes over much of the ground covered in Exodus. The intense concern with sacrifice and purity points to priestly authorship; the work was probably begun in the days of the first temple but not finished, so most scholars claim, until the second temple had been built and its cult established. It seems clear, though, that whoever wrote Deuteronomy knew many of the laws recorded in Leviticus, which must have existed in some earlier version by the seventh century. If Deuteronomy is, as Moshe Weinfeld has argued, the work of royal scribes (or of some group of scribes patronized by reformers in the court), then we have to imagine two contemporaneous but rival schools of secret legislators, writing new laws, revising old laws, and claiming that their work, too, had been delivered by God to Moses at Sinai.[7]

Deuteronomy is the crown of Israel's law: so, at least, academic commentators commonly conclude, sensing perhaps that the book is the work of writers rather like themselves. Principles of inclusion and order are no more evident here than elsewhere, but the book as a whole has the form of an intellectual composition, elaborately rhetorical, somewhat verbose, didactic, and—the anachronism is useful—ideological.[8] Leviticus reads like a record of priestly practice, no doubt idealized. Deuteronomy is more programmatic, aiming self-consciously at religious, perhaps also at political, reformation. Its laws have been called prophetic, humanitarian, secular, liberal, redistributive, and even feminist—though many seem remarkably unsuited to such adjectives. In any case, if Exodus is the law of the tribes, and Leviticus the law of the temple, then Deuteronomy is the law of the nation or, more specifically, the law of the royal court and the capital city, which stand for the nation. We might

In God's Shadow

think of it (anachronistically again) as one of the earliest examples in Western history of the work of urban intellectuals.

It has often been said that Israelite law—the three codes taken together—is more "advanced," that is, more humanitarian, liberal, and so on, than that of other ancient peoples. The Deuteronomists themselves make a similar claim when they have Moses ask the assembled Israelites: "And what nation is there so great, that hath statutes and judgments so righteous as all this law, which I set before you this day?" (Deuteronomy 4:8).[9] Moses acknowledges here that other nations have laws, even if these are less righteous than Israel's; the others are not outside the law, not barbarians. But they apparently don't receive their laws directly from God. Except for the commandment of Genesis 9—"Whoso sheddeth man's blood, by man shall his blood be shed: for in the image of God made he man"—there is no divine revelation to humankind generally or to the "nations," but only to Israel.

Curiously, it is just this universal law against murder, as Moshe Greenberg has shown, that distinguishes Israel's criminal code from all the others that we know of in the ancient world. The other codes allow for monetary compensation in cases of murder, while the Bible insists on capital punishment.[10] Whether this law is more righteous or more humanitarian is an open question, though the apparently related refusal of biblical legislators to punish crimes against property with death certainly appeals to modern readers. Human life is an absolute value for the biblical writers, which leads them paradoxically to condemn murderers to death. But property has only relative value, so theft is never a capital crime. This distinction, Greenberg argues, is a biblical innovation and a human advance.

Still, the discovery and translation of more and more legal codes from both Mesopotamia and Asia Minor require us to be skeptical of analyses, less rigorous than Greenberg's, that attempt apologetic and moralizing comparisons. The reiterated argument that the experience of slavery in Egypt requires social justice in Israel has no precedent elsewhere. But the substance of the biblical laws, especially the laws dealing with family and economy, isn't in any sense singular or original; Israel's legislators were clearly working within a common Near Eastern legal tradition.[11] The protection they provided for the weak—slaves, strangers, women—is sometimes greater and sometimes lesser than that provided in other ancient codes. The penalties they prescribed for violations of the laws are sometimes more lenient, sometimes harsher. Social differentiation is considerably more rigid in, say, the Babylonian laws than it is in Israel's, but national differences make more of a difference in Israel than in Babylonia.

I shall return to the question of what justice and injustice meant to the biblical writers in the last chapter. What is most important here is not the substance of the law but its provenance and presentation. I have already commented on the unexpectedly pluralizing effects of God's sole authorship. But there is also a more narrowly political point to be made about divine provenance—and then two points about the textual presentation of the law. Though I have denied the claim that the three codes are substantively superior to other ancient codes, the points that I now want to make will give modern liberal and democratic readers reasons to admire the biblical legislators. I will try, however, to avoid the apologetic style.

First, then, Israel's law is God's alone; it has no other possessive modifier. Above all, and in contrast to other Near Eastern codes, it isn't the king's law. Despite the rich narrative accounts of Israel's monarchic period, writes Martin Noth, "we nowhere hear of the law-giving activity of the kings."[12] Nor is the law ever described as the work of an assembly of elders; nor, again, as a priestly codification, or a philosophical construction, or a judicial invention. Justice Oliver Wendell Holmes's maxim, that law is what the judges say it is, may in fact apply to ancient Israel as well as to the modern United States, but the proposition would have been literally inadmissible among biblical writers. Politically, this means that everyone—kings, elders, priests, judges—is subject, indeed equally subject, to the authority of the law. Equality is a matter of principle; the actual power relations prevailing in the community at any given time would obviously qualify and distort the working out of the principle. Nonetheless, principles are important, as we can see from the story of Ahab and Naboth in First Kings 21.

Ahab, who rules the northern kingdom of Israel, covets the vineyard of Naboth, which adjoins his palace grounds. He offers Naboth a "better vineyard" or a money payment. Naboth refuses, saying, "The Lord forbid it me, that I should give the inheritance of my fathers unto thee." Indeed, the Lord does forbid it, according to laws delivered to Moses in the wilderness (Numbers 27 and 36). Ahab can do nothing: he goes home "dispirited and sullen," takes to his bed, and turns his face to the wall. His wife, Jezebel, a Phoenician woman who worships Baal rather than Yahweh and doesn't know or respect Israel's law, contrives Naboth's murder. Ahab then seizes the vineyard and is confronted by the prophet Elijah, who asks, "Hast thou killed, and also taken possession?" (1 Kings 21:19). It is a wonderful scene, and I will return to it in the chapter on prophecy. I am more interested here, however, in Ahab's dispiritedness than in Elijah's righteous anger. The king implicitly acknowledges the laws of land tenure and thinks himself constrained by them. No way of changing the law is available to him.

The only people who might openly challenge and change the law are the prophets, who claim a direct relation to God. Moses, the first prophet, with the most direct relation, does add to the law he originally delivered—but only by bringing a case "before the Lord" (Numbers 27:5) and waiting until "the mind of the Lord might be shewed them" (Leviticus 24:12). The first of these passages is especially interesting because the case in question is initiated by the "daughters of Zelophehad," who speak before the congregation of Israel defending their right to inherit their father's land. God tells Moses that their plea is just and commands him to announce a new inheritance law.[13] The daughters seem more important here than the prophet, and the scene in which they appear suggests how the writer views the accessibility of legal procedures and the popular character of legal argument. But the law is never again disputed so publicly. Nor did the later prophets have the authority to revise it in this open way.

Indeed, I know of only one passage in all the prophetic writings that seems to set the living word against the written law. Here is the prophet Jeremiah speaking to the people of Jerusalem:

> How do ye say, We are wise, and the law [*torat*] of the Lord is with us? Lo, certainly . . . the pen of the scribes is in vain. The wise men are ashamed, they are dismayed and taken: lo they have rejected the word of the Lord; and what wisdom is in them? (8:8–9)

The meaning of these lines is obscure, since there is no specific "law" that the prophet denies or cancels. He is probably concerned more with scribal "wisdom" than with the legal code. A better example of the prophet's relation to the law is provided by Jeremiah 17:21–22, where the laws of the Sabbath are amended or, as Jeremiah claims, elaborated: "Take heed to yourselves and bear no burden on the sabbath day, nor bring it in by the gates of Jerusalem." No prohibition of "bearing burdens" is recorded in the three legal codes. But Jeremiah quickly adds: "Hallow ye the sabbath day, as I commanded your fathers," thus reading his amendment back into the original law. The prophet, too, is bound by the law; he cannot play the part of Max Weber's charismatic leader who proclaims: "The law is thus and so, but I say unto you . . ." Still, prophets do change the law without acknowledging what they are doing; and so do priests, judges, and scribes. Kings can't even do that; they can only break the law. They can put their hands on it, violently, but they can't leave their intellectual or moral mark on it. (One "statute," having to do with the equal division of booty, is attributed to David in First Samuel 30:25, but David here was not yet king.)

The second distinctive feature of Israelite law is its radical embeddedness in a historical narrative. Since this narrative, recorded in Exodus and Numbers and recapitulated in Deuteronomy, stretches only from the deliverance of the Egyptian slaves to the death of Moses on the eve of the invasion of Canaan, Israelite kings play no part in it, and except in Deuteronomy 17, which anticipates and regulates kingly rule, they make no appearance in the legal texts. So it isn't surprising that they are not among the acknowledged or even the unacknowledged interpreters of the law. (Solomon is celebrated for wisdom, not legal knowledge.) The deliverance story is the textual setting for an anti-authoritarian and justice-oriented legalism. Future generations of Israelites are enjoined not only to study the law but also to retell the history. The legal texts refer regularly to the historical narrative and so invite interpretation in its terms—hence the special force (whatever the substance) of the commandments about slaves, strangers, the poor and needy, widows, and orphans. Babylonian and Assyrian kings, in the preambles to their own law codes, insist upon the protection they offer to these same groups, perhaps with reason. But their protection is noblesse oblige, the special task of the mighty. Only in Israel is the task democratized, rooted in a common experience of oppression.

But this experience did not lead Israelite legislators to abolish slavery. According to the covenantal and Deuteronomic codes, Hebrew slaves cannot be held longer than six years, a rule that effectively turns slavery into a form of limited indenture (Exodus 21:2–6; Deuteronomy 15:12–18). Nothing is said of foreign slaves, however, for whom the sabbatical year presumably brings no release. Leviticus is explicit in permitting the permanent enslavement of foreigners: "they shall be your bondmen forever" (25:46). This must also be the way Egypt's pharaoh thought about the children of Israel. Curiously, the Levitical standard for the treatment of the Israelite "bondman" is set by reference to what appears to be an ethnically undifferentiated class: he is to be treated "as a hired servant and a sojourner." He must serve and sojourn, however, for forty-nine years, until the jubilee rather than the sabbatical release. He can't be treated as harshly as a (foreign) slave, since he belongs, along with all "free" Israelites, to God. Deuteronomy also recognizes the inter-ethnic class of "hired servants" (wage workers) and explicitly demands equal treatment for all its members: "Thou shalt not oppress an hired servant that is poor and needy, whether he be of thy brethren or of thy strangers" (24:14). Here the experience of Egyptian bondage is given a general application: "But thou shalt remember that thou wast a bond-man in Egypt." The Deuteronomic commandment not to return a fugitive slave ("He shall dwell with thee, even among you, in that place which he shall choose in one of thy gates, where it liketh him best" [23:15–16]) seems also to apply to foreigners, though scholars disagree about its exact meaning.[14]

The differences among the laws of slavery suggest an extended and serious argument—which is entirely appropriate in a community with a shared memory of bondage. And the argument must have been as much about the experience as about the laws themselves: What moral and legal consequences followed from the remembrance of Egypt? What did it mean to be a vassal nation, a community of divine servants? To answer questions like these was to justify one or another understanding of the laws.

And these questions bring me to the third distinctive feature of Israel's codes: many of the laws that they include are laws-with-reasons, justified laws. Apparently, justifications are rare in the other Near Eastern legal codes. The great kings of Mesopotamia didn't have to provide arguments for their laws. Nor does God, and many of his laws, like theirs, are delivered without justification and seem entirely arbitrary—the laws of holiness and purity provide the clearest examples. By contrast, the social and economic laws often come with reasons attached. Sometimes

In God's Shadow

these refer directly to the historical narrative: "Also thou shalt not oppress a stranger: for ye know the heart of a stranger, seeing ye were strangers in the land of Egypt" (Exodus 23:9). Sometimes the justifications appeal to a more ordinary morality or, simply, to common sense:

> If thou . . . take thy neighbour's raiment to pledge [i.e., as a pawn], thou shalt deliver it unto him by that the sun goeth down: For that is his covering only, it is his raiment for his skin: wherein shall he sleep? (Exodus 22:26–27).

> When thou buildest a new house, then thou shalt make a battlement for thy roof, that thou bring not blood upon thine house, if any man fall from thence. (Deuteronomy 22:8)

The distinction between justified and unjustified law is, from a theoretical perspective, more interesting than the standard scholarly distinction between casuistic and apodictic law. Scholars have argued that case law is common to the Bible and other ancient codes, whereas the sharp imperatives of the apodictic form ("Thou shalt not . . .") are more likely to be unique to Israel. But this assessment is much disputed and of uncertain significance even if true. What David Weiss Halivni has called the "Jewish predilection for justified law" is, if it exists, more genuinely important.[15] In the biblical texts, the predilection is only intermittently displayed. (The reiterated phrase of Leviticus, "for I am the Lord your God," may provide a reason for obeying the laws, but it doesn't provide a substantive justification of their content.) Laws-with-reasons appear often enough, however, to call for an explanation: What is the reason for the reasons? One possible answer to this question is the strength of the covenantal idea. The laws must be justified, we might say, because the covenant requires the people's consent. Even though the people have already given a wholesale consent—"All that the Lord hath spoken we will do" (Exodus 19:8)—Israel's legislators seem unwilling to rely entirely on it. They seek in addition something more specific and particularized, as if they have in mind a genuinely consensual community whose members know exactly what they are doing and why.

But perhaps the legislators are giving reasons first of all to one another and only incidentally to other members of the community. Another explanation for the justifying clauses in the biblical codes is that they reflect the actual discussions that went on within priestly or scribal or judicial circles. They are the textual residue of oral advocacy—of what was actually said in defense of legal reform and revision. The argumentative style of the Talmud stands, on this view, at the end of a continuous development that has its beginnings here. But the beginning is very different from the end—and much harder for us to understand. How can we reconstruct the mind-set that governed the earliest Israelite legal arguments? Whatever the sophistication and, as modern readers are likely to think, the humanism revealed in, say, the law of the pledge, biblical legislators were clearly open, as the rabbis generally were not, to the idea of divine intervention. And when God intervened, speaking directly to Moses, or through the mysterious urim and thummim, or via his prophets, he did not give reasons. The word *torah*, which usually means "instruction," "testimony," "law," or "decision," also means "oracle." Both priests and prophets delivered oracles, often unclear and always unargued. Like the answers to specific questions provided by the urim and thummim, these usually have to do with policy, not law. They are pronouncements about the future, warnings and foretellings, not legal rulings. Still, biblical law was worked out by people who believed in the warnings as well as the rulings, who had a sense of God's mysterious immediacy that was largely lost by the rabbinic age. The rabbis, some of them anyway, were openly skeptical about the possibility (and even the desirability) of divine intervention in their decision-making.

Mind-set aside, however, laws-with-reasons are not mysterious; whether they are aimed at fellow lawmakers or at ordinary citizens, they aim to persuade. From this aim, two things seem to follow about the biblical understanding of the law. First, the biblical understanding isn't in any simple sense a legal positivist understanding. No doubt, God's law is authoritative because God is omnipotent, the sovereign of the universe. But no particular rendition or interpretation of the law is authoritative for this reason. Legal positivism works only when sovereign power is regularly and visibly deployed. But God's deployments, despite his omnipotence, are irregular and usually invisible. Hence his authority is effectively taken over by Israel's secret legislators. None of them (since the king is excluded) possess anything like sovereign power, so they are led to think about the law as something that requires argument.

And if there are arguments, there must also be standards to which the arguments appeal. Justified law implies the previous existence of ideas about justification; in the case of civil and criminal law, of ideas about justice. It appears that God himself is bound by these ideas, as Abraham tells him at Sodom: "Shall not the Judge of all the earth do right?" (Genesis 18:25). If God's power does not make his decisions authoritative, neither does his righteousness make them just. The biblical writers were not moral positivists any more than they were legal positivists. Moses' boast in Deuteronomy about the value of Israelite law carries the same implication as Abraham's rebuke: though the law is divinely delivered, divinely commanded, it does not determine but only realizes what is right. Or, alternatively, it fails to realize what is right, for it is always possible that the reasons given for this or that law will be disputed (though never explicitly).

The effect of the disputes is, again, to pluralize the law. Old laws are not canceled; rather, new laws or revised versions of old ones are added. I have already suggested that the process of replacement rather than addition characterizes other Near Eastern legal codes. Only among the Hittites, apparently, are the replacements made explicit (and only in a code without the usual royal preamble, apparently designed for the use of jurists): "If someone blinds a free man or knocks out his teeth, formerly he would give one mina of silver, now he gives 20 shekels of silver and pledges his estate as security."[16] No reasons for the change are given, either because ordinary Hittites had no need to know or because the legislative authority of the king or his judges was never in question. Among the Israelites, since the additions and revisions were unacknowledged, they were also mostly unjustified. We have to reconstruct the arguments that were probably made on the basis of justifications offered in other cases. But there is one very nice example of an addition with reasons attached.

In Exodus 21:2–6, it is required that a "Hebrew servant" (slave) be set free in the sabbatical year. He shall "go out free, for nothing." The law is repeated in Deuteronomy with an important addition:

> And when thou sendest him out free from thee, thou shalt not let him go away empty: Thou shalt furnish him liberally out of thy flock, and out of thy floor, and out of thy winepress: of that wherewith the Lord thy God hath blessed thee thou shalt give unto him. And thou shalt remember that thou wast a bondman in the land of Egypt. (15:13–15)

The historical reference is especially appropriate here since the Israelites did not "go away empty" from Egypt (Exodus 12:35–36). Surely they should behave toward their own kinfolk at least as well as the Egyptians behaved toward them! But this argument was apparently not entirely convincing, for the Deuteronomic authors add another: "It shall not seem hard to thee, when thou sendest him away free . . . for he hath been worth a double hired servant to thee" (15:18). I am not sure exactly what this means, perhaps that well-treated servants worked especially hard. Or it may refer to a provision of Hammurabi's Code that sets the debt slave free after three years rather than the six that Israelite slaves served. If so, this is a more specific comparative reference than Deuteronomy 4:8—though it might suggest that Babylonia had statutes and judgments as righteous as Israel's, or more so. In any case, legal revisionism clearly involved economic as well as historical arguments.

And sometimes revisionism involved arguments of the sort that we would call ideological, arguments that reflect systematic religious-political disagreements. The slavery laws of Deuteronomy, for example, are clearly intended to improve the status of women, though the improvements are neither plainly marked out nor explicitly defended. The six-year limit, from which women were excepted in the Exodus code, now covers them in exactly the same way as men are covered (compare Exodus 21:7 and Deuteronomy 15:12). Male and female slaves are to be similarly treated, though nothing is said against their dissimilar treatment in times past. An even more intriguing example of what has been called Deuteronomy's "feminism" is the revision of the Tenth Commandment. Here is the Exodus version:

> Thou shalt not covet thy neighbour's house, thou shalt not covet thy neighbour's wife, nor his manservant nor his maidservant, nor his ox, nor his ass, nor anything that is thy neighbour's. (20:17)

And here is the Deuteronomic version:

> Neither shalt thou desire thy neighbour's wife, neither shalt thou covet thy neighbour's house, his field, or his manservant, or his maidservant, his ox, or his ass, or anything that is thy neighbour's. (5:21)

In the revised commandment, the wife is set apart, deliberately taken out of the list of possessions, assigned, as it were, a verb of her own. Again, no reason is given for the small but significant change; this, the text suggests, is what God really said at Sinai. But it seems obvious that someone reading the earlier version did not like it. We can only imagine what he, or she, said to his, or her, fellow legislators.

The existence of three codes means that Israel's legal tradition was pluralist in character, encompassing (with what degree of strain we don't know) argument and disagreement. Given the "predilection for justified law," we can see what the arguments were probably like. I suggested in the previous chapter that ancient Israel did not have a culture of citizenship; the biblical texts provide no doctrinal defense of—they hardly seem to take an interest in—political participation. But there clearly was a legal culture. I don't mean, necessarily, a culture of litigation, though access to the courts appears to have been easy and the judges fairly busy, if not always fair in their business. The frequency with which they are criticized by the prophets suggests the everyday importance of their decisions. So does the commandment that comes at the very beginning of Deuteronomy, set apart from all the others: "Ye shall not respect persons in judgment; but ye shall hear the small as well as the great" (1:17). Babylonian and Egyptian judges were probably similarly enjoined; I don't know whether they had to listen to anything quite like a jeremiad when they failed to live up to their responsibilities. But for our purposes here, litigation and judicial integrity are less important than legislation and interpretive authority.

Here is what gives Israel's legal culture its distinctive—and, I might add, its enduring—character. It seems that from fairly early on, a significant number of people, virtually the whole of the nation's intelligentsia, such as it was, were engaged in arguing about the law. The fact that priests, judges, elders, prophets, and scribes assigned their arguments to God we can take as piety or presumption. Either way, the assignment legitimized their own activity. In principle they were articulating the content of the Sinai covenant; in practice they were deciding—more than once—what that content should be. Certainly, the decision-making process was political (and moral) as well as legal. But it was never understood or defended in political terms. Nor are procedures specified by which individuals were admitted to the process. Priests were born to their tasks, but there were many priests, and some of them played a greater role than others. Judges were appointed; we don't know by whom, probably the king. The elders of the people or, more likely, the patriarchs of the clan, served in local courts or sat in the city gates.

In God's Shadow

Prophets were called by God, but we have only their own accounts of their calling. About the scribes we know little. These are the people I have called the secret legislators of Israel—an elite, no doubt, but a very loosely structured elite, whose covenantal/legal consciousness was probably not entirely different from that of the nation at large.

The looseness of that elite had something to do with the tripleness of the codes—and both looseness and tripleness had something to do with the divine singularity, which could not be imitated or even authoritatively represented anywhere in Israelite society. None of this, needless to say, gave rise to a pluralist *doctrine*. No biblical writer argued for the legitimacy of rival interpreters or of rival interpretations of the law. None of them were pluralists in the modern sense of that word. Nor does anything in the Bible resemble the saying in the Talmud that refers to the contradictory teachings of the schools of Hillel and Shamai: "These and these are the words of the living God" (BT Eruvin 13b). Still, as a group, the biblical writers, authors and editors alike, left behind in the canonical texts a legacy of multiple and inconsistent codes and a record of unacknowledged interpretations and revisions. We can only speculate about their reasons; perhaps they had what Geoffrey Hartman calls "a respect for friction."[17] In any case, they rejected the two possible resolutions of the friction—serial replacement and full-scale editorial harmonization—and instead chose to live with multiplicity and inconsistency. The result of their choice was a written law that made possible those strange open-ended legal conversations that constitute the oral law of later Judaism.

THREE

Conquest and Holy War

For the modern reader, the conquest of Canaan, with all its attendant slaughter, is the most problematic moment in the history of ancient Israel. There is no reason to think that it was similarly problematic for the biblical writers, none of whom undertook to construct an argument on behalf of the seven Canaanite nations comparable to Abraham's argument on behalf of Sodom and Gomorrah (two Canaanite cities). Both the priestly authors of Leviticus and the Deuteronomists are careful to give God moral reasons for his commandment to drive out or exterminate the seven nations—"Not for thy righteousness or for the uprightness of thine heart, dost thou go to possess their land: but for the wickedness of these nations" (Deuteronomy 9:5)—and the argument is repeated and insisted upon in a way that has led some commentators to conclude that Israel had a bad conscience about the conquest.[1] But there are so many other explanations for doubled and tripled passages in the Bible, and they support such different theses, that the conclusion is weak. Moreover, as we shall see, the commandments seem to reflect a religious doctrine, which is also repeated a number of times without a trace of bad conscience. One might more easily argue that conscientious Israelites were duty-bound to join in the bloody business of the conquest and to show no mercy.

The religious doctrine of holy war—the phrase isn't biblical but it also isn't anachronistic—does not seem to have any intrinsic connection to Israel's covenantal faith. There have been efforts to connect holy war with monotheism or with the idea of election. Only a jealous God and a chosen people, it is argued, could inspire a *religious* defense of genocide.[2] Polytheism, by contrast, made for coexistence, first of gods, then of peoples. But this claim has been implausible ever since the discovery almost a hundred years ago of the Moabite stone, dating from the eighth century, which provides an account of the wars of Israel and Moab directly parallel to the early chapters of Second Kings. The account is in the first person, as if written by Mesha, king of the Moabites:

And Chemosh [the national god of Moab] said to me, 'Go, take Nebo against Israel.' And I went by night and fought against it from the break of dawn till noon; and I took it and slew all: seven thousand men, boys, women, and [girls,] and female slaves, for I had consecrated it to Ashtar-Chemosh.[3]

The passage sounds remarkably like the biblical accounts of holy war, and since Hebrew and Moabite were mutually intelligible dialects of the same language, the warring nations may have exchanged ideas about holiness. In any case, Mesha proclaims a doctrine that must have been known also to the biblical writers: some wars are commanded by the national god and fought for his exclusive benefit; captives and booty are offered to him and not kept by the victorious soldiers. I don't quote the Moabite inscription here in order to excuse Israelite warfare—as if to say, that is how people behaved in those days. After all, Israel is repeatedly commanded not to copy the customs, especially the religious customs, of the surrounding nations. Why, then, did it make the idea of consecration, or something like it, where what is consecrated is also doomed, into one of its own doctrines?[4]

There were alternative doctrines. Moabites and Israelites fought secular and limited wars as well as holy and total wars, and the biblical texts include rules for limited wars alongside, even entangled with, the laws of the *herem*, the ban, which consigned entire cities to utter destruction. The alternatives don't quite match the divine simplicity of the *herem* (since they are adapted to the actual circumstances of national coexistence), and there doesn't appear to be an explicit critique of holy warfare in any of the biblical books, though there are some explicit refusals to engage in it. Nonetheless, if the authors of Deuteronomy make the *herem* central, they seem to do so against strong opposition—from kings, for example, who commonly wanted to enjoy the fruits of their victories and to reward their soldiers with something more than divine approval. Perhaps the kings also saw no point in religiously prescribed slaughter: a midrashic story has King Saul asking Samuel whether it was really necessary to kill the innocent (BT Yoma 22b). One might expect a similar query from the Deuteronomists, for they were the party of reform. One of the hardest questions about biblical politics is how to explain the cruelty of their book: In what sense is the *herem* a reformist doctrine?

I won't address that question until I have considered the conquest narratives within which the cruelty is or isn't acted out. For these texts are doubled; there are two very different versions of the conquest. Some rough attempts at harmonization are also evident, but the differences are not erased. They are the subject of intense debate among scholars trying to figure out what cannot be figured out, short of some dramatic archaeological discovery: the actual process that brought Israel into Canaan. I am more interested here in the ideas the different writers had about what might have, and what should have, happened.

The first version, and what reads like the official version, of the conquest story is provided in the book of Joshua, chapters 1–11, ending with the lines "So Joshua took the whole land, according to all that the Lord said unto Moses . . . And the land rested from war" (11:23)—a claim that actually fits only some of God's sayings to Moses as we now have them. The land's "rest" comes at the end of a systematic campaign marked by miraculous victories, when city walls came tumbling down and the sun stood still. The *herem* law was rigorously applied throughout—from the first battle, the siege of Jericho, where "they utterly destroyed all that was in the city, both man and woman, young and old, and ox, and sheep, and ass, with the edge of the sword" (6:21), to the battle for the hill country, where they "destroyed all that breathed, as the Lord God of Israel commanded" (10:40), to the battle for the north, the valley of Jezreel and the lower Gallilee: "neither left they any to breathe" (11:14).

The conscientiousness of all this is attested by the story of Achan, which takes up the whole of Joshua 7. Achan seems to have been an ordinary Israelite soldier, no leading figure, who took some gold and silver and a "goodly Babylonian garment" from a house in Jericho and hid the booty in his tent. Looting was a violation of holy war doctrine, which required total destruction, and it brought Achan and his family under the ban—evidence that the ban transcended all national distinctions. The entire family ("sons and daughters") and all their possessions, including the tent, were brought to a place outside the camp and stoned and burned. I need hardly point out that the *herem* was not a prohibition against looting of the sort that later figures in international law. The purpose of the more modern prohibition is to leave a conquered people its possessions so that something like ordinary life can be resumed. Looting here is a crime against living men and women. Achan, by contrast, sinned only against God; no one was left alive in Jericho to wear the goodly garment that he stole.

Indeed, according to this version of the story, no Canaanites were left anywhere in Canaan by the end of Joshua's campaign—with the exception of the Gibeonites, who made a covenant with Israel and lived for many centuries among the Israelite tribes. They alone remained of the original population, their survival explained by an elaborate tale of an unlikely diplomatic trick, which I will have more to say about below. But this totalizing story of successful genocide is immediately contradicted by its own authors, who were forced to acknowledge an alternative tradition—or perhaps to recognize the obvious fact that Canaanites still lived in the land. Thus Joshua 16:10: "And they drave not out the Canaanites that dwelt in Gezer; but the Canaanites dwell among the Ephraimites unto this day." Again in Joshua, the same acknowledgment is made with reference to a number of cities in the Jordan and Jezreel valleys, as if the triumphant campaign described only a few chapters earlier had never taken place:

> Yet the children of Manasseh could not drive out the inhabitants of those cities; but the Canaanites would dwell in that land. Yet it came to pass when the children of Israel were waxen strong, that they put the Canaanites to tribute; but did not utterly drive them out. (17:12–13)

The authors or editors of Exodus and Deuteronomy have included some verses, attributed directly or indirectly to God, that are obviously intended to account for the continued Canaanite presence—verses that sit uneasily alongside the commandments to drive out or destroy. "The Lord thy God will put out those nations before thee by little and little," Moses tells the people in Deuteronomy; "thou mayest not consume them at once, lest the beasts of the field increase upon thee" (7:22). This text says nothing about imposing taskwork on the remaining Canaanites (the same sort of work, apparently, that Pharaoh imposed on the Israelites in Egypt); its programmatic formula is consistently more radical: "Thou shalt smite them and utterly destroy them; thou shalt make no covenant with them, nor shew mercy unto them" (7:2). But the invading Israelites were not able to enforce this program, and though God himself is said to have delayed its enforcement in order not to leave the land desolate, the length of the delay ("unto this day") must have made the explanation seem thin and unpersuasive. The Deuteronomic editor of Judges offers another explanation, much stronger but also very strange: to punish the Israelites for adopting Canaanite religious practices, God announces that he "will not henceforth drive out any from before them of the nations which Joshua left when he died" (2:21). But the whole purpose of driving them out—indeed, as we shall see, the reason given by the authors of Deuteronomy for holy war—was to prevent them from teaching Israel their religious practices. God seems to have given up for exactly the wrong reason.

The second version of the conquest is most clearly set forth in the opening chapters of Judges, though it is hinted at earlier. It is an unsystematic account of an unsystematic process. Now the Israelites seem to have infiltrated rather than invaded the country, settling where they could, fighting when they had to, signing treaties, collecting tribute, intermarrying, absorbing the Canaanite nations and in the process learning of their ways. A conquest of this sort does not preclude the ban, though it requires a much more flexible application of it—which is exactly what the texts of the second version suggest. "The *herem* in war could go to varying lengths," writes Max Weber, "and the rules of the division of booty indicate that the tabooing of the total booty, of men, women, children, cattle, horses, furniture, was not the rule."[5] The ban is only sometimes applied in Judges (see 1:17 for the only explicit reference to the *herem* law), and there is no talk of slaughtering "all that breathes." This second conquest narrative concludes not with a victory claim but with a confession of failure, presumably by the hand of the Deuteronomic editor:

> And the children of Israel dwelt among the Canaanites, Hittites, and Amorites, and Perizzites, and Hivites, and Jebusites: And they took their daughters to be their wives, and gave their daughters to their sons, and served their gods. (3:5–6)

But the failure is religious, not political, for in both these versions of the story Israel succeeds in establishing itself in Canaan—killing or dispossessing many of the inhabitants and, whether rapidly or gradually, coming to rule over the others. A few of the old Canaanite city-states managed to hang on (Jerusalem apparently one of them) until David's time, but the power of their kings was replaced by that of the Israelite tribes, their elders, and their charismatic warrior-judges. At some point, wars with the Canaanites simply cease to be reported; the tribes are now engaged (and, presumably, the remnants of the seven nations alongside them) with external enemies, Midianites, Moabites, Philistines, and so on. When in response to these new wars, the people of Israel establish a monarchy of their own, it is tribal and national in character, not city based; whatever the fate of their gods, the political regime of the Canaanites is no longer an option.

The second conquest story seems more likely than the first, if only because it acknowledges a reality that its authors profess to find unattractive. We are more prone to believe reports of failure than of triumph. Moreover, a doctrine of warfare—not so explicitly formulated as the holy war doctrine but visible in the texts—fits the second story. This doctrine doesn't exclude the occasional use of the ban, but it establishes an alternative norm: limited war, respect for treaties, tribute and the corvée rather than deportation and slaughter. It is reflected in Deuteronomy itself, a seventh-century composition that refers back to the age of the conquest, but its clearest expression comes in texts that deal with the early monarchy. The kings of Israel and Judah apparently did not consider themselves bound by the *herem* laws. They may have invoked the holy war doctrine in this or that instance, just as Mesha of Moab did, but they knew of another law and seem to have regarded that, too, as ancient law.

The prophet Amos, who lived in the eighth century, provides the best indication of what this other law required. In his indictment of the nations around Israel, he lists a series of war crimes (as we would call them) that are virtually identical with the pious acts of holy warfare.

In God's Shadow

Here is a partial summary, in the prophet's own, sometimes metaphorical language:

> the people of Damascus "have threshed Gilead with threshing instruments of iron"
> the people of Gaza "carried away captive the whole captivity to deliver them up to Edom"
> the people of Tyre "remembered not the brotherly covenant"
> the king of Edom "did pursue his brother with the sword, and did cast off all pity, and his anger did tear perpetually"
> the Ammonites "have ripped up the women with child of Gilead"
> the king of Moab "burned the bones of the king of Edom into lime" (Amos 1 and 2)

All these things it was wrong to do, and wrong, presumably, no matter who did them. Amos's list reflects, Weber thinks, a kind of international law that was recognized, if not consistently observed, by both Israel and its neighbors.[6] If we imagine the prohibitions that lie behind the prophet's indictments, we have a code for coexistence, not necessarily peaceful; indeed, it assumes ongoing warfare. What it aims to guarantee is the survival of the parties, if only so that they can fight again. Even the most radical defeat is not to be followed by the exile of a nation or the killing of women and children.

This code doesn't figure in either Exodus or Leviticus, both of which show little concern with foreign policy. The tribal confederation for which the covenant code of Exodus was probably designed had no stable or coherent foreign policy, and the priestly authors of Leviticus left such questions to Israel's kings (and, later on, to foreign emperors). But the Deuteronomic authors are distinctly interested, and we shall have to look closely at what they say. Deuteronomy 20, the crucial text, shows signs of revision, and I shall argue, following Michael Fishbane, that limited war and holy war doctrines have been uneasily joined—the second added to the first without erasing or superseding it.[7] But interpretive arguments of this sort, which make claims about the provenance not of whole books, or legal codes, or narrative sequences, but of individual verses, are speculative and highly uncertain; I shall try not to build too much upon them.

The rules for military engagement begin at Deuteronomy 20:10, following upon a list of men exempt from battle (the exemptions don't fit an invading army of nomadic tribes and presumably date from and apply to a later time). Standing, supposedly, on the banks of the Jordan, Moses commands the people:

> When thou comest nigh unto a city to fight against it, then proclaim peace unto it. And it shall be, if it make thee answer of peace, and open unto thee . . . that all the people that is found therein shall be tributaries unto thee, and they shall serve thee. And if it will make no peace with thee, but will make war against thee, then thou shalt besiege it: And when the Lord thy God hath delivered it into thine hands, thou shalt smite every male thereof with the edge of the sword: But the women, and the little ones, and the cattle, and all that is in the city, even all the spoil thereof, shalt thou take unto thyself. (20:10–14)

This is a summary statement of the limited war doctrine. It is entirely consistent with Amos's indictments and with much of the historical material in First and Second Kings. The limits will seem inadequate from a contemporary perspective—and the war as a whole most likely aggressive: "when thou comest nigh" does not suggest self-defense. (The rabbis later called this sort of war "optional," whereas a holy war is "commanded.")[8] But the *herem*, at least in its more radical versions, is excluded by this account. The same exclusion is even more apparent in 21:10–14, which lays down rules for the treatment of captive women. Triumphant soldiers are given only two options: they must marry their captives or set them free. *Herem* law, by contrast, requires that the women be killed;

and the reason for the slaughter is the fear of intermarriage (and religious syncretism—the two, as we shall see, are persistently connected).

Since these laws were proclaimed, according to the text, on the eve of the crossing of the Jordan, they would seem to apply to the immediately forthcoming battles. But Deuteronomy 20:15 emphatically denies this, introducing instead the law of holy war:

> Thus shalt thou do unto all the cities which are very far off from thee, which are not of the cities of these [seven Canaanite] nations. But of the cities of these people, which the Lord thy God doth give thee for an inheritance, thou shalt save alive nothing that breatheth: But thou shalt utterly destroy them . . . That they teach you not to do after all their abominations. (20:15–18)

The order of the verses is distinctly odd, suggesting, as Fishbane argues, "the addition of the law of *herem* to an older siege law," which had achieved sufficient authority so that it could not be dropped from the text. Perhaps the rules about captive women had a similar authority; or they may reflect the supposed feminism of the Deuteronomic authors, a little incongruous here, since respect for women would seem to depend on a prior respect for life itself. In any case, the qualifying clause about cities "very far off" is not repeated in chapter 21, leaving its rules radically inconsistent with 20:18.

So there is a law that fits the second version of the conquest, and another law, radically different, that fits the first. The uneasiness of the link between them is illustrated by the story of the Gibeonites, a Canaanite nation with which Israel signed a treaty of peace in accordance with the "older" law. The treaty must have been well known, and the Gibeonites still around or still remembered when the book of Joshua was written, for the authors feel compelled to explain this apparent disregard of the *herem* in the very time and place it was meant to apply. Their story is artful, if a little hard to believe. The Gibeonite elders, having apparently read the book of Deuteronomy, dress themselves in the clothing of travelers and claim to be from a far-off land. Joshua and the "princes of the congregation," without seeking an oracle from the "mouth of the Lord" or, for that matter, consulting their own scouts and spies about the location of Gibeon, "made a league with them, to let them live" (Joshua 9:15). "Using the biblical law so as to circumvent it," as Fishbane writes, the Gibeonites escape the *herem*.[9] The clear argument of the authors or editors of Joshua, good Deuteronomists writing long after the fact, is that this Canaanite nation, like all the others, should have been destroyed.

Looking back from the last years of the monarchy, the Deuteronomists insisted that all Israel's troubles had a single cause: the worship of Canaanite gods, the imitation of religious practices abhorrent to Yahweh. And the reason for this endlessly reiterated sin was the continued presence of Canaanites in the land and the sexual intermixing of the two peoples. Hence the invention of the totalizing *herem* was probably a retrospective response to the dangers of miscegenation. The doctrine presumably derives from some older practice—we have seen it described on the Moabite stone—in which the men and women, the animals, and even the material artifacts of conquered cities were sacrificed to the god of conquest. Traces of the idea of sacrifice can still be found in Deuteronomy (13:17), but its authors also provide an explicit rationale of an entirely different sort for the *herem*, making it something like a functional equivalent of the ban on intermarriage. When the two appear together, as in Deuteronomy 7:2–3, one or the other is superfluous. Had the Canaanites been exterminated, the anxiety about intermarriage would have had no object; had the ban on intermarriage worked, genocide would have had no religious purpose. That its purpose was religious, not ethnic or racial, is demonstrated by the law of the seduced city (13:12–17), which subjects Israelite idolaters to the same collective destruction as Canaanites. But the biblical texts do suggest a peculiar fear of alien women, the carriers of religious pollution. Canaanite wives beguile and bewitch their husbands and lure them into idol worship; the daughters

In God's Shadow

of Israel are, by contrast, so demure and chaste as to be incapable of similar behavior on behalf of Yahweh (see Deuteronomy 7:3–4, where the distinction is clear).

The *herem* is a possible policy in Deuteronomy because Israel, in Joshua's time and in Josiah's, six hundred years later, when the book was probably written, actually possessed an army capable of carrying it out—though Josiah's army must have been made up in large part of mercenaries, hence an unsuitable instrument for holy war. The literary prophets of the eighth and seventh centuries describe war in general as a divine enterprise. God will fight on Israel's behalf; the king's army is superfluous (see Chapter 6). By the time of Ezra and Nehemiah, after the return from Babylonia, there was no army at all; Israel had been radically demilitarized.

In truth, it had never exactly been militarized, at least in the biblical writers' view. Warrior heroes make virtually no appearance in the traditions of either total war or limited war, and the Bible does not celebrate the military virtues anywhere. Jonathan and the young David hint at an "alternative ideal," which makes in the end, as Oliver O'Donovan has written, "rather little headway in Israel."[10] Still, there was an army in Joshua's time and in the time of the kings; after the exile and until the rebellion of the Maccabees, there was not. And so the *herem* makes no appearance in post-exilic biblical texts; nor is there any talk of a new conquest modeled on the old one. Now the argument focuses narrowly on intermarriage. Ezra and Nehemiah and the writers we call the Chroniclers, who probably produced the books or the final version of the books that bear their names, were heavily influenced by Deuteronomy. But they had all given up, or been forced to give up, the fantasy of a genocidal solution to the problems they faced. Their goal was still the same, the holiness of Israel; it was now to be reached, however, by separation from the surrounding nations, not by a total war against them.

Of course, genocide wasn't a real option for the Deuteronomists either, for the Canaanites had been subjugated and absorbed by their time. Intermarriage, combined with political power, had in fact worked to produce a single nation that was more Israelite than Canaanite, though its religious practices were clearly syncretistic in character. As the prophets understood, it was no longer possible for a holy Israel to destroy an idolatrous Canaan. They were forced instead to summon up the unholy Assyrians and Babylonians to punish an idolatrous Israel. Fortunately, neither the Assyrians nor the Babylonians, cruel as they were (the Assyrians especially), were committed to the *herem.* How can we explain the commitment of the authors of Deuteronomy? Theirs was the radicalism of the writing desk, says Moshe Weinfeld in one of the best readings of Deuteronomy.[11] And there is some truth, I suppose, in Weinfeld's suggestion that the brutality of intellectuals is a function of their distance from actual political or military engagement (but we should remember that intellectual pacifism is commonly attributed to the same cause). In the seventh century, writes Max Weber, "just as today, in all countries, we find the highest measure of war thirst among those strata of literati who are farthest from the trenches and by nature least military."[12] The kings of Israel, by contrast, though they fought many wars, did not favor holy war.

This argument merely pushes the problem away, inviting us to distance ourselves from these distant and ineffectively fierce literati (who are, in so many other ways, very close to us). It seems better to acknowledge the power of the Deuteronomic writers and to confront their political/religious ideas more directly. The book of Deuteronomy works out in considerable detail a view of Israel as a "holy people," a community of "brethren." Its steady tendency is to intensify the closeness and mutual commitment of the people. Hierarchy is minimized (relative, at least, to the priestly writings), and religious obligations are imposed more equally on all Israelites. Women are incorporated more fully into the community; they participate in the covenantal ceremonies (whereas in Exodus 19:15 the men of Israel are commanded to avoid all contact with women for three days before the Sinai covenanting: "Come not at your wives"), and women also, apparently, join the festal pilgrimages to Jerusalem. The authors of Deuteronomy express a heightened concern for the weaker members of the community, and the social and economic practices they design are clearly intended to minimize the cruelties of class. Even the sacrificial system is reconceptualized, Weinfeld argues, so that it might serve welfarist ends: "The constant emphasis on the obligation to share the sacrificial repast with indigent persons creates the impression that the principal purpose of the offering is to provide nutriment for the destitute elements of Israelite society."[13]

This provision is extended to the stranger (*ger*, meaning "resident alien," not "foreigner"), as well as to widows, orphans, poor people generally, and the landless Levites. But the emphasis of the text is on the internal obligations of the covenantal-kinship community: "Thou shalt open thine hand wide unto thy brother, to thy poor, and to thy needy, in thy land" (Deuteronomy 15:11). The possessive pronoun is important here (see also Deuteronomy 24:14: "thy strangers . . . within thy gates"), as is the word "brother," repeated again and again—fifty or more times in the book of Deuteronomy, only nineteen times in Leviticus. It is important, too, that the laws of ritual purity (holiness) are imposed only on brethren in Deuteronomy, though Leviticus requires purity of anyone living in the holy land. All this together makes for an intensity of connection that is missing in other biblical texts. The intensity is largely notional, no doubt, given the civil wars described in the book of Judges, the later division of the kingdom, and the social conflicts to which the prophets testify. But it provides the background necessary for any understanding of Deuteronomic warfare.

Holy community and holy war are related ideas—not necessarily because holiness makes for hostility toward foreign nations, more probably because community does. The relation is not essential, only persistent. Holiness might well have similar effects. But a holy people could aim (as we shall see) to convert and incorporate foreign nations; tightly bound communities, by contrast, commonly resist expansion of this sort, which might dilute their brotherhood. "By uniting with some men," wrote Jean-Jacques Rousseau, "we become the enemies of mankind."[14] The stronger the union, the greater the enmity. Rousseau dealt with this problem—it *is* a problem, though never recognized as such in Deuteronomy—by imposing a radical separatism upon his republic. He would have banned commerce with foreign nations and travel abroad, thus making marriage out of the political community highly unlikely. His ideas about education are strikingly reminiscent of Deuteronomy 6:7, which requires a "diligent" and virtually full-time teaching of Israel's history and laws. "I wish," Rousseau writes in his *Government of Poland*, "that when [a child] learns to read, he should read about his own land . . . that at fifteen, he should know its whole history, at sixteen all its laws."[15] Hardly anything more needs to be known or taught. The world outside is a great temptation, and since Rousseau doesn't want to wage war against it, he recommends isolation and ignorance instead.

These last were not options for Israel at the time to which Deuteronomy refers—nor realistic options even in Ezra's time, when something like Rousseau's program was actually proposed. Hence the holy war, which aimed to remove or exterminate the Canaanites before they corrupted the holy nation. The aim was retrospective, after centuries of corruption, first in the age of the judges who fought what were mostly unholy wars against Israel's new neighbors and also married their daughters (Samson is the classic example), and then in the age of the kings, who seem, most of them, to have systematically copied the religious practices of the Canaanites. The books of Judges, Samuel, and Kings have little to say about the holiness of Israel or about the brotherly bonds that hold the community together. What they report about the common life is often unattractive, so they provide a realistic background for the Deuteronomic reform program. But their authors (or the authors of the tales and chronicles out of which the histories were composed) were capable, as the authors of Deuteronomy were not, of a wholly nonideological view of warfare, as in the account of the wars with Aram (see Chapter 4). The most interesting example comes from Judges, and since it is also the last of the Bible's conquest narratives, it makes for a nice conclusion here.

According to Judges 18, the tribe of Dan had failed to establish itself in the portion of the land originally assigned to it by Joshua. So the Danites send out scouts in search of a new place, and the scouts find a Canaanite people living in and around Laish: a peaceful people, without hereditary rulers (in this regard, like the Israelites) and without close ties to neighbors. The scouts report back, and the Danites organize a war party of six hundred men—a more likely number than any other in the exodus and conquest narratives; the whole story has a realistic air. The outcome is briefly told: they "came unto Laish, unto a people that were at quiet and secure: and they smote them with the edge of the sword, and burnt the city with fire. And there was no deliverer" (18:27–28). The author of these lines, Martin Buber suggests, intended to make a pro-monarchic argument: "A people without a king plunders; a people without a king is plundered."[16] That may well be right, but to make this argument, he had to adopt a critical attitude toward the first people (his own) and a sympathetic attitude toward the second (his enemy). The Deuteronomic writers, for reasons we should worry about, were incapable of either the criticism or the sympathy.

FOUR

∞

The Rule of Kings

The biblical account of the history of Israel is marked by two radical disjunctions. It begins as family history, with Abraham, Isaac, and Jacob, their wives and concubines, their sons and daughters. Familial conflict is its first theme: Abraham's break with his father, Sarah's quarrel with Hagar, the struggle of Jacob and Esau, the rivalry and then the reconciliation of Joseph and his brothers, and much else that might be counted as domestic politics. What is at issue is birthright and inheritance, divine and patriarchal favor, the local and immediate forms of power. Then, as a result of Egyptian oppression, the focus shifts to the history of a people. Its leaders—Moses, Aaron, Joshua, and the successive judges—have families, no doubt, but we are told very little about them. Moses' children are never considered as possible heirs; the Aaronite priesthood passes to Eleazar and Phinehas without any interesting familial intrigues (the killing of Nadab and Abihu in Leviticus 10 is extrafamilial). Joshua's children are never mentioned; none of the judges makes any effort to pass on his or her power. Does Deborah have sons or daughters? We know only the name of her husband. Now political struggle within Israel takes place between rival leaders and would-be leaders like Moses and Korah, who are not related to one another except as Israelites, and among the recalcitrant tribes, whose members are joined by covenant and only distantly by blood. A mostly undifferentiated but powerfully present people murmur against their leaders, turn again and again to idol worship, reaffirm their faith on solemn occasions.

Then the focus shifts again, back to family history. This time the families are dynasties or would-be dynasties, but the conflicts are the same as before: sibling rivalries, the intrigues of wives and concubines, the struggle for an inheritance that is now also a royal succession. Kingship recapitulates patriarchalism (except for the usurper Athaliah [2 Kings 11], Israel had no queens).[1] The people fade into the distance; they are courted sometimes by ambitious princes (like Absalom), but mostly they appear only after the succession has been decided, to hail the victor. The king is accompanied by military commanders and political advisors, who figure significantly but always secondarily in his story; they are the rough equivalents of the patriarch's family servants and retainers. Our attention is focused in both cases on the household.

This focus makes for a certain practical and tough-minded realism. Gideon, Samson, and Deborah are legendary heroes. But David, who slew the giant Goliath and became the greatest of Israel's kings, is at the same time a fully realized literary-historical character, human, all too human. We see him castigated by his wife Michal, seducing or seduced by Bathsheba, conniving at the death of Uriah, unable to respond to the rape of his daughter Tamar, desolated by the death of Absalom. In David's story as it is told in Second Samuel, there is no hint of the conventional magnifications of monarchy: no mysteries of state, no divine descent, no royal magic, no healing touch. His unhappy family is like a thousand others, except that its unhappiness is publicly acted out—without a script but on a stage, and with a historian standing in the wings to record the action. The action has wide-reaching effects, but its focus is always familial. In royal as in patriarchal households, birthright and succession are at stake. Gideon, Samson, and Deborah have no heirs. But it is David's whole purpose, as it was Saul's, to establish a throne upon which his son can sit. Families aim at continuity; parents labor for their children's sake (though some of the children, like Absalom, are impatient for the labor's end). Here, too, David is ordinary enough, and Moses and Joshua, who labored for the nation, are decidedly unusual. Why should *this* family rule over all Israel?

The transition from judges to kings, charismatic individuals to royal fathers of families, is historically contested. The origins of the contest, or of the arguments used in the contest, extend far back in time, to the very beginning of Israel's national history, to the Egyptian oppression: for wasn't Pharaoh a king and the escape from Egypt a liberation from royal servitude? But the arguments also have a more immediate origin in the centuries between the exodus or, better, the conquest, and the establishment of the monarchy, centuries when "there was no king in Israel [and] every man did that which was right in his own eyes" (Judges 21:25). Why should these Israelite men, free to choose what was right, who never served Moses or Joshua or any of the judges, become the subjects and servants of Saul's or David's household?

Israel before its kings is often described as a tribal confederation, on the model of a Greek amphictyony. In a style characteristic of much biblical scholarship, Martin Noth writes that "undoubtedly, a fixed constitution existed" and insists that "the Israelite twelve-tribe confederacy . . . conducted its affairs according to regular rites and according to prescribed forms of conduct."[2] Maybe so, but we know from the accounts in the book of Judges how rarely the various tribes acknowledged their connection and fought together against a common enemy; the last war described in the book, and the bloodiest, is a civil war. There is painfully little evidence of regular rites or prescribed forms. The only thing that is undoubtedly true about the "constitution" of the confederacy is its doubtfulness.

Israel is also a covenantal community or, following the book of Joshua, an association of heads of families, bound by a kind of treaty to God and one another. "Choose you this day [which gods] ye will serve," Joshua tells the elders, commanders, magistrates, and officers assembled at Shechem, "but as for me and my house, we will serve the Lord" (Joshua 24:15). The other houses are immediately pledged to the same service, and this covenant seems to provide the underlying—now broken, now renewed—unity of the confederation. Political rule is radically decentralized and intermittent even in its local manifestations. God is the only center. When there were no kings in Israel, God was king.

This period of Israel's history—when no family was singled out, chosen by God or men to be dominant over all the others—is remembered in the Bible as an age of heroes, but also as a dangerous, even chaotic, time. The successive chiefs/judges/commanders don't seem to have occupied anything that could be called an institutionalized office; titles change, individuals come and go; there are no authorized successions; even the priesthood, supposedly hereditary, is subject, as the example of Eli and his sons indicates, to divine disposition. "During the confederacy," Weber writes, "there was only the intermittent, varying sway of the charismatic war heroes"—each one "raised up," as the Bible tells us, by God.[3] That the tribal confederation and the covenant of family heads survived for two hundred years with leadership of this sort is testimony to divine favor or rare good luck. In fact, the kingship of God over Israel coincided with the eclipse of empire in Egypt and Assyria. According to the biblical histories, a politically decentered Israel faced only local enemies. But one of these, the Philistines, finally succeeded in dominating most of the hill country that the Israelites had conquered, or infiltrated, two centuries earlier. Philistine triumph and the disunity of Israel's tribes brought on the crisis out of which monarchy emerged.

The story is told in the first book of Samuel, chapter 8, and it is a famous story—the beginning, we might say, of the age-long debate over the virtues of kingly rule. There is no written evidence of any similar debate in Egypt or Mesopotamia or in the cities of the Canaanites or the Philistines. Even the Greek discussions about the best regime lie far in the future. In all the countries of the ancient Near East, monarchy is regarded as the divine and natural form of government; the king is a god or a deputy or servant of the gods, connecting politics to nature, the state to the cosmos, ensuring the fertility of the fields and the reproduction of humankind. Now, sometime around the year 1000 BCE, the elders of Israel come to Samuel, the established judge and seer, and ask him to "make us a king to judge us like all the nations" (8:5) and to lead Israel in battle. The request is impossible in this important sense: the fact that the people imagine a king being made at their instance means that he can't be a king like the kings of all the other nations. And Samuel demonstrates how different the making of this king will be by disputing the request.

Both the request and the dispute have a precedent. In Judges 8:22–23, "the men of Israel" come to Gideon, who has just led them in a successful war against the Midianites, and say, "Rule thou over us, both thou and thy son, and thy son's son also." Kingship is not mentioned here, but the emphasis on the succession makes the point. As it is understood in Israel, kingship is the successive rule of fathers and sons; the contrasting regime is the intermittent rule of leaders unrelated by blood, representatives of an eternal God. Gideon's response affirms the contrast: "I will not rule over you, neither shall my son rule over you: The Lord shall rule over you." His words remind the "men of Israel" of the commitment that makes them Israelites; Gideon addresses them as men of the covenant.

Samuel might have responded in the same way had he himself been asked to become king. Faced with the more impersonal request for a new political regime, he attempts what is perhaps a more politic, certainly a more pragmatic and secular, response. He addresses the elders as fathers of families and describes to them the consequences of submitting themselves to the father of a particular family. He will take your sons and daughters into his service, Samuel says, "and appoint them for himself . . . to be his horsemen . . . [to] run before his chariots . . . to reap his harvest . . . to make his instruments of war . . . to be cooks and . . . bakers." And he will tax you for his own benefit, seizing "your fields, and your vineyards, and your oliveyards, even the best of them." "And ye shall be his servants"—as you were the servants of Pharaoh, before you became servants of God, free among your fellow men (8:11–18). But the elders are not persuaded; freedom is too dangerous; they want a ruler in their own image, and they are willing to pay the price and allow one household, initially like all the others, to become a royal court.

It isn't that they think, naively, that the king won't behave as Samuel suggests. Saul and David are, after all, men like themselves, and the extraordinarily realistic account of the successive royal courts was written, presumably, with Israel's elders in mind. In a sense, the rabbis were right, centuries later, when they declared (in the name of a later Samuel, one of the leaders of Babylonian Jewry), "All that is set out in the chapter of a king, he is permitted to do" (BT Sanhedrin 20b). The people have been warned, and they or their representatives have agreed; therefore the behavior predicted by Samuel is permissible, even though neither Samuel nor the God with whom he speaks believe that it is necessary. "The Holy One said to Israel: My children, I endeavored that you be free of the monarchy."[4] The elders had a different plan, but that doesn't mean that they intended to enslave themselves to the kings into whose service they had voluntarily entered. They did not accept Samuel's arguments, but they were as protective of their households as he thought them to be. When Solomon conscripted too many of their children, turning the royal corvée into something like a *levée en mass*, he put his succession at risk. Representatives of the northern tribes now bargained with his heir, Rehoboam, demanding that he promise to "make the grievous service of thy father, and his heavy yoke which he put upon us, lighter." And when Rehoboam refused, the many households of Israel deserted the royal household, repeating the battle cry of an earlier rebellion: "What portion have we in David? neither have we inheritance in the son of Jesse: to your tents, O Israel: now see to thine own house, David" (1 Kings 12:16). The northerners turned to Jeroboam, who had been one of Solomon's officials, "and called him unto the congregation and made him king over all Israel." They *made him king*, as if to say that they would serve him only so long as he served them.

We may take the Deuteronomic law of kings (which derives, some scholars think, from the northern kingdom) as a kind of fallout from the debate that Samuel began and from the rebellion that was its practical expression. The text (Deuteronomy 17:14–20) is in no sense a theoretical statement, but it is nonetheless a reflection upon Samuel's warnings and Solomon's oppressive policies. It recounts the initial request of the elders, permits (some say, commands) the setting up of a monarchic regime, and establishes a set of limits on kingly rule designed perhaps to rule out "grievous service" and "heavy yokes"—though there is no direct reference to the corvée. "But he shall not multiply horses to himself . . . Neither shall he multiply wives to himself . . . neither shall he greatly multiply to himself silver and gold . . . That his heart be not lifted above his brethren." In other words, the king is not to expand his household or increase his power or wealth—this is the reading of the rabbis of the talmudic period—beyond what is absolutely necessary for the performance of his duties.[5]

The reiterated phrase "to himself" suggests that what is at issue here is personal and dynastic aggrandizement. The authors of Deuteronomy want a king who will, when necessary, lead Israel into battle— *and do nothing more.* Perhaps they mean to repudiate imperial warfare ("horses" stands in here for chariots), though that is by no means certain from the Deuteronomic text as a whole. More likely, they mean to deny the king anything like a Praetorian guard. They are not all that different from the elders who came to Samuel, but they write after the experience of actual kings and their mercenaries. The medieval commentator Nahmanides probably captures their meaning: "You will set a king over you like all the nations that surround you—only he should not be like their kings . . . for the main desire of kings is to increase horses and horsemen for themselves."[6]

Chapters 17 and 18 of Deuteronomy read something like a constitutional text, and it is notable that they treat the judicial function as separate from the monarchy.[7] The elders had asked for a king to "judge us" as well as to "fight our battles" (1 Samuel 8:20), but nothing is said in Deuteronomy about the king sitting in judgment (as Solomon, for example, famously did) or appointing judges. Adjudication is centralized in Jerusalem. When the elders "within thy gates" are unable to decide a case, because the "matter [is] too hard," they are to go up into

> the place which the Lord thy God shall choose; And thou shalt come unto the priests the Levites, and unto the judge that shall be in those days, and enquire; and they shall shew thee the sentence of judgment. (17:8–9)

The king is unmentioned here, but no one else is given the task of choosing the "judge that shall be in those days." So this is an incomplete constitution, and exactly how constrained the king is remains unclear.

Nor is it clear, as I have already suggested, that the Deuteronomic historians regarded Deuteronomy 17–18 as a constitutional text. The sole biblical reference back to this text comes in the account of Solomon's reign (but the reference may work the other way), which deals explicitly but not always critically with horses, wives, and silver and gold. Though Solomon "had forty thousand stalls of horses for his chariots, and twelve thousand horsemen" (1 Kings 4:26), he is actually praised for his military prowess, since it made for peace: "And Judah and Israel dwelt safely, every man under his vine and under his fig tree . . . all the days of Solomon" (25). Solomon also acquired great wealth, but not only "to himself": "The king made silver to be in Jerusalem as stones" (10:27). These two passages are clearly not critical. Solomon is condemned because he "loved many strange [foreign] women" and took many wives, who "turned away his heart after other gods" (11:1–4). He is also criticized, though only after his death, for the "heavy yoke" that he laid upon the people (12:4)—which might be taken as a violation of the closing injunction in Deuteronomy that the king should not lift his heart above his brethren (which NJPS translates as "act haughtily toward his fellows").

But in the rest of the Deuteronomic histories, covering some three hundred years of monarchic rule, kings are criticized only for religious failings—never because they built too large an army (acquired too many horses and chariots), or amassed too much wealth, or lifted their hearts (or acted haughtily). Perhaps the Deuteronomic text was meant to be authoritative, but in practice, even in the practice of historical judgment, it seems to have had no authority. The writers of the historical books are monarchists but, not in any obvious way, constitutional monarchists. Nonetheless, the passages in First Samuel and Deuteronomy provide a distinctive view of kingship—and, over the long history of monarchic government, an unusual view.

The king's household is raised above the other households, but his heart is not. He is in his person no different from any other Israelite; his elevation, such as it is, is purely practical and instrumental. "The relation between the Hebrew monarch and his people," writes Henri Frankfort, "was as nearly secular as is possible in a society wherein religion is a living force."[8] Indeed, the argument that I have just rehearsed is entirely secular, but it is shadowed by two religious arguments, one rejecting and the other exalting monarchic rule. I have set these two aside for the moment in order to stress the most remarkable feature of Israelite kingship, which is a negative feature: the absence of cosmological significance. The king is a human artifact, made by the people for their own purposes: that's why awe and reverence are absent from First Samuel.

In God's Shadow

"The Hebrews knew that they had introduced kingship on their own initiative . . . and under the strain of emergency"—as a political solution to political problems.[9] I will come back to this point later on. Despite the desire for likeness, this regime is unlike that of Israel's neighbors.

Many Israelites, beginning with Samuel himself, aspired to a regime even more radically unlike "all the nations." Resistance to kingship did not come only from people like the northern tribal representatives, worrying about their sons and daughters; nor was it only secular in its reasons. The more radical resistance came from Israelites who felt that only God should rule in Israel. Their central claim is put by God himself. "They have not rejected thee," he tells Samuel, "but they have rejected me, that I should not reign over them" (1 Samuel 8:7). In fact, the two rejections are simultaneous and identical; God's rule can be overthrown only by overthrowing his designated agents; and whenever his agents are overthrown, so is he. Israel had been and, Samuel thought, should have remained a kingdom of God, ruled by men and women who were God's servants and nothing more, solitary figures without significant family ties, "raised up" only for a time. This is apparently a minority position among Samuel's contemporaries and for the next four or five centuries; it is not revived until a wholly new understanding of divine service is worked out, first among the priests after the Babylonian exile and then among the sages after the destruction of the temple. In the monarchic period, we find the theocratic view directly expressed only occasionally, by one or another of the prophets. "They have set up kings," says Hosea in God's name, "but not by me" (8:4).

To capture the meaning of the kingship of God is not easy. This is a regime without archives; we have stories, like the Samson stories, which read very much like folktales, but we have no official records, no court chronicles. In practice, God's rule made for decentralized government; according to the kings and their scribes, it made for anarchy: "every man did that which was right in his own eyes." I quoted that line earlier as a description of the pre-monarchic regime; it was no doubt intended as an indictment. And yet the picture presented in the book of Judges is not, until the end at least, wholly unattractive.[10] A community of covenanted men, heads of families, peers, responsible for their own conduct, subject to divine intervention at critical moments, otherwise left to their own devices—this could as easily be utopian as dystopian. But the collected stories are too brutal, the civil war at the end too bloody, to serve the purposes of idealization. When the prophets want to contrast their own (monarchic) moment with an earlier time, they choose the rule of God through Moses, the wilderness period, rather than the period of the judges. "There was no king in Israel" then either (Moses is called a prophet in Deuteronomy), but divine rule was more steady, divine intervention less sporadic; and though Moses was often opposed, anarchy was not his or Israel's problem.

Nonetheless, the transition from judges to kings is remembered as a rejection of God. Despite the work of royal scribes, there survives in the biblical text an account not only of the elders' request for a king but also of Samuel's condemnation of the request—and even of the elders' later acknowledgment that they had added to all their previous sins "this evil, to ask us a king" (1 Samuel 12:19). The idea that God's rule is better than the rule of kings survives the highly problematic experience of divine governance and reappears, again and again, in Israel's history. This survival probably accounts for the failure of monarchy to achieve cosmological status. Kings may serve human purposes—perhaps even human necessities—but they are only dubiously servants of God. At least, this is one of Israel's political traditions. There is, of course, another tradition, assiduously cultivated by the kings themselves, immensely popular, with a long post-monarchic afterlife, according to which kings are indeed God's servants and even something more.

The high theory of monarchy is probably the work of scribes/priests/ prophets (we know neither the names nor the social roles) attached to

Solomon's or some later king's court. The theory is read back to the time of David, but the biblical historians suggest that whatever David's own ideas, his presentation of himself as king was cautious and, relative to his son's, unpretentious. Though picked out by God and anointed by Samuel, he was also confirmed and anointed again by the elders: "So all the elders of Israel came to . . . Hebron; and king David [he was already king over Judah, his own tribe] made a league with them in Hebron before the Lord: and they anointed David king over Israel" (2 Samuel 5:3). Covenanted with the elders, he was bound by their traditions—hence, probably, his inability to build a temple in Jerusalem, his new capital city. The God of the old covenant had never dwelt in a "house"—so the prophet Nathan tells David—nor had he ever asked the judges of Israel to build him a house; rather, he had "walked in a tent and in a tabernacle" (2 Samuel 7:5–6). The portable ark that held the Torah was the most important religious symbol of the decentralized kingship of God, and it is hard not to believe, as Frank Cross has written, that "the insistence on this old symbolism . . . was directed against the Canaanite ideology of kingship . . . which developed immediately . . . with the building of the Temple."[11]

The opposition isn't only symbolic. The wilderness tabernacle had been built with gifts from the people—from "whosoever is of a willing heart" (Exodus 35:5). So many people were willing that Moses had to call a halt to the gift-giving: "the people bring much more than enough for the service of the work" (36:5). The twice-repeated account of the construction emphasizes its popular character. Though Bezalel is "singled out" by God to lead the work, he is accompanied by "every one whose heart stirred him up" (36:2). By contrast, when it came to building the temple, "Solomon raised a levy out of all Israel" (1 Kings 5:13; NJPS: "imposed forced labor on all Israel."). This is the corvée that Samuel warned the people against, which led eventually to the northern secession. We see here, very concretely, what it meant to have a king like all the other kings. This kind of kingship might be justified in practical terms, but it needed a more ideological justification, and the necessary ideology was taken, Cross suggests, from Israel's Canaanite neighbors.

But Canaanite ideology had to be mediated by a new version of Israelite ideology; the high theory of monarchy had to be naturalized into the covenantal tradition, a process that set limits on the full development of a Canaanite royalism in Israel. The crucial mediating idea was the covenant itself, which was now transformed from a conditional pact between God and the people of Israel to an unconditional pact between God and the house of David. This transformation is the subject of lively scholarly debate and I shall offer only a simplified account, more controversial than I shall acknowledge as I go along.[12] The debate is sustained by disputed readings of obscure passages in a much-edited text; it has no foreseeable conclusion. I shall follow the scholars who argue that conditionality is the earlier idea. The Sinai covenant has the form of an if-then mutualism; if you keep my commandments, God tells Israel, then you will live in peace and prosperity in the land to which I will bring you; and if not, not. This conditionality is then acted out: the people fail to keep the commandments, and God punishes them, sometimes directly with fire and plague, more often indirectly, with military defeat. But he does not abandon them; after every episode of transgression and punishment, the old relationship is restored. So, at least, goes the account in the history books (Judges, Samuel, Kings), and it suggests that early on, some notion of a permanent tie, eternal divine love for Israel, must have come to figure in the covenantal tradition. But the emphasis (visible in Deuteronomy, for example, with its blessings and curses) was on conditionality.

Solomon's servants, or some later king's, discover or invent an alternative tradition. Appropriately, they trace this tradition back to Abraham rather than to Moses, for they mean to describe a covenant in which the people or nation has only a secondary role, first place being assigned to patriarchs and kings. What God promises now is less importantly peace and prosperity for Israel than an endless succession, heir after heir, for Abraham and David. There is still a shadow of the old conditionality, but the emphasis has changed. We see it in the promise to David set forth in one of the royal psalms, number 89, probably written to be sung or chanted in Solomon's, or some later king's, temple:

> I will set his hand also in the sea
>> and his right hand in the rivers . . .
> I will make him my firstborn,
>> higher than the kings of the earth.
> My mercy will I keep for him for evermore,
>> and my covenant shall stand fast with him.
> His seed also will I make to endure for ever,
>> and his throne as the days of heaven.
> If his children forsake my law,
>> and walk not in my judgments;
> If they break my statutes,
>> and keep not my commandments;
> Then will I visit their transgression with the rod,
>> and their iniquity with stripes.
> Nevertheless my lovingkindness will I not utterly take from him,
>> nor will I suffer my faithfulness to fail.
> My covenant will I not break,
>> nor alter the thing that is gone out of my lips . . .
> His seed shall endure for ever,
>> and his throne as the sun before me.
> It shall be established forever as the moon,
>> and as a faithful witness in heaven.[13]

This claim is very strong indeed, and it is further strengthened by the witness of sun and moon, deities to Israel's neighbors, though the Psalmist is careful to avoid implications of divinity here. His treatment of other Canaanite themes is similar, trespassing cautiously on alien and forbidden ground. "I will set his hand also in the sea / and his right hand in the rivers" suggests without quite saying it that the gods of sea and rivers have been defeated by the Lord's anointed. "I will make him my first-born" names David and then Solomon divine sons—but only by adoption. Another psalm is more forthright:

> The Lord hath said unto me, Thou art my son; this day have I begotten thee. (2:7)

Even these lines claim only a post hoc fathering, divine sonship without direct divine descent, but the meaning is clear enough: all the other men of Israel are merely the fathers of their own sons; the king is the son of a heavenly father. These claims embellish the covenantal relationship without entirely replacing it. Embellished in this way, however, the covenant and the monarchy it establishes take on a radically new character.

The king's family is still central (though Solomon succeeds in escaping or repressing any realistic familial history: despite his many wives, we have no account of domestic intrigue in his household). But the king's family is no longer one family among many. It now replaces the others in at least this sense: Israel's history is mediated through it alone. Insofar as the high theory of monarchy is successful, the king stands in for the people, who suffer for his sins and are, more rarely, rewarded for his righteousness. When the prophets castigate the people as a whole, they are abandoning the high theory; when the author or final editor of Kings focuses narrowly on the sins of Manasseh, he is writing the high theory into the historical record. But he writes with the assurance that even a very bad king, if he is David's heir, will have heirs of his own to whom God will remain committed.

We can best grasp the full meaning of the new doctrine if we look again at the Deuteronomic law of kings. Deuteronomy presumably is later than the psalms I have quoted, but it probably represents, as I have argued, the view of the Israelite elders who first asked for a king and of those other elders who deposed Rehoboam and set Jeroboam on Solomon's throne (and insisted that David was only the "son of Jesse"). The account of the law ends with a statement of its purpose: "That he turn not aside from the commandment to the right hand, or to the left: to the end that he may prolong his days in his kingdom, he, and his children, in the midst of Israel" (Deuteronomy 17:20). This is no promise of prolonged days, only a hope and a program. The medieval commentator Rashi is certainly right to see here the old if-then argument: "From the positive statement," he writes, "you may derive the negative, and so indeed do we find in the case of Saul." On this view, there can't be a guaranteed succession, for each king will be judged by his own performance. The high theory of monarchy also holds that David's heirs will be judged—and even chastised with plagues and wars. Indeed, Psalm 89, quoted above, ends with the plea of a king who has been "cast off and abhorred" that God remember "thy former lovingkindnesses, which thou swarest unto David in thy truth." But the succession is still said to be eternal. Each individual king partakes in the mystery of permanence, divine favor, adoptive sonship, mythic triumph.

What happens when the succession fails? The seizure of King Jehoiachin by the Babylonians in 597 and the deposing, blinding, and exile of Zedekiah, whom they had set in his place, brings the Davidic dynasty to an end. After that, God's steadfast love for the house of David is nowhere in evidence. Zerubbabel may have harbored hopes for a restoration after the return from Babylonia; if he did, his hopes were in vain; he seems to have had a hand in the rebuilding of the temple, and then, abruptly and without explanation, he disappears from the historical record. The next kings of Israel were from another family and ruled without the support of a divine covenant. They were kings in the Hellenistic rather than the Canaanite style, but did not dare attempt the Hellenistic version of mythic embellishment.

David's line lived on in Israel's imagination, however, and eventually the high theory of monarchy found expression in one of the versions of prophetic messianism. How this came about I cannot try to explain here. It is enough to say that messianism is the heir of mythic kingship, just as the messiah himself will be the heir of the house of David, the adopted son (or, among Christians, the actual son) of God. For many centuries, Israel's political hopes were focused on this figure, who would come in God's time, in the fulfillment of his promise. There were occasional attempts to force the end, to impose a messianic regime (perhaps a failed attempt accounts for Zerubbabel's disappearance). But messianism is, most of the time, a politics of passivity and postponement, as Gershom Scholem has argued—an apolitical politics (see Chapter 10). With the advent of the monarchy, the royal household replaced the people as the carrier of Israel's history; in the afterlife of monarchy, the people wait for the miraculous return of the heir of David's house.

An apolitical ending, however, is not the whole story of Israelite kingship, for it can also be said that the critical moment when the elders come to Samuel and demand a king is the dawn of politics or of political understanding in Israel. The doctrine of God's earthly kingdom, like later messianism, is an apolitical doctrine: it denies autonomy to political actors. If we think of politics as a form of human coping with the problems of individual and group coexistence, then Israel's politics had been preempted, as it were, by God himself, who supplied judges to the people and fought directly on their behalf. If "the Lord is a man of war" (Exodus 15:3), what need is there for more ordinary men of war? The reduction of Gideon's army to a tiny band is designed to make this point—"lest Israel vaunt themselves against me, saying, Mine own hand hath saved me" (Judges 7:2).

To be saved by God's hand is undoubtedly a sign of favor. But it also represents a loss of political control. And how can Israel depend on divine assistance when it stands so often in violation of divine law? In any case, God's interventions are intermittent and long delayed; he waits until the last possible minute. What the elders ask of Samuel is a different kind of government, visibly embodied in a king, institutionalized in a royal court and army, stabilized through hereditary succession. The vesting of authority in one family is at the same time a collective seizure of power—from God himself!—and a replacement of charisma by politics, or, since kings are ritually anointed, a political routinization of charismatic rule. The result is a special kind of normality, man-made rather than natural or divine, subject therefore to an ongoing critique, but normal nonetheless: Israel's kings face the same realities as other kings, and unlike God, they must attempt some reasonable accommodation.

Henceforth God's interests are represented by his prophets, while the full and often contradictory set of human interests—personal, dynastic, and national—is represented by the king. Prophecy is born together with monarchy lest divine law have no voice in the world. This double birth sets up the central conflict of the new regime, usually construed, following the argument of the Deuteronomic historians, as a conflict between royal immorality and prophetic admonition. The conflict takes exactly this form in the famous cases of David and Uriah, and Ahab and Naboth. The prophet facing down the king, the king obviously in the wrong, penitent (like David) or irrevocably condemned (like Ahab): this is what we have been taught to expect from prophets and kings. Prophecy is at war with personal wrongdoing, later on with social wrongdoing. But prophecy is also at war with politics itself—not only when politics is a form of self-aggrandizement but also when it is a form of self-reliance and self-help.

The clearest examples of this latter opposition come from the experience of war. The elders wanted a king to "go out before us, and fight our battles" (1 Samuel 8:20). But it is also the responsibility of kings to avoid battles when that is possible and to make peace when battles end. The earliest conflict of king and prophet is brought on by Saul's refusal to kill the Amalekite ruler Agag after a successful war (15:8–30). Here Samuel, in the role of prophet, upholds the laws of holy war—which, since they require the extermination of the enemy, will not seem to many of us the proper subject of prophetic advocacy. Saul opposes the holy war for reasons that remain obscure until the opposition is repeated by

Ahab in a war against the Syrians (Aram). Ahab's position is clear: he spares the Syrian king and his people for the sake of peace. He calls King Ben-hadad "brother," and as soon as the battle is over, the two kings enter into negotiations:

> And Ben-haded said unto him, The cities, which my father took from thy father, I will restore; and thou shalt make streets [markets] for thee in Damascus, as my father made in Samaria. Then said Ahab, I will send thee away with this covenant. So he made a covenant with him, and sent him away. (1 Kings 20:34)

An unnamed prophet condemns this sensible behavior, claiming that God had "appointed" the Syrians "to utter destruction" (20:42). Ahab has a better idea. Acknowledging that Israel had not been destroyed by Ben-hadad's father, he seeks only a limited victory over the son. This is the politics of accommodation, and it represents the triumph of the elders who came to Samuel: Israel is indeed a nation "like other nations" when its kings call other kings "brother."[14]

So monarchy is a form of normal politics, whereas the prophets defend an abnormal politics that is sometimes admirable and sometimes not. The opposition is reenacted again and again. When Solomon marries "strange women"—that is, the daughters of foreign princes—builds them temples and shrines, and permits them to "burn incense and sacrifice unto their gods" (1 Kings 11:8), he is neither defending religious toleration nor advocating idol worship. He has no ideological intentions at all; he is simply pursuing what must, again, have seemed a sensible and was certainly a conventional foreign policy, aimed at peace with his neighbors. But he is condemned by the prophets and, as we have seen, by the Deuteronomic historians. Similarly, when the last kings of Israel, a motley crew of usurpers and murderers, seek alliances with Egypt or Assyria, they are acting as the weak must act in the company of the strong. Every actual alliance entailed risks, no doubt, but it was hardly foolish to think that the risks of relying on divine intervention, as several of the prophets demanded (see Chapter 6), were even greater—and not only because of the moral character of these particular kings. Necessity must be served, and kings are appointed for just that service.

That kings defend politics against divine law is likely to seem to us a Machiavellian idea, the product of religious (and perhaps moral) skepticism. It is in fact a biblical idea, and if it is reported in negative terms, from the side of the law and not of the king who breaks the law, there is nonetheless some grudging recognition of its realism. That is the upshot, surely, of the argument in First Samuel as it has come down to us: that kings have their purpose and value even though they are likely to behave badly. The biblical authors and editors hope at the same time, of course, for a perfect king (David is the model despite his imperfections), who will not resist but enact the law. In Deuteronomy 17, the king is commanded to write out for himself a copy of the law and "to read therein all the days of his life." The covenant between king and God is meant to sustain this commitment: the king promises to keep the divine statutes, *to do them.* But the king is also covenanted with the people, on at least one of the Israelite understandings of kingship, and the implicit law of this covenant is *salus populi suprema lex.*

That last formula has no biblical equivalent that I know of, though there is among the biblical authors and editors some sense of possible tensions between popular well-being and divine command. Within the Jewish tradition, an explicit argument along these lines comes only much later, from medieval rabbis and commentators. One of the most astute and politically sophisticated of these is Nissim Gerondi, who lived and wrote in fourteenth-century Spain. I want to look very briefly at his account of biblical kingship, which reflects a very different political experience but is not, it seems to me, wholly anachronistic. In Gerondi's view, God's laws, as delivered to Moses at Sinai, constitute a "perfect" legal system; they make for "absolute justice." But this kind of perfection is often at odds with the requirements of normal human life, that is, with "social and political order." Judges like Samuel are required to act in accordance with the law, to further, so to speak, God's cause "whether or not the ordering of . . . society has been accomplished." Strangely (or perhaps not), gentile laws often prove "more pertinent" to social order "than some of the laws found in the Torah." Kingship was instituted, by God as by the elders, to remedy this deficiency. The sin of the elders, according to Gerondi, was to want Israel to be like other nations *in all respects* rather than only minimally, with respect to social order alone. But the elders were entirely justified in seeking a political antidote to divine perfection.[15]

The king is in charge of politics, and therefore he is freed from the law: he is "not subject to the laws of the Torah, as the judges are." The only example Gerondi supplies is taken from criminal law. The king is permitted to punish his subjects with death "in accordance with the needs of the moment rather than absolute justice." He can ignore the biblical requirement of two witnesses and the many additions to this requirement made by the talmudic sages (and designed, it seems, to abolish capital punishment altogether). Gerondi has nothing to say about the biblical accounts of kingly behavior, and I don't mean to present him as justifying what is there condemned—Solomon's marriages, say, or Ahab's disregard of the holy war. But were these kings to speak on their own behalf, what better justification could they offer than this: that they were bound to meet the requirements of domestic law and order and of international peace—and therefore they were exempt from the commands of God?

Gerondi recognizes the dangers of this position, and so he stresses the Deuteronomic command that kings copy and study the law. Kings must be learned and pious so that their violations of the law will be limited. Still, this requirement conceals a radically secular conception of kingship. In some respects, Israel is exactly like other nations; and it is for the sake of this likeness, and the political necessities it reflects, that kingship is instituted. Gerondi has simply elaborated in rabbinic style what the elders (but not Samuel) already understood. And the king that he defends, like the king that they accepted, will probably conscript and tax (and kill) his subjects for his own benefit as well as for theirs. Personal piety is no adequate barrier to royal excess; nor are the various prohibitions of the Deuteronomic account effective barriers—for the king will surely need horses and chariots, and gold and silver, to fulfill his secular purposes. The Bible does not provide, nor can Gerondi imagine, any effective constitutional or political check on the power of kings. Still, finding a constitutional check will be easier if it is clearly understood that the king is not God's adopted son but rather the people's choice, not the servant of divine law but of social order. Society can always find other servants.

Kingship, then, arises in Israel as an entirely practical response to the dangers of theocratic (charismatic) rule. The high theory of monarchy, with its myths of divine sonship and unconditional covenant, comes later. It represents a royal effort to escape the practicalities, and the escape is so successful that the house of David survives the death of its last son and lives on in impractical, apolitical, messianic fantasy. The kingship that the elders asked of Samuel thus stands precariously between theocracy and messianism. The charismatic judge comes at the last minute; the messiah comes at the end of time. But the king and his sons are there continuously, year after year. They exist in what we might call the space of secular time, which is the space of normal politics. Insofar as there is any recognition of an autonomous political realm in biblical thought, it has its beginning and perhaps its only location there.

FIVE

Prophets and Their Audience

The prophets are most commonly read as moral teachers, and read that way, their books (or selected parts) are the biblical texts most accessible to contemporary men and women. For us, the prophets are poets of social justice, utopian visionaries. I don't mean to dispute that reading here, only to complicate it. For prophecy had a political (or antipolitical) role in ancient Israel, and the importance of the prophets has as much to do with the way they played their part as with the lines delivered, however wonderful the lines. I want to consider what the biblical writers tell us about the audience of the prophets and the public spaces in which they spoke, and I want to ask what it might mean, to the writers and to us, that they spoke in public, to an audience.

In a book about political morality, the philosopher Stuart Hampshire claims that a certain kind of public speech is a universal feature of human societies: "Wherever and whenever human societies exist, whether they are primitive or technologically advanced, issues of policy will be debated in some assembly of chosen persons . . . The institution of articulating and reviewing contrary opinions on policy is of necessity species-wide."[1] What Hampshire is describing here is deliberation, practical reasoning, the essence of politics according to the Greeks— according, also, to contemporary theorists of ideal speech and deliberative democracy.

Is there anything like deliberation in the Bible? Certainly, the kings of Israel and Judah had advisors, but we are told very little about what the advisors said or about how or where they spoke. Mostly, the search for knowledge of God's will replaces the articulation of human policy; oracle replaces argument. The Greeks also consulted oracles, but doing so was secondary to the processes of public debate and decision. I assume that there was debate and decision in ancient Israel, too—"of necessity," as Hampshire says—but we get only glimpses of the process in the biblical texts. The author of the post-biblical First Book of Maccabees expresses admiration for the Roman republic, where "every day three hundred and twenty senators constantly deliberate concerning the people" (8:15).[2] Perhaps he hoped to see a similar regime established in Jerusalem. But nothing like "constant" deliberation is described for the previous thousand years.

Samuel argues with the elders about the advantages and disadvantages of kingship; Absalom consults his advisors on the strategies of rebellion; Rehoboam receives the conflicting advice of the old men and the young men; a group of officials in Jehoiakim's court discuss Baruch's scroll before bringing it to the king. But there aren't many other examples. At best, this sort of thing is simply taken for granted by biblical writers, a background politics that doesn't arouse their interest. What is up front is very different.

We read almost nothing in the Bible about assemblies and councils, though both probably existed, and there must have been conventions about the forms of speech appropriate within them. Curiously, God is sometimes said to preside over a council or assembly or host of heavenly beings (the key references are in the Psalms: see 89:6 and 8), and the prophet Micaiah, whom we shall meet again, actually describes a discussion between God and "all the host of heaven" about how to deal with one of Israel's kings (1 Kings 22:19).[3] But the biblical writers don't seem interested in reporting on earthly discussions of this sort, and they never suggest the existence of a council or assembly meeting regularly for political debate. We find instead a typically one-sided discourse that has its origin not in divine deliberation but in divine revelation: God speaking at Sinai, Moses' orations in Deuteronomy, prophetic declamation. Abraham and Moses talk back to God, arguing against his destructive fury, Abraham for the sake of the people of Sodom, Moses for the sake of Israel itself. Amos, reporting a vision, claims briefly to have played Moses' part (7:1–6). And Jeremiah asks God to "remember that I stood before thee to speak good for them, and to turn away thy wrath from them" (18:20). But mostly when the prophets plead Israel's cause, they don't do so in a dialogue with God; nor do they speak independently of his instigation. Their claim to be listened to derives from a previous claim, that they speak the "word of the Lord."

The stories about the prophets nonetheless provide some of the most interesting dialogues in the Bible: Samuel and Saul, Nathan and David, Elijah and Ahab, Amos and Amaziah, Jeremiah and Hananiah, Jeremiah and Zedekiah, Haggai and the priests. Much of what the prophets say, though not deliberative, is certainly argumentative; we can readily imagine what the text rarely provides: the opposing positions, the word that is not the word of the Lord. In the case of Moses, who is called the first prophet, the opposing positions (the "murmuring" of the people, Korah's challenge) are actually recorded in the text; it is Moses' arguments that are mostly missing; since he can call for miracles and terrible punishments, he doesn't need to argue. Later prophets have no such intimate connection with God and so lack anything like Moses' authority. They are commonly resisted, disputed, denied their title. And the prophet's title can be vindicated only by his words. Though other tests are proposed, as we shall see, the true test is this: by his words—

rhetoric, eloquence, poetic power, argumentative skill—shall you know him.[4] In the prophetic books we find the most important forms of public speech in ancient Israel. But is this public speech also political speech?

Excluding Moses, whose position is unique in biblical history, the prophet as a political figure first appears together with the king. As I suggested in the last chapter, we can think of the two as a double replacement for the charismatic judges. Kings take on the military and judicial roles of the judges, though in a less personal, more institutionalized way. They hire mercenaries and create standing armies; and although they don't often sit in judgment, they probably appoint or confirm the men, increasingly likely to be professionals, who do. Prophets take on (most of) the charisma of the judges, the immediate divine connection. They are "raised up" by God, while the kings, after David, are born to their tasks and raised at court. (In the northern kingdom, where dynastic rule was never firmly established, new kings were anointed by prophets, or they were usurpers, without legitimacy.) The appointments of David the king and Amos the prophet are strikingly similar:

> I took thee from the sheepcote, from following the sheep, to be ruler over my people. (2 Samuel 7:8)

> And the Lord took me as I followed the flock and . . . said unto me, Go, prophesy unto my people. (Amos 7:15)

But David is the last king so "taken," while Amos is only the first of a series of prophets who have left a written record of the moment when they were called by God.

The existence of court and temple prophets notwithstanding, prophecy was not an office but a calling. Each prophet was individually called; there was no prophetic covenant like the priestly covenant with Aaron or the royal covenant with David. Hence there are no prophetic genealogies (only Zephaniah is traced back to a possibly royal great-great-grand-father; but there are no prophets in his past). Mostly, we are given only a father's name, sometimes only a place: "Amos, who was among the herdsmen of Tekoa" or "Micah the Morasthite." Elijah is the only prophet to appoint a successor. Among the literary prophets, there are no authorized successions. If there were prophetic schools or circles, if prophets had followers, they had no heirs—at least, no heirs with names. No prophet after Elisha was the son or disciple of another prophet. Kings and priests were uniformly members of a ruling or upper class (the new kings of the northern kingdom were not taken from the sheepcote; they were royal officials or military commanders). Prophets, by contrast, were drawn from every social stratum; the social range of prophecy was determined by the radical inclusiveness of the national covenant. The divine call could come to anyone—even to women, who rarely take public roles in the Bible. There were no female priests and no queens except the usurper Athaliah, but women were called, though rarely, to be judges and prophets. This means that anyone could claim that he (or she) had been called. It also means that any claim could be disputed.

What were the stakes in the dispute? The prophets of Israel made no claim to rule; nor did they ever organize anything remotely resembling a political party or movement or even a sect. When power is at stake, strict standards of legitimacy are normally worked out: kingship and priesthood were subject, at least in principle, to genealogical proof. The standards were looser for prophets, no doubt because the stakes were lower. The prophets demanded only to be heard, and significant numbers of them were no doubt listened to if not harkened to in the centuries that stretch from Samuel's time to Malachi's. Kings chose their favorite prophets, in much the same way that presidents and prime ministers choose their policy advisors today. The kings wanted favorable forecasts, just as their contemporary counterparts do, and this seems to be what prophets had to offer. The crucial asset that they derived from their calling was the ability to read the future. If they could not make policy, they were indispensable advisors to policy makers. But their advice, again, was always disputed.

Deuteronomy 18:22 provides the official—and obvious—standard by which these disputes about callings and foretellings were to be resolved:

> When a prophet speaketh in the name of the Lord, if the thing
> follow not, nor come to pass, that is the thing which the Lord hath
> not spoken, but the prophet hath spoken it presumptuously.

The Deuteronomic rule isn't much help at the moment of prophecy, but I suppose that war prophets, in an age of frequent warfare, might acquire a reputation for accurate forecasts (or for inaccuracy and "presumption"). But long-term prophecies, dealing with the future of the dynasty or the kingdom, are essentially untestable by this standard. Prophecies of disaster have a way of being fulfilled if one waits long enough, and it may be that prophets like Amos were remembered, their words preserved and finally canonized, because of such fulfillments. I suspect, however, that the Deuteronomic rule worked only in the short run and was probably overridden even there, often enough, by the king's preference for favorable oracles.

Some prophets were certainly ready to provide what the king preferred. Consider the story in First Kings 22 about Ahab and his four hundred prophets, all of whom recited in unison whatever the king wanted to hear. King Jehoshafat of Judah, Ahab's ally in a war against the Syrians, was skeptical, apparently, about such recitations, and asked for one more prophet, a second opinion. "There is yet one man," replied Ahab, "Micaiah the son of Imlah, by whom we may inquire of the Lord: but I hate him; for he doth not prophesy good concerning me, but evil." Micaiah is called and prophesies defeat at the hands of the Syrians; the kings march into battle anyway and are indeed defeated. From this case the rabbis derived another standard of prophetic reliability: the authentic prophet speaks in his own voice and his own manner.[5] Beware, then, the multitude of prophets, all of whom say the same thing. Conformity is the mark of inauthenticity.

This standard is best applied to prophets who speak at length and in public. Micaiah himself, like other war prophets, has very little to say and nothing at all of larger political significance. What makes prophecy truly significant is not the oracle, the military forecast, but the moral admonition. The two are connected, for admonitions can be understood as conditional oracles: you (the king) will lose the war, or your dynasty will fall, or your kingdom will be destroyed—so speaks the prophet in God's name—unless you repent of your sinful acts and cleave henceforth to the covenantal law. Now the prophet is less foreteller than censor. He will have to speak in his own voice, for the censorial role requires courage, which most of his fellow prophets, like Ahab's four hundred, clearly lack. And since the people he is censoring won't want to listen, he will have to insist upon his calling and find some way to vindicate it. How can he prove that his words are divine? Only by speaking them divinely: the prophet is dependent upon his eloquence.

We can see this dependency even in the case of court prophecy, which can be dramatic and powerful even as it is brief and unelaborated: thus the parable that Nathan uses to condemn David after the seduction of Bathsheba and the murder of Uriah, culminating in the line (decoding the parable) "Thou art the man" (2 Samuel 12:7), and thus Elijah's confrontation with Ahab after the murder of Naboth: "Hast thou killed, and also taken possession?" (1 Kings 21:19). But eloquence rises to its occasions, and the decisive occasions come when the prophet leaves the relative privacy of the royal court and speaks at large to the people. The great poetry of the prophetic books is all spoken in public. The books themselves were probably added to and revised in the course of oral or written transmission (and some of the specific foretellings may have been amended to meet the Deuteronomic test). But even today, when many of the references are unknown and many lines obscure, the prophetic writings are best read out loud.

At the time they were spoken, they were also contested out loud, in public, by other prophets, by royal officials, and even by ordinary Israelites. Some of the contestations are recorded or described in the prophetic books; only occasionally, however, do we hear two or more voices, the priest Amaziah as well as Amos (7:10–17), the enemies of Jeremiah as well as the prophet himself (26:7–19). More often, we have only one-sided denunciations of other prophets: conformists, flatterers, time servers, the authors of the "smooth things" that, says Isaiah (30:10), the people want to hear. Since the "smooth things" also sometimes come true—as in the victories of Jereboam II, foretold by Jonah the son of Amitai, a contemporary of Amos and presumably an opponent—the speakers were not without credibility as prophets. Still, the cacophony of prophetic voices must have generated a considerable distrust, so that *our* prophets, the authors of the biblical books, sometimes dissociate themselves from the whole enterprise. "I was no prophet," says Amos; "neither was I a prophet's son [the member of a prophetic school]; but I was a herdsman, and a gatherer of sycomore fruit" (7:14).

Those words from the first of the literary prophets are echoed by one of the very last, Second Zechariah, who seems to warn his listeners against Amos's strategy of dissociation: "And it shall come to pass in that day, that the prophets shall be ashamed every one of his vision . . . But he shall say, I am no prophet, I am a husbandman; for man taught me to keep cattle from my youth" (13:4–5). Exactly what prompted these last words, we can only imagine; they come at the end of a long history of acrimonious and often ad hominem arguments between "true" and "false" prophets. In the case of the prophets, however, in contrast to the anonymous legislators of Israel, a few recorded instances of argument ease the way for our imaginations. What these texts suggest is something rather different from Hampshire's review of policy options. Though policy was at stake—mostly foreign policy: whether to march to war or join a military alliance or negotiate a surrender—the immediate focus was on the prophet's credentials, his divine authorization. If he really spoke in God's name, there was no point in soliciting other opinions. But could someone who prophesied disaster for God's people possibly be speaking in God's name? This is the form the arguments commonly took—public speech, certainly, but a very indirect kind of deliberation. The authors of the prophetic books were fully engaged in these arguments, and there is no evidence (except for the preservation of their books rather than the books of their opponents) that Amos's strategy of dissociation worked. Prophets they undoubtedly were, a small group among the hundreds of others; they spoke more truthfully perhaps, or more eloquently, but they were of the same number. Together with their opponents, they made the northern shrines and the streets and courtyards of Jerusalem lively places, if not yet genuinely political.

We don't know precisely when the prophets left the royal court and moved into the public spaces of Israel's cities and towns. Elijah and Elisha travel around the country, but they are more like miracle workers—legendary heroes, the disarmed successors of the warrior-judges—than public speakers. Amos is the first prophet of whom we can say with certainty that he delivered his prophecies to a general audience—at the shrine in Beth-el. But he refers to earlier figures, unnamed, who tried to do the same thing and were silenced: "But ye . . . commanded the prophets, saying, Prophesy not" (2:12). His contemporaries, Jonah son of Amitai in the north and an earlier Zechariah in the south, were still courtiers, speaking (so far as we know) only to kings. Later prophets still had court connections: Isaiah advised King Hezekiah; Jeremiah, who had friends among royal officials, was consulted by Zedekiah at the very end. But these two, and all the others now, had another place to speak:

Run ye to and fro through the streets of Jerusalem. (Jeremiah 5:1)

Stand in the gate of the Lord's house and proclaim there his word. (7:2)

Shrine and city, the streets, the gates, even the temple courtyard: the importance of these new locations cannot be overemphasized. When the prophet spoke only to the king, he was working, presumably, on the assumption that the king's decision was the only one that mattered. The history books seem still to reflect this view: the fate of Israel as a whole is tied, relentlessly, to the failures of its kings. But when the prophet speaks in public, the working assumption shifts. Now it appears to matter that ordinary men and women think this way or that way, live or don't live in accordance with the law. If they have no part to play, no responsibility for the moral life of the kingdom, why is the prophet commanded to speak to them? From Amos on, the prophets have less and less to say about the sins of kings alone. They address the whole society, though they always recognize its hierarchical character. Some of the people are more responsible than others.

Amos denounces the rich, with their summer houses and winter houses, couches of ivory, wines and perfumes: they take interest on loans to their brethren, falsify weights and measures, bribe judges, and sell the poor into debt slavery. Isaiah and Jeremiah refer more directly but also more obscurely to the political power structure. We have a picture in our mind of the people described by Amos. They are the local bourgeoisie. But when Isaiah says, "The Lord will enter into judgment with the ancients of his people, and the princes thereof: for ye have eaten up the vineyard" (3:13–14), we are on less familiar territory. The ancients (elders) and the princes are men of the state, not men of the market, and we know only in a rough way how the state functioned, how its functionaries were selected, and exactly what their functions were. Here the biblical texts provide fewer details, an imagery far less rich—as if the writers were uninterested in the textures of political life or were relying on the all-too-intimate understanding of their audience. In any case, the crucial point is this: all these rich and powerful people are denounced in the hearing of the others, the poor, the weak, the needy.

Not that the others are exonerated. When Jeremiah foretells the destruction of Jerusalem, he leaves no one out, from the top to the bottom of the political hierarchy:

> Because of all the evil . . . which they have done to provoke me to anger, they, their kings, their princes [or officers], their priests, and their prophets, and the men of Judah; and the inhabitants of Jerusalem. (32:32)

And in the standard prophetic trope of the divine law suit, it is Israel as a whole that sits in the dock, charged with violating covenant law.

> For the Lord hath a controversy with his people, and he will plead with Israel. (Micah 6:2)

But the prophets never call upon ordinary Israelites to act politically, to take responsibility for public policy. As Max Weber says, "No prophet was a champion of 'democratic' ideals." They were concerned for the welfare of the people, especially the poorest of the poor, but they had no interest in the opinions of the people. They did not believe in "a right to revolution or to self-help [by] the masses oppressed by the mighty."[6] All that their indictment requires is a moral reformation: an end to idolatrous worship, fair dealing in the marketplace, Sabbath observance, compassion for the poor. The demands made on the powerful leave them in place and in power: honest law enforcement from royal officials, justice from judges, pious instruction from priests, truth from prophets. What is subversive in the prophetic books is not most immediately the message but the speaking of the message—and the person of the messenger, the divinely called, self-appointed prophet, the embodiment of charisma without power, which is always a threat to power without charisma.

But the threat went both ways, and it seems likely that (true) prophets were as much threatened as threatening. We can get some sense of their political impact, or lack of it, by looking closely at two recorded confrontations, outside the royal court, between prophecy and authority. The first brings Amos face to face with the priest Amaziah at the shrine in Beth-el. Amos takes the initiative, uninvited, prophesying the destruction of the northern kingdom; the priest responds in what is to us an all-too-familiar way:

> Then Amaziah the priest of Beth-el sent to Jereboam king of Israel, saying, Amos hath conspired against thee in the midst of the house of Israel: the land is not able to bear all his words. For thus Amos saith, Jereboam shall die by the sword, and Israel shall surely be led away captive out of their own land. Also Amaziah said unto Amos, O thou seer, go flee away into the land of Judah, and there eat bread and prophesy there. But prophesy not again any more at Beth-el: for it is the king's chapel and it is the king's court. (7:10–13)

Amos answers Amaziah with the lines I have already quoted, denying that he is one of the prophets (that's not the way he earns his bread). Then, defying the ban, he prophesies once more in Beth-el, foretelling the destruction of the priest and all his family, and leaves the shrine or is forcibly removed—he is not reported there again.

Amaziah's conspiracy charge was almost certainly false; nothing in Amos's book, or in any other of the prophetic books, suggests so forward a political move. In any case, Amos is acting publicly, not secretly, "in the midst of the house of Israel." Presumably, what really worried the priest was the possible effect of Amos's oracles and admonitions on the listening people. But this worry, too, may have been misplaced; the land seems to have borne the prophetic words easily enough. We are not told how the actual worshippers at Beth-el responded to Amos; they did not at any rate rally to his defense or protest his banishment. Nor does he, responding to Amaziah, make any appeal to the people. Amos is not a popular tribune, even though, more than any of the other prophets, he speaks out of a deep sympathy for the oppressed. He is God's representative, no one else's, and had God sent him back to Beth-el, he would have returned and accepted whatever punishment the king ordained. But "conspiracy" was someone else's business.

Some prophets actually conspired against kings. Ahijah had a role in the rebellion of the first Jereboam against Solomon's son, and Elisha sent one of his followers, an unnamed prophet, to anoint Jehu and perhaps also to plan his coup d'état (1 Kings 11:29–39; 2 Kings 9:1–10). But these were not speaking prophets; in neither case did they warn the king against whom they plotted, and they seem entirely unconcerned with the sins of elders, officers, priests, or people. In Amos's case, given his account of Israel's condition, it would hardly have helped to anoint a new king. What was necessary was moral reform and—though he never says so—social transformation, and to effect change on this scale Amos had no agents or, at least, no new agents. He relied on the very people he condemned.

The second confrontation between prophecy and authority is sometimes called the trial of Jeremiah, though the account (chapter 26) reads more like a religious or political dispute than a judicial procedure. The prophet, standing in the temple courtyard, delivered a prophecy of doom for the shrine and the city—holding open, however, the possibility that God would "repent" if the people "hearken and turn every man from his evil way." As soon as he finished, "the priests and the prophets and all the people took him, saying, Thou shalt surely die." Jeremiah's crime, they believed (or hoped), was false prophecy. The princes or officers of Judah, hearing of the incident, came from the palace to the temple "and sat down [in judgment?] in the entry of the new gate." The priests and prophets repeat their charge, with the people now among the listeners: "This man is worthy to die; for he hath prophesied against this city." Jeremiah in turn repeats his (conditional) prophecy, addressing himself to both officers and people. "As for me, behold, I am in your hand: do with me as seemeth good . . . unto you"—though if they kill him, he says, they will kill an innocent man, "for of a truth, the Lord hath sent me." The officers and the people now support Jeremiah against the priests and prophets, and additional support comes from "certain of the elders of the land," who remind the assembly that the prophet Micah prophesied doom for Jerusalem and was not put to death by King Hezekiah (Micah is quoted in the only instance of explicit interprophetic citation in the Bible). But then another case is cited, of a prophet named Urijah, who prophesied "according to all the words of Jeremiah" and who was "fetched forth . . . out of Egypt," where he had fled, and killed by King Jehoiakim. At this point, the narrative breaks off with a summary note that is not quite the report of a verdict: "Nevertheless, the hand of Ahikam the son of Shaphan was with Jeremiah, that they should not give him into the hands of the people to put him to death."

The story is extraordinary: what actually happened, and who was on which side, and what it all meant has been the subject of much scholarly debate.[7] I want to make only one point: though the prophet's speech is taken very seriously by all the parties who join in the discussion, his call for a "turning" away from evil is never discussed. The question of interest is whether this man, Jeremiah, speaks in God's name. The classic political question—What ought to be done?—doesn't arise. We can guess that it did in fact arise from the involvement of Ahikam, who was one of the reforming officials in Josiah's time and who must have had a lively interest in policy matters. But even in Josiah's time, all that we are told about Ahikam is that he, together with other royal officials, carried the newly discovered "book of the law" to the prophet Hulda for authentification. The question of interest, then, was whether the book was God's book, not whether its laws made political or moral sense. Still, Ahikam was probably engaged in answering the latter question, too, and he may have been an advocate of reform, in opposition perhaps to the priests and prophets of the temple.

But from which evil ways did Israel have to "turn" in order to escape God's anger? The prophets offer a full catalogue of possibilities, and we can read their lists as programs and therefore as political arguments of a sort. But they don't suggest priorities, or propose a strategic ranking, or do any of the other things that political activists have to do. What the royal officials finally choose, very late in the day, with the Babylonian army nearing Jerusalem, is a turning away from oppression: a release of debt slaves. The release is accomplished, interestingly, by a covenant rather than a decree: "king Zedekiah made a covenant with all the people . . . to proclaim liberty" (Jeremiah 34:8). So Israel "turned" or returned to the codes of Exodus and Deuteronomy, apparently long neglected. When the Babylonian army was diverted by an Egyptian attack, the covenant was broken, and the former slaves were forced back into servitude. Jeremiah immediately protested, and his words suggest that he was one of the instigators of the release (34:13–18). But how the choice was made, who opposed it (apart from the slaveholders) and who supported it, what they said at the necessary meetings—all this is concealed from view. The trial is reported; the deliberations are not.

The prophets were social critics, perhaps the first social critics in the recorded history of the West. It is their sense of a divine calling that makes the criticism possible. Thus Jeremiah, describing God's word as it "came to me":

> Behold, I have made thee this day a defenced city, and an iron
> pillar, and brasen walls against the whole land, against the kings
> of Judah, against the princes thereof, against the priests thereof,
> and against the people of the land. And they shall fight against
> thee; but they shall not prevail against thee; for I am with thee,
> saith the Lord, to deliver thee. (1:18–19)

Though the attention of the biblical writers is focused unwaveringly on claims like this one, on the authority of the prophets or the lack of it, the texts also provide, at great length, their critical arguments: invocations of Israel's history, references to the law codes, descriptions and indictments of current practices, including ritual practices (the province of the priests) and legal practices (the province of royal officials), and sharp attacks on the foreign policies of both northern and southern kings. The substance of these arguments I must leave for the next chapter. I want only to insist that the substance must also have been addressed by the prophets' contemporaries in some institutional setting—and also in city streets and temple courtyards. For the authority question—Did this prophet speak the word of the Lord?—was never settled and, indeed, could not have been settled. It isn't only that religious charisma breaks through all authority structures and calls into question all processes of authorization; equally important is the fact that social criticism can never be authoritative. Once the prophet is in the streets, all we can do is listen to whatever he has to say and judge its value for ourselves.

Court and temple prophets speak with the authority of court and temple, which reinforces and, we are likely to think, constrains their divine calling. But the streets add no authority; now the prophet is on his own. He has to convince us that his words are God's, that his indictments are true, and that his reforms will work. I have already said that the prophet is known by his eloquence. But by eloquence here I don't mean merely his choice of words or the rhythm of his sentences. He has to use language in a way that engages the minds and touches the hearts of his listeners; he has to remind them of what they know, evoke their historical memories, play on the nerves of their commitment, their guilt, their hopes for the future. Eloquence is not primarily linguistic but cultural.

The culture on which the prophets drew, whose resources they deployed, was a religious (and a legal) culture rather than a political one. When kings and prophets divided the functions of the charismatic judges, the kings took on the political work, for which there was very little cultural support or reinforcement (even David and Solomon are celebrated more for writing psalms, cultivating wisdom, and building the temple than for organizing, expanding, and running the state). The prophets became the representatives of God in the world, with no practical tasks except criticism. They spoke for the tradition: a history of miraculous interventions, a covenantal law divinely revealed. The more they stressed the miracles and the revelations, the less value there appeared to be in the work of kings. A royal reformer might be welcomed by the prophets (though Jeremiah doesn't seem to be fully engaged with the Josianic reformation), but a serious alliance was unlikely; no prophet, once prophecy had emerged from the court into the streets, showed any interest in the actual politics of reform or any readiness for the compromises this might require.[8] The prophets' unreadiness, indeed, was what made them so radical. But theirs was—in ways that will become more clear when we examine some of their substantive arguments—a fiercely antipolitical radicalism. Prophecy was a kind of public speech that militated against deliberation. God's message overrode the wisdom of men.

"They have spoken words," declared Hosea scornfully, thinking of the rulers of Israel and their courtly advisors, "swearing falsely in making a covenant: thus judgment springeth up as a hemlock in the furrows of the field" (10:4). The judgments of the prophets, or at least of the "true" prophets, were entirely different. But if anything is to come of those judgments, some people, the prophets themselves or the men and women in their audience, must "speak words," must argue about what ought to be done, and listen to counterarguments, and work toward "covenants" or agreements, even if these require compromise and accommodation. Politics lies just beyond prophecy, but the biblical prophets, judging from their texts, did not go there.

SIX

Prophecy and International Politics

rophecy in Israel emerges with kingship, but it reaches its full development only with empire. The greatest prophets were, as Weber writes, "world political demagogues and publicists," which is to say that they were continually engaged by imperial politics and warfare.[1] So were their fellow Israelites, and not only or most importantly because ordinary men and women still remembered David's empire. In the tenth century BCE, a unified Israel had been the strongest power between Mesopotamia and the Nile—so, at least, the biblical historians tell us. Since that time, the two Israelite kingdoms and their neighbors had fought and negotiated with one another, always in the shadow of greater and more ambitious states to the east and southwest. By the eighth century, when the first of the literary prophets were at work, Assyria and Egypt had become the effective contenders for power and plunder in all the countries of Syria-Palestine. What was left to states like Israel and Judah was alliance politics—with neighboring states against one of the empires or with one of the empires against the neighbors. The risks are high in a politics of this sort, and they were greatly heightened by the cruelty of the Assyrians: "Blood fairly drips," says Weber, "from the cuneiform inscriptions."[2] We know very little about how these risks were conceived or confronted in Moab or Aram or the Philistine cities. In Israel and Judah, by contrast, we have a historical account of how the kings dealt with their neighbors and with the more distant and threatening imperial powers. And we have an even more interesting parallel account—the "world political" arguments of the prophets.

The prophets were caught up in questions of international politics, and they sometimes sound like little more than partisan ideologues. Whether they wished it or not, Weber argues, "the prophets . . . actually always worked in the direction of one or the other furiously struggling inner-political clique, which at the same time promoted definite foreign policies."[3] The king was the focus of these struggles, waged chiefly by court counselors and "wise men," but sometimes also by demagogues in the streets. Competing factions favored this or that imperial power, urged alliance or appeasement, or rebellion or war. The aim of the factions was not only to win the king's ear, power in the palace, and status and wealth in the country at large. The foreign policy of the nation was also at issue, and everyone had an interest in sustaining whatever degree of independence was compatible with safety and security—hence the politics of the eighth and seventh centuries: sending and receiving ambassadors, calculating the balance of power, fortifying cities and preparing armies, paying or refusing to pay tribute. The prophets were involved in all of this, and yet the central purpose of the greatest of them was to deny its value. Rejecting Weber's description, they would have said that they were partisans only of God.

Israel's kings might have said the same thing—or, more probably, they would have claimed that God was *their* partisan, the chief advisor, encourager, and supporter of the king's party. This is the message of the royal psalms, in which fantasies of David's empire seem to survive: "He teacheth my hand to war . . . a bow of steel is broken by mine arms" (18:34). As a result of this divine instruction, the king triumphs over his enemies; strangers submit themselves to him; he becomes "chief of the nations" (*rosh goyim*—18:43). Here is a further example of the high theory of monarchy, as it is revealed to us in temple song. The king is God's anointed, his adopted son, and whenever the rulers of the nations take counsel together and plan war against him, he shatters their strength with a "rod of iron" and breaks them in pieces "like a potter's vessel" (2:9). These are prophetic images too, but the rod of iron (in God's hand, not the king's) is Assyria (Isaiah 10:5) and the broken vessel is Israel itself (Isaiah 30:14). The prophets did not accept the high theory.

But they were also at war with what we might think of as the low theory of monarchy, the more secular account, according to which the people of Israel set up a king so that he would "go out before us and fight our battles" (1 Samuel 8:20). The king must hope for divine support, but he seeks at the same time the counsel of wise men who know about affairs of state, and he trains and organizes an army or finds generals like Abner and Joav to teach his (mostly hired) hands to fight.

Kingship was, as I have argued, a form of self-reliance. It constituted the state as the agent of its own destiny, or, more exactly, it put the state into the hands of its own agents—kings, counselors, ambassadors, soldiers. Everything depended on their insight and skill—or *almost* everything, since prophets were still consulted before Israel went to war to learn if God looked favorably on the battle plan. I don't think that Gerhard von Rad is right to claim that Israel under the monarchy had "written off" God as the determining force of its present and future—though that is God's suggestion, when he tells Samuel that "they have rejected me, that I should not reign over them" (1 Samuel 8:7).[4] Despite this rejection, Israel's kings thought of themselves as God's allies. At the same time, however, they opened up room for their own alliances and political determinations. And so long as the Israelite kingdoms were surrounded by kingdoms of roughly the same sort, with similar populations and resources, the politics of self-reliance worked fairly well. As in any monarchy, there were strong kings and weak kings, military victories and military defeats, good treaties and bad treaties. The Deuteronomic historians regard political fortune as the product of divine reward and punishment, but the kings and their advisors may well have had another, not implausible view: that fortune was their own work. Though this latter view is never fully articulated in the biblical books (and there is certainly no celebration of the strategic acumen or courage in battle of any of Israel's kings), we need to assume its existence if we are to understand the contrasting view of the literary prophets.

The rise of the warrior-kings of Mesopotamia probably made Israelite kingship obsolete, though the kings, understandably, were slow to recognize this. Self-reliance was an increasingly dangerous business. Decisions still had to be made: to seek an alliance with this imperial power or that one, to look to Egypt for help, to resist an advancing army or to surrender, to pay or refuse to pay tribute. But now the time and space for maneuver were mostly determined not in Samaria or Jerusalem but in capital cities far to the east. The odds on any local determination succeeding were not very good. Israel's fate was no longer in its own hands.

What about the God who once taught those hands war? The astonishing innovation of the prophets was to claim that he was now the teacher of foreign armies. He was still the God of war; he still, sometimes, acted directly, miraculously, in warfare, just as he had done in the time of the exodus, when he drowned the Egyptian army, and in the time of the conquest, when he made the sun stand still. But his activity was no longer limited to Israel; he was now a global warrior, controlling the entire course of international politics. In the book of Judges, God's power is displayed within a more limited compass; his concern is focused narrowly on Israel, even when he uses other nations to punish Israelite sinfulness:

And the children of Israel did evil in the sight of the Lord: and the Lord delivered them into the hand of Midian seven years. And the hand of Midian prevailed against Israel. (6:1–2)

In the prophetic books, by contrast, God takes an active interest in nations other than Israel—indeed, in all the nations of the world—not only punishing them for the evil they do but also showing compassion for them and bringing them back to their heritage and land (see, for example, Jeremiah 12:14–15 on Israel's neighbors). He still uses other nations in much the same way that he used the Midianites, as instruments of Israel's punishment (and, later on, of Israel's restoration); but now he enters into a different, and steadily closer, relationship with them. The king of Assyria is the "rod" of God's anger (Isaiah 10:5); the king of Babylon is God's "servant" (Jeremiah 27:6–7); the king of the Persians is his "shepherd" and even his "anointed" (Isaiah 44:28 and 45:1—these epithets are otherwise applied only to Israelite kings).

God's sovereignty now extends to the whole of world history, but it isn't entirely clear just what the nature and purpose of the extension is. What does this sovereign God do and why does he do it? "Strange is his work," says Isaiah (28:21—NJPS), and certainly the biblical accounts of that work are often obscure and enigmatic. God is a lawgiver to Israel, but none of the prophets describes him in a legislative role vis-à-vis any other nation. And the Psalmist explicitly denies that God is a universal lawgiver:

He sheweth his word unto Jacob, his statutes and his judgments unto Israel. He hath not dealt so with any [other] nation: and as for his judgments, they have not known them. (Psalm 147:19–20)

With regard to the others, God's sovereignty encompasses only two of the three branches of government familiar to us: he is first of all judge of the nations (though they don't know this) and then the executive enforcer of his own decisions.

> For the Lord hath a controversy with the nations, he will plead
> with all flesh. (Jeremiah 25:31)

The Hebrew word here translated as "controversy" (*riv*) commonly implies litigation, and litigation takes place against a background of law. Israel's law is provided and legitimated by the Sinai covenant, hence God's "controversies" with Israel (see, for example, Micah 6:1–5) are called "covenant lawsuits" by modern scholars. Is there a covenant with the nations? Or does some universal law underlie God's judgments of their behavior? It appears that Israel's covenant is unique. But God's original judgment of the nations, manifest in the Flood, suggests that there is indeed a universal law, though we are never told when it was revealed or how it is to be known (the rabbis later invented the Noahide Code to deal with these questions). In any case, the nations are judged harshly, and not only for their crimes against Israel. Amos, the first of the literary prophets, who can hardly have had more than a dim premonition of world empire, is already clear about this: God punishes the nations for their crimes against one another:

> For three transgressions of Moab, and for four, I will not turn
> away the punishment thereof; because he burned the bones of
> the king of Edom into lime. (2:1)

Writing a century later, the prophet Nahum pictures the whole world celebrating God's destruction of the Assyrians—"for upon whom hath not [their] wickedness passed continually?" (3:19).

God is a universal judge. He judges the nations now without their knowledge or consent, but Isaiah imagines a future age when they will come willingly to receive his judgments. The vision of Isaiah 2 ("they shall beat their swords into plowshares") is probably the best known of prophetic texts; it is mostly read, as I shall read it in Chapter 10, as an expression of messianic hope. But it is also a first account, not wholly fantastic, of post-imperial international politics. The prophet seems to envisage a federation of peoples, each one free from all the others, united only by their mutual recognition of divine sovereignty. Though the law goes forth from Zion, there is no hint here of Israelite political triumph; there is no new empire except the empire of God, who "shall judge among the nations" (2:4). Norman Gottwald has argued that this can only mean, in practice, that God's prophets deliver his judgments, which the nations voluntarily accept.[5] Jeremiah claims exactly this role; he is a "prophet unto the nations," to whom God says: "See, I have this day set thee over the nations and over the kingdoms, to root out, and to pull down, and to destroy, and . . . to build and to plant" (1:10). All this is accomplished by the prophetic word alone. The prophets make no claim to political rule—not in Israel, not in the world at large. And when they describe an ideal ruler, a Davidic king, he is king only over Israel; other nations still have kings of their own.

The idea of a God in total control of world history and politics opens the way to universalist visions of this sort. It doesn't sever the connection between God and Israel, but it does lead the prophets to imagine additional connections. Perhaps the most startling example is a fragmentary oracle in Isaiah 19, of much-disputed provenance, which seems to describe an alliance of Israel, Egypt, and Assyria, bound together in the service of God:

> In that day shall Israel be the third with Egypt and with Assyria,
> even a blessing in the midst of the land: Whom the Lord of hosts
> shall bless, saying, Blessed be Egypt my people, and Assyria the
> work of my hands, and Israel mine inheritance. (19:24–25)

Isaiah's more famous vision is of a wider and looser union of all the nations, great and small, who have learned the truths of monotheism and who gather for worship and judgment in Jerusalem.

The prophets understand this extraordinary gathering as the end-product of what can only be called divine intention. It isn't the result of a political program that Israel or anyone else has adopted. God is in full control even before his sovereignty is universally recognized. What exactly is his intention? Here we encounter the same difficulties as when we asked about the nature of his "work." It seems that he wants what he has wanted ever since the days when he confronted Pharaoh in Egypt: that the whole world see his power displayed, understand its awfulness, and accept his sovereignty. The God of the Bible is omnipotent; yet, at the same time, he is angry and frustrated. Having created men and women with finite minds and free wills, he suffers from their ignorance and wickedness. Still, the prophets believe that God will eventually get what he wants, fulfilling himself, as it were, in world history. He will achieve universal honor and obedience by subduing all the other rulers—by ruling alone. A sovereign God "bringeth the princes to nothing" (Isaiah 40:23), so that all of them, in the end, accept him as their sole judge.

The passage about God "bringing the princes to nothing" comes from Second Isaiah, who writes at a time when the princes of Israel had already been brought to nothing. Perhaps it was easier to recognize God's world-historical sovereignty when Israel had no sovereign of its own. But many of the most important prophetic passages dealing with "the nations" and hence with international society probably predate this time. In fact, the prophet's understanding of divine politics did not replace some earlier understanding of royal politics. The first coexisted with the second—and challenged it. The challenge takes two very different forms. I have already described how several of the pre-literary prophets castigated Israelite kings for failing (or refusing) to carry out the dictates of holy war doctrine. Here were kings who pursued sensibly secular policies, fighting limited wars and signing treaties of peace, when they should have consecrated their enemies to God and slaughtered them all. God had made these kings his agents, but they had acted according to their own understandings, on their own or their country's behalf.

The challenge of the literary prophets is very different, for they seem to have given up the idea that Israel was in any sense a political agent acting at God's command among the nations. We find in their writings the first hints of an alternative conception: that Israel is a victim nation, always at the wrong end of someone else's agency. I shall not consider here how this victimization might be thought to serve God's purposes. A suffering servant (see Isaiah 53) is a servant still, but his service is not political. Nor is it likely to be voluntary; one would expect suffering servants to drag their feet. What must be stressed, however, is that Israel's suffering is politically managed by God himself, which makes an autonomous political response hard to imagine. God's "is the hand that is stretched out upon all the nations" (Isaiah 14:26)—and, above all, upon Israel. Even when it is not stretched out directly but only through the mediation of Assyrian or Babylonian armies, the resistance of Israel's kings seems morally and militarily senseless. These armies come at God's instance, even when they attack Jerusalem itself, where his house stands and his anointed rules.

The point is difficult: the Assyrians and Babylonians are indeed sent by God; their world-historical role is purely instrumental. And yet, at the same time, they have their own willfulness; they come up against Israel freely. So Isaiah can say of Assyria that it is the "rod" of God's anger (10.5):

I will send him against an hypocritical nation. (10:6)

But he adds immediately that this "sending" does not consist in command and obedience. The king of Assyria does not know that he has been sent:

Howbeit he meaneth not so, neither doth his heart think so; but
it is in his heart to destroy and cut off nations not a few. (10:7)

And so the Assyrians, once they have served God's purposes by punishing Israel, will themselves be punished by another "rod." They, too, will suffer, though they will never be suffering servants; they serve God only in their triumphs.

Why will they be punished? What is wrong with destroying nations that God wants destroyed? I have already suggested that the Assyrians never made a covenant with God, and we have no record of their reception of divine law. If that is so, how are the Assyrians to know that their wars and conquests are wrong? As the rabbis would say, When were they warned? The prophets do not explicitly pose questions of this sort; perhaps they have in mind some version of a natural law that might provide answers. The texts don't suggest that it is their cruelty that makes the Assyrians wicked. God's punishments require cruelty: all sorts of horrors figure in the prophetic accounts of divine justice or, as it more often appears, divine vengeance. And here in Isaiah, God not only sends the Assyrians against Israel but also explicitly authorizes their predictable behavior:

> I will send him against an hypocritical nation, and against the people of my wrath will I give him a charge, to take the spoil, and to take the prey, and to tread them down like the mire of the streets. (10:6)

The only crime of the Assyrian king, according to Isaiah, is to do all this as if it were his own idea, "the fruit of [his] stout heart" (10:12):

> For he saith, By the strength of my hand I have done it, and by my wisdom. (10:13)

The king claims to be an agent, and in some sense he is, for he plans his own conquests. And yet it is this very claim that displays his wickedness—and also his ignorance: he is like an axe that boasts itself self-moved against the hand that moves it (10:15).

This passage in Isaiah might be considered the source or first instance of what G. W. F. Hegel called the "cunning of reason." Here it is God's cunning to use the Assyrians for purposes they cannot imagine, let alone endorse. They serve a cause they do not know. But it is a special feature of the prophetic argument, which Hegel did not pick up (and which the replacement of God by reason might well make inconceivable), that the Assyrians are punished for their service. They are not punished for what they do, but for the arrogant intention with which they do it—though it is hard to see what other intention would lead them to perform as God requires. They can't obey commands that they have not received, hence the conclusion that the prophet seems to suggest: they are punished for acting intentionally, in accordance with their own will and reason.

Agency is a sin, even though God created agents. But this can't be right, since the prophets consistently demand moral action—the reform of Israelite society, for example. They call upon kings, judges, priests, and elders to act in accordance with the covenant. The strange doctrine that action itself is sinful holds true only in international society and only in an age of empire. Did the prophets believe, though they never say it explicitly, that imperial politics and warfare were inherently ugly? Certainly, their visions of the future are visions of peace, even if this is a peace realized by military means: the successive defeat of one arrogant emperor after another, until the hand of God behind the terrible destruction is finally recognized, and, as Oliver O'Donovan writes, "a family of humble nations [creeps] out from under the wreckage of the empires."[6] In the end, the prophets suggest, the wreckage will be God's own work; no other agent will be involved. Apparently, he can be terrible in ways that human beings should never be. In international politics, *imitatio dei* is no virtue. Action on that scale, action of that awfulness, tempts kings and emperors to put themselves in God's place, to lay claim to a power like his—which is the wrong sort of imitation. Here is a sphere of action where human beings are better off not doing what God does, indeed, not *doing* anything.

Again and again, the prophets recall how God laid waste to Sodom and Gomorrah (Abraham's protest is not remembered) and how he annihilated the Egyptian army at the Red Sea. In these cases, there was no human rod or axe between his hand and its destructive effects, no human agents who might boast of their cruelty. Perhaps this is what the prophets believe about the latter days: if God alone is cruel, cruelty can be brought to an end; no Assyrians or Babylonians will require punishment in their turn. Where there are human agents, however, they are of necessity unattractive—arrogant, bloodstained, criminal. The work that they do, though it is part of God's great design, is not good work for human hands. It cannot be commended; it must not be celebrated.

This grim view of international politics may explain why the prophets never assign an instrumental role to Israel in God's world-historical plan. So far as I can tell, Israel is never described as a rod or an axe (in Psalm 2, the king carries a rod; he isn't himself the rod of God). Nor is Israel ever sent to enforce God's judgments upon the nations. Indeed, there are virtually no prophetic descriptions of Israel as a nation-in-arms and no expressions of admiration for warrior or diplomat kings. This is international politics seen from the perspective of the weakest nations. The prophets hope, sometimes, for a grand reversal of fortunes, and the ressentiment of the weak is by no means absent from their visions of future time. But the triumphs they look forward to are God's triumphs; the military or political efforts of Israel's kings seem entirely irrelevant. God has no need for their work, and if they do nothing at all, they will at least be protected from his righteous anger.

Do nothing: this is the prophetic idea of a religiously sanctioned foreign policy, and it constitutes the prophetic challenge to the kings of Israel and Judah, who were as likely as Assyrian kings to rely on the strength of their hands and the wisdom of their counselors. Stay out of international politics, which belongs to God alone and to his instruments—who are also, mysteriously, his enemies. Only he can oppose and overthrow them, in his own good time:

> Then shall the Assyrian fall with the sword, not of a mighty man [*lo ish*]. (Isaiah 31:8)

The prophets may have made a virtue out of necessity—Israel's sword will never bring the Assyrians down—but this is by no means the whole story of their new doctrine. For it would be a powerful counterargument to that doctrine that diplomacy, alliance, and even war itself are necessary means of self-defense in an age of empire. Why not make a virtue out of these? But the prophets see God's hand behind the empires, and so they deny the value, indeed, the very possibility, of self-defense. Assyrians and Babylonians misunderstand their agency; Israel must not even attempt to be an agent. This is not only an argument against some Israelite king's improbable imitation of Ashurbanipal or Nebuchadnezzar. It is an argument against the actual policies of Ahaz, Hezekiah, Manasseh, Josiah, and their successors in the last days of the southern monarchy. I want now to examine the argument in detail. How should Israel act or not act in an age of empire?

In the year 735, only thirteen years before the Assyrian destruction of Samaria and the exile of the northern tribes, a coalition of Israel and Syria "went up toward Jerusalem to war against it" (Isaiah 7:1). Ahaz, king of Judah, mobilized his forces to resist the attack and sent ambassadors to Assyria, asking for help—a dangerous but by no means irrational request. This is the moment that Isaiah chooses for his first political, or antipolitical, intervention. He seeks out the king and urges him, in God's name, to give up the mobilization and the embassy:

> Take heed, and be quiet [*hashkait*]; fear not, neither be faint-hearted. (7:4)

The plan of Ahaz's enemies "shall not stand, neither shall it come to pass" (7:7) so long as the king has faith in God's help and seeks no other help. The prophet's words are probably meant to recall the moment at the Red Sea when Pharaoh's army drew near and the people fearfully gathered around Moses:

> And Moses said unto the people, Fear ye not, stand still and see the salvation of the Lord. (Exodus 14:13)

"Be quiet," "stand still"—the message is the same, and in both cases it represents a radical denial of the doctrine of self-help.

Indeed, it is a leitmotif of the Hebrew Bible that self-help is unnecessary. The Israelites need not provide food for themselves in the wilderness: God provides manna. Moses doesn't need to look for ways of asserting his authority against the rebellious people: again and again, God punishes the rebels. Joshua doesn't have to organize the siege of Jericho: the walls come tumbling down. Isaiah is doing little more than reiterating the lesson of these stories.

Commentators on Isaiah often praise the prophet's shrewdness, as if political circumstances dictated his words. The prophet's arguments are driven not only by faith but also by prudence and calculation. "Isaiah's main concern," writes Joseph Blenkinsopp about the prophet's response to a later and more frightening military threat, "was to dissuade the young king [Hezekiah] from being drawn into an anti-Assyrian alliance that would predictably lead to disaster." Norman Gottwald is a little more cautious: Isaiah's advice to the king, he argues, was not "a narrowly religious judgment." Rather, "he believed that what was religiously requisite was also politically practical." The prophet was one more royal counselor or wise man, wiser than the others.[7] But we hardly know enough to make judgments of this sort. We cannot say what was in Ahaz's mind when he declined to "be quiet" or, later on, in Hezekiah's mind when he joined the alliance against Assyria. No doubt, they made their own calculations. Why should we assume that Isaiah was politically shrewder? It seems more likely that his advice, as Weber argues, "was purely religiously motivated through Yahwe's relationship to Israel"— which made prudence and calculation irrelevant.[8] That is why Isaiah gives the same advice to successive kings, reiterating his views in different circumstances, taking no notice of the differences.

The most dramatic moment comes in 701, when the Assyrian army was on the march, destroying the cities of Judea and nearing Jerusalem. This time the king—Hezekiah, one of the best Israelite rulers, according to the Deuteronomists—contemplates an Egyptian alliance, planning, as Isaiah says,

> to strengthen [himself] in the strength of Pharaoh, and to trust in the shadow of Egypt. (30:2)

The prophet argues against the alliance, denying the saving power of Egypt. But his denial is not based on any military or political analysis of Egyptian strength relative to Assyrian strength. Indeed, if we count horses and chariots, we might incline toward the Egyptians. But doing so would be a mistake:

> Woe to them that go down to Egypt for help; and stay on horses, and trust in chariots, because they are many; and in horsemen because they are very strong; but they look not unto the Holy One of Israel, neither seek the Lord. (31:1)

The Egyptians are men, not God, their horses flesh, not spirit (31:3), and it is for this reason that the alliance with them should be rejected. But this reason would mean rejecting every conceivable alliance: it isn't only Egyptian horses that are made of flesh. What, then, should Hezekiah do?

Isaiah's argument in 701 is the same as it was in 735, expressed in the same words:

> In return and rest shall ye be saved; in quietness [*b'hashkait*] and in confidence shall be your strength. (30:15)[9]

Once again, *do nothing:* but what does this mean? What the prophet urges upon the king, according to Martin Buber, is "a special kind of politics, theopolitics." This is a politics easier to explain negatively than positively: it requires the rejection of any alliance that "involves the people [Israel] in other nations' wars of expansion."[10] That these wars are planned by God doesn't matter; it is wrong for men to plan them and therefore wrong for Israel to associate themselves with any of the imperial plans. Isaiah never quite says this, but it isn't an implausible account of his argument. *Do nothing* means at least this: do not participate in imperial politics or warfare.

What follows from this refusal? Here is Buber's positive account of Isaiah's "theopolitics":

> He who has dealings with the powers renounces the power of powers . . . and loses its help; whereas he who confides and keeps still thereby gains the very political understanding and strength to hold his own.[11]

The expected parallelism is missing from the second clause here: he who confides and keeps still thereby gains the help of "the power of powers"—God's help. Buber doesn't want to say this, but it is surely what Isaiah means. Isaiah is not recommending a new "political understanding" but a radical withdrawal from politics:

> For through the voice of the Lord shall the Assyrian be beaten down. (30:31)

Buber's argument is closer to that of contemporary pacifists, who claim that there is a nonstandard, nonimperial, nonviolent politics with which we can hold our ground. On this view, the prophet does not intend to criticize self-reliance but rather to give an alternative account of what it means—or, better, an alternative account of the "self" upon whom we can reasonably rely. The faithful Israelite is a person of inner strength, unwilling to fight but not necessarily unwilling to act politically—in, for example, some ancient equivalent of civil disobedience. Perhaps this is also what Norman Gottwald has in mind when he says that Isaiah's "be quiet" does not mean "to fold the hands and wait."[12]

So far as foreign policy is concerned, however, "folding the hands and waiting" is exactly what Isaiah means, and the narrative account of the events of 701 is carefully shaped to fit and vindicate this recommendation. Hezekiah did not sit still but actively prepared Jerusalem for an

Assyrian siege. The Siloam tunnel that brought water into the walled city dates from this time; Isaiah himself refers to it and records also that the king broke down houses to fortify the walls (22:9–11). According to the account in Second Kings, Hezekiah negotiated with the Assyrians and paid a large tribute, even stripping the gold from the temple doors and pillars (18:14–16). But these negotiations are omitted from the narrative in Isaiah, which otherwise follows Second Kings closely. In the prophet's book, Hezekiah prays to God and does nothing else, and God sends a plague that destroys the Assyrian army (37:36).

A different version of the same events is suggested by the Assyrian chronicles, which record only victories and plunder and the "reduction" of the Judean kingdom—and which imply that the Assyrian army withdrew in good order. Hezekiah clearly remained a tributary, probably having negotiated, as Second Kings suggests, a near surrender that saved his capital and his kingdom. Perhaps the strength of Jerusalem's walls and the newly secured water supply made the negotiations possible. But none of the prophets would have thought that foresight in preparing for a siege or skill in diplomatic dealings were worth boasting about. Divine assistance was the only true sign of a good king.

What happens when there are no good kings and no hopes for divine assistance? A century after the Assyrian withdrawal, in the very last days of the southern kingdom, the prophet Jeremiah offers advice rather different from Isaiah's. He, too, opposes an Egyptian alliance and a rebellion against the imperial power of the east, now Babylonia. His view of alliance politics in general is entirely familiar: to seek help from any worldly power is to forsake God (2:17–18).[13] But, at the end, when the Babylonian army has laid siege to Jerusalem and food is running out in the city, Jeremiah does not tell the king to "be quiet" and do nothing. He urges a prudent and intelligent policy, though of the most passive sort:

Then said Jeremiah unto Zedekiah, Thus saith the Lord, the God of hosts . . . If thou wilt assuredly go forth unto the king of

Babylon's princes, then thy soul shall live, and this city shall not be burned with fire. (38:17)

"Go forth" and surrender: here is political advice that aims to save what can be saved. Jeremiah is the architect of the politics of defeat and exile, a politics of accommodation to the powers that be. The differences with Isaiah are important, but I shall not emphasize them here, for surrender is also a way of escaping from statehood and political responsibility. When Jeremiah gave Israel into the hands of Babylonia, he believed that he was giving it into God's hands. He promised at the same time a future redemption for which the people had nothing to do but wait. God will punish the Babylonians as he punished the Assyrians (50:18)—but not by the hand of Israel.

These arguments of Isaiah and Jeremiah hold, once again, only in international politics. Only with regard to other nations are the kings of Israel measured by what they don't do, by their refusal to use whatever power they have. By contrast, the books of both these prophets are full of recommendations for reform at home. These never quite add up to a political program, as I have already argued, but that is not what we should expect from prophetic discourse. It is clear enough that the prophets' judgments on Israel, unlike their judgments on the other nations, are also calls for action. Standing still, keeping quiet, surrendering to the local powers that be—these are not the expected or the right responses. "Justice, justice shall you pursue," says the author of Deuteronomy (16:20—NJPS), and the prophets understand that "pursue" is an active verb. Even if it doesn't require political action, it certainly requires work in the world.

The pursuit of justice is the sort of work that we most readily associate with the Hebrew prophets. It is important to note that it doesn't involve any of the standard ways of "seeking the Lord" or any of the ritual expressions of faith in God. The pursuit of justice is the very opposite of fasting and sacrifice. Thus Isaiah:

In God's Shadow

Is not this the fast that I have chosen? to loose the bands of wickedness, to undo the heavy burdens, and to let the oppressed go free, and that ye break every yoke? Is it not to deal thy bread to the hungry, and that thou bring the poor that are cast out to thy house? (58:6–7)

Years earlier, Amos had spoken even more directly:

I hate, I despise your feast days, and I will not smell in your solemn assemblies. Though ye offer me burnt offerings and your meat offerings, I will not accept them: neither will I regard the peace offerings of your fat beasts . . . But let judgment run down as waters, and righteousness as a mighty stream. (5:21–24)

What the prophets require at home is care for the oppressed, the hungry, and the homeless; judgment; and righteousness. And if the people of Israel meet these requirements, they will be safe in international society— even in the age of empire. The classic statement of assurance comes from Jeremiah, speaking, I assume, before the Babylonian onslaught:

Thus saith the Lord of hosts, the God of Israel, Amend your ways and your doings, and I will cause you to dwell in this place. Trust ye not in lying words, saying, The temple of the Lord, The temple of the Lord, The temple of the Lord . . . For if ye thoroughly amend your ways and your doings; if ye thoroughly execute judgment between a man and his neighbour; If ye oppress not the stranger, the fatherless, and the widow, and shed not innocent blood . . . [and] neither walk after other gods to your hurt: Then will I cause you to dwell in this place, in the land that I gave to your fathers, for ever and ever. (7:3–7)

This is the prophetic message with regard to the world of nations: the only good foreign policy is a good domestic policy. Act justly at home, and your home will be secure. The position is immediately recognizable, for it has often been adopted in modern times by the political left, the party of domestic reform. But the modern version of the prophetic message is driven not only by leftist ideology but also by prudence and calculation, for a society ruled by principles of justice and solidarity will also be a strong society, whose citizens are prepared to risk their lives in its defense. Clearly, the prophets intend no such argument. For them, social justice at home guarantees divine protection abroad; there is no need for citizen soldiers. This position is, however, deeply unsatisfactory, for it denies what cannot be long denied: the autonomy of international politics and the dangers it poses. We might well ask Jeremiah why he condemns Israelites who say "the temple of the Lord, the temple of the Lord," implying that reform is unnecessary so long as the rituals of worship are maintained, when all that he and his fellow prophets have to say in the global arena is "the God of Israel, the God of Israel," implying that diplomacy and defense are unnecessary so long as faith remains firm. "The failure of the politics of the prophets," Moshe Halbertal and Avishai Margalit write in their book on idolatry, "is inherent in the uncompromising requirement of God's exclusivity in the political realm." The prophets would bar Israel's rulers from "playing the game of earthly politics."[14] But the game of heavenly politics has its own difficulties. Job's claim that the righteous suffer as much as the wicked is as true in international as it is in domestic society.

In any case, the prophetic position with regard to domestic reform is not consistently held. At some point in the pre-exilic period—exactly when is in dispute—the prophets begin to talk about a dramatic divine intervention into Israel's own affairs. God's local instrument, as it were, will not be a "rod" but a "branch" of the stock of Jesse; this messianic king will accomplish what ordinary kings have failed to do. Once one is thinking along these lines, it is possible to say to all of Israel what Isaiah said to Ahaz and Hezekiah: "Take heed, and be quiet; fear not." In Chapter 10, I will try to describe how this prophetic message, first delivered in the context of international politics, was eventually brought home.

SEVEN

Exile

I am not going to tell sad stories about the fall of the house of David and the years of exile in Babylonia, but I want to begin my account of exilic politics by recognizing the extent of the disaster that struck the people of the southern kingdom in 587. It was the fulfillment of the curses of Deuteronomy—and also of God's promise that what had happened to the Canaanites would happen to the Israelites, too, if they committed similar "abominations." In fact, however, the fate of the two nations was not the same. If we accept the version of the conquest presented in the book of Joshua, Israel fared better than Canaan, for its people were not exterminated, merely transported. If we accept the version in Judges, Israel fared worse, for its defeat was not gradual and partial, but sudden and total. Its capital city was destroyed, its temple was burned, many of its leaders were killed, and a significant part of the nation—the entire political and religious elite and the skilled craftsmen of its cities and towns—was carried away to Babylonia. Only the peasants were left, and the poorest of the city dwellers, and the unknown poet, sometimes said to be

Jeremiah, though that seems unlikely, who wrote the great lament for Jerusalem:

> How doth the city sit solitary, that was full of people! (Lamentations 1:1)

Defeat and exile are human tragedies, but in this case they were also events in a political history that somehow they failed to terminate. After the fall of Samaria to the Assyrians in 721, the ten northern tribes were transported, literally, into oblivion; they vanish from the historical record. The southerners, by contrast, were able to shape a common life in exile—perhaps because of the earlier achievements of Davidic kings, or the Deuteronomic reformers, or the later prophets, or the temple priests—or perhaps because the Babylonians provided easier conditions than the Assyrians had. While the exiles sat and wept by the rivers of Babylon, they also maintained some sort of communal organization and, in time, prospered economically. They worked out new ways of worshipping God, resisted the local religions, argued about politics and theology, produced new versions of old books, listened to and preserved the work of two of the greatest prophets, Ezekiel and Second Isaiah. Whether all this would have made for steadfastness and survival in a foreign land had there been no return to Jerusalem, no rebuilding of the temple, is radically uncertain. As it was, the exile lasted only half a century. But Cyrus's edict of restoration did not restore either kingship or political independence; except for the Hasmonean interlude, Israel was henceforth a vassal people, Judea an imperial province. So exile was a long-term loss, and the years in Babylonia were the beginning of a long-term adjustment.

The immediate political loss is nicely illustrated by the prophet Ezekiel in the introduction to one of his extraordinary visions: "And it came to pass in the sixth year [of the exile] . . . as I sat in mine house, and the elders of Judah sat before me" (8.1). Amos went to the shrine of Beth-el to prophesy; Isaiah went to the palace of the king or the gates of the city; Jeremiah spoke in the temple courtyard. But in Babylonia, the elders come to Ezekiel's house. Prophecy has retreated to the living room. Now there are no public spaces such as an independent state affords, within which people freely assemble for political, social, or religious purposes and listen or don't listen to the itinerant prophet. I take Ezekiel's house, so far removed from God's house and the king's house, to be a symbol of statelessness. It is understandable that prophecy in such a setting should become more mystical, also more personal— though both Ezekiel and Second Isaiah retain an intense interest in international politics, statelessness being a recent and, they hoped, temporary condition. The gatherings in Ezekiel's house, and presumably in many similar places, marked the beginning of a deep transformation in the common life of Israel—the process through which Israelites were turned, or turned themselves, into Jews.

The unavoidable question among the exiles was the question of responsibility. How did the disaster happen? What led God to desert his people, to allow his temple to be destroyed? Who was to blame? Some Israelites must have concluded that God had failed them or definitively abandoned them and that the most prudent course now was a shift in religious allegiance. A small number of passages written by the prophets of the exile seem to respond to this view. But most of the exiles looked for answers within the parameters of the covenantal faith. The first answer is reflected in the final writing and editing of the book of Kings. From the standpoint of Davidic ideology, the doctrine of the royal covenant, no one could be held responsible except the kings themselves. Here was the inner weakness of the high theory of monarchy: it hardly allowed for any distribution of blame. The attention of the historians focused on Manasseh, who reigned some forty years before the exile:

and Manasseh seduced [the people of Israel] to do more evil than did the nations whom the Lord destroyed before [them].

And the Lord spake by his . . . prophets, saying, "Because
Manasseh . . . hath done these abominations . . . I will wipe
Jerusalem as a man wipeth a dish, wiping it, and turning it up-
side down. And I will forsake the remnant of mine inheritance."
(Kings 21:9–14)

But why Manasseh alone? Few of the kings of David's house could
be called blameless, and it seems that the very idea of monarchy suffered
a partial eclipse in the aftermath of the Babylonian triumph. Judging
from the last chapters of Ezekiel and from the post-exilic writings, neither the exiles nor the early returnees had any great enthusiasm for a full
political restoration. Haggai and Zechariah placed their hopes in Zerubbabel, a grandson of the last Judean king, but it is unclear how far his
ambition reached and how much support he was able to muster. After
that, though descendants of David were apparently known to be living in
Judea, they had no recorded political following. Perhaps Second Isaiah's designation of Cyrus as the Lord's anointed (45:1) signaled what
was coming: the country's destiny would not be placed again in the uncertain hands of Davidic kings.

The second answer to the question of responsibility can already be
found in the pre-exilic prophets. Working from their own understanding of the Sinai covenant, according to which the whole people had
sworn obedience to God's law, the prophets blame the people themselves for the disaster that is about to befall them. They uphold the doctrine of collective responsibility. The doctrine is elaborated in two very
different ways. Sometimes the prophets suggest that guilt is distributed
throughout the collectivity: each and every Israelite has sinned against
God. This is the implication of Jeremiah 5:1, a passage that refers back, I
think, to Abraham's argument with God about Sodom and Gomorrah:

Run ye to and fro through the streets of Jerusalem . . . and seek in
the broad places thereof, if ye can find a man, if there be any that
executeth judgment, that seeketh the truth; and I will pardon it.

God would have pardoned Sodom for the sake of ten righteous men, Jerusalem for only one; but the prophet cannot find even one. The more specific social criticism of the prophets, however, carries a very different implication. When Amos, for example, criticizes the rich for oppressing the poor, he seems to suggest the innocence of the poor. Surely they can't be blamed for their own oppression. Or, again, when the writer of Lamentations, in the days immediately after the exile, says that "Judah is gone into captivity because of affliction, and because of great servitude" (1:3), he is probably referring to persistent violations of the law that required the release of slaves (see the story in Jeremiah 34). Whoever was to blame for that, the slaves were not to blame. And yet the poor and the slaves, together with all other Israelites, suffered the consequences of divine wrath.

The earliest biblical doctrine of responsibility makes guilt hereditary: God "[visits] the iniquity of the fathers upon the children, and upon the children's children, unto the third and to the fourth generation" (Exodus 34:7). Jeremiah rejects this view, but only for the future age of Israel's redemption:

> In those days they shall say no more, The fathers have eaten a
> sour grape, and the children's teeth are set on edge. But every-
> one shall die for his own iniquity. (31:29–30)

In "these" days, by contrast, God "recompensest the iniquity of the fathers into the bosom of their children after them" (32:18). What is the difference between these days of Jeremiah's present and those days of future redemption? It is politics, I think, that makes the difference. Now the covenantal law must be taught and enforced, and this requires kings, priests, and judges, authority structures and communal decisions. The state and all its members either live up to the covenant or fail to do that, and failure leads to collective punishment, which the prophet represents in the conventional language of heredity. It is in any case more plausible to say of collectivities than of individuals that coming generations will suffer for the sins of this one. In the future, however, God will deal directly with individuals; the mediating apparatus of political rule, of kingship and priesthood, will no longer be necessary:

> And they shall teach no more every man his neighbour and every
> man his brother, saying, Know the Lord: for they shall all know
> me. (31:34)

Compare this passage with Exodus 32:27, when Moses comes down from the mountain, finds the people worshipping the golden calf, and orders the Levites to go through the camp and "slay every man his brother, and every man his companion, and every man his neighbour." When people "know the Lord," the slaying won't be necessary, nor will the teaching—and collective responsibility will disappear along with political authority itself.

But as things turned out, it was exile, not redemption, that brought with it the end of politics or, at least, of national sovereignty and authoritative teaching and judging. And it is "by the river of Chebar" in Babylonia, not in Jerusalem, in his own house, not in the temple courtyard, that Ezekiel announces a strong doctrine of individual responsibility. He repeats Jeremiah's line about sour grapes and then repudiates it for the present, the biblical here and now: "Ye shall not have occasion anymore to use this proverb in Israel" (18:3). Every soul, the prophet says, is God's—the son's as much as the father's—and only the "soul that sinneth, it shall die." The argument that follows is of a kind very rare in the prophetic writings, first because of its directness and specificity, and second because of its substantive emphasis on personal rather than national right- and wrongdoing. The prophet speaks in prose, avoids metaphor (except for the sour grapes), reports no visions. He speaks only about individual Israelites, "every one according to his ways" (Ezekiel 18:30), and never refers to political intermediaries: kings, officials, priests, or prophets. The sins for which individuals are held responsible are the sins of everyone, and the reward for avoiding them is distributive rather than collective: personal well-being, not national success or triumph.

> If a man be just and do that which is lawful and right, And hath not eaten upon the mountains, neither hath lifted up his eyes to the idols of the house of Israel, neither hath defiled his neighbour's wife, neither hath come near to a menstruous woman, And hath not oppressed any, but hath restored to the debtor his pledge, hath spoiled none by violence, hath given his bread to the hungry, and hath covered the naked with a garment; He that hath not given forth upon usury, neither hath taken any increase, that hath withdrawn his hand from iniquity, hath executed true judgment between man and man, Hath walked in my statutes and hath kept my judgments, to deal truly; he is just, he shall surely live. (18:5–10)

The list of sins is not new (nor is the mixing of references to the laws of purity and of justice), and Moshe Greenberg, in his commentary on Ezekiel, has argued that its partial repetition in the more conventional chapter 22 is evidence that it wasn't "tailored for individuals or for exiles" and doesn't suggest a "shift in focus from national community to individual souls."[1] But I would stress the differences between chapters 18 and 22 rather than the similarities. The later chapter repeats the argument of the pre-exilic prophets, though now in the past tense, as if to explain the recent catastrophe: "Their own way have I recompensed upon their heads, saith the Lord God." Recompense here is not, as in chapter 18, "every *one* according to *his* ways." The use of the plural pronoun in 22 is politically significant; the sins of the city are hierarchically attributed to priests, officials, prophets, and the mysterious "people of the land," and the punishment is collective: "the house of Israel is to me become dross" (22:18). The *whole* house is condemned, for its sinners represent all Israel, unlike the individualized "souls" or "persons" of chapter 18.

Ezekiel in chapter 18 does not provide a third answer to the question about political responsibility—it wasn't Israel's kings who brought about the destruction, nor was it Israel collectively; it was individual Israelites. Instead, he asks another question. He replaces "Why was the city destroyed?" with "How should a man live?" This question is certainly not new: we can read the well-known lines of Micah that begin "He hath shewed thee, O man, what is good" (6:8) as an earlier answer. Ezekiel's answer is no different, only more elaborated and detailed, drawing upon the legal codes in a manner appropriate, as Greenberg says, to the priestly-prophetic character of Ezekiel's work as a whole.[2] But prophecies like Micah's lack the explicit individualizing thrust of Ezekiel 18. The reassurances and consolations of earlier prophets are standardly addressed to Israel as a whole, whereas Ezekiel reassures the individual: if a person is righteous, that person will be rewarded. The most obvious parallel to this claim comes not in the other prophets or in the historical writings but in the wisdom literature—Ezekiel's argument is like that of the friends of Job. Job himself makes the obvious rejoinder, but like his friends, he is focused on his own case; he doesn't see himself as the member of a moral and national community.

Israel in exile was still a community, but it was no longer in control of its own destiny; only individual Israelites could exercise such control, and unless they were favored by the gentiles, they could control only their own divergent destinies. The politics that follows from this loss of collective control is most clearly revealed in the book of Esther. The book is, as Robert Alter says, "a kind of fairy-tale"; scholars continue to argue about whether there is some historical core to the story, but for our purposes that doesn't matter.[3] The author had a view of exilic politics that obviously resonated with his earliest readers, and it is that view that I shall try to explicate. At its very beginning, the book provides a second symbol of Israel's statelessness: it reports that Esther in the king's harem did not reveal "her kindred nor her people" (2:20). Ezekiel prophesying in his house, Esther silent in the palace: the two together suggest what exile must have felt like. They don't necessarily suggest the full reality, for Nehemiah did not conceal his national identity in the king's palace. But Esther and Nehemiah have something else in common: they were not the chosen representatives of their people. At critical moments, both of them speak on the people's behalf, but they were chosen by a foreign king, served the king, and were utterly dependent on his favor. They weren't the heirs of royal or priestly covenants; they had not been called by God; they did not seek the advice of a council of elders. We may think of them as the first court Jews (though Joseph is a distant model).

What is politically decisive about the book of Esther, marking its radical newness, is the absence of any attributions of responsibility to the exiled Israelites (identified throughout as Judeans or, perhaps, as Jews). These Israelites are not first-generation exiles; the author does not describe them as a guilty nation deserving of expulsion from the land of Israel and of the doom that Haman is planning; Haman is not an agent of divine retribution. Nor, however, are the Israelites described as members of a self-confident nation, capable of defending themselves. They are not responsible for what is about to happen to them, and they are not responsible for preventing what is about to happen to them. Until Esther wins from the king a decree permitting self-defense, the people are helpless and despairing: "there was great mourning among the Jews, and fasting, and weeping and wailing" (4:3). All this was doubtless a way of calling upon God, though God is never mentioned in the story, nor does he come to the people's aid. The weeping and wailing is in anticipation of grief to come; there is nothing to do. The description of Jewish self-defense later on is in the same vein, with the affect reversed: it is a fantasy of revenge rather than a realistic account of political (and military) action.[4] The people do not save themselves; they are saved by Esther's beauty and courage. Escape from doom is a piece of luck, not likely to be repeated.

Note the contrast with the Joseph story. Joseph tells his brothers that it is God who has made him Pharaoh's chief minister—and for one reason only: so that he can save his family. "And God sent me before you to preserve you a posterity in the earth and to save your lives by a great deliverance" (Genesis 45:7). Joseph's career is providential; Esther's is not, though she saves a whole nation. Hers is a secular story. It is Mordechai, not God, who gets her into the king's palace and, to the astonishment of some medieval rabbinic commentators, into the king's bed.[5] God is more distant in this exilic tale. Mordechai tells Esther that if she does not speak to the king, help will come to the Jews from "another place" (4:14)—heaven, presumably, but the reference is oddly restrained.

Haman is the first anti-Semite, and although he is called a descendant of the Amalekites, he is unlike all the previous enemies of Israel—the Egyptians, who feared the growing number of Jacob's descendants; the neighboring tribes and peoples who fought with the Israelites for land and wealth; the rival kings who competed for empire; the priests and prophets who served alien gods. Haman's enmity is excited by the vulnerability of the Jews, strangers in a strange land, who cling to their own ways. His charge to the king against them is remarkably prescient. The author of this fable, if that's what it is, has grasped the deepest meaning of the Jewish exile. "There is a certain people scattered abroad and dispersed among . . . all the provinces of thy kingdom; and their laws are diverse from all people; neither keep they the king's laws" (3:8). Mark the two elements in the accusation. The people are "scattered abroad," whereas most other conquered nations live clustered within a bounded territory, where they are at home, settled, and subject to the familiar forms of social control. There is something insidious, something dangerous, in the very dispersion of the Jews. And, moreover, they keep their own laws, separating themselves from all the king's other subjects. There is something vicious in their difference.

Much of Jewish exilic politics is addressed, not only defensively, to that second charge (the first is unanswerable). How was the nation to survive, scattered abroad and profoundly different from the nations among whom it was scattered? How could it maintain its identity under

In God's Shadow

alien rule without its own kings, officials, and priests? How should it regard the laws of foreign kings? The earliest answer to these questions, and in a way the definitive answer, was provided by the prophet Jeremiah in a letter sent from Jerusalem to the exiles in Babylonia:

> Thus saith the Lord of hosts, the God of Israel, unto all that are carried away captives . . . Build ye houses, and dwell in them; and plant gardens, and eat the fruit of them; Take ye wives, and beget sons and daughters; and take wives for your sons, and give your daughters to husbands, that they may bear sons and daughters; that ye may be increased there, and not diminished. And seek the peace of the city whither I have caused you to be carried away captives, and pray unto the Lord for it: for in the peace thereof shall ye have peace. (29:4–7)

Jeremiah probably did not intend that daughters of Israel should be "given," like Esther, into a foreign king's harem, even if that sort of thing made for the peace of the city or, as the author of the book of Esther meant to suggest, the safety of the exilic community. But the prophet does recommend a political as well as a material accommodation to the conditions of captivity—arguing against rival prophets like Hananiah and Shemaiah, and many royal officials too, who favored conspiracy and revolt in Jerusalem and urged a stubborn hostility to the peace of the city upon the Babylonian exiles. Jeremiah's arguments went unheeded at home, but they seem to have been taken to heart in Babylonia. Even today, Jewish commentators on the book of Esther cite his letter as evidence that Haman's charge against the descendants of the exiles was false. Their difference posed no danger.[6]

But what exactly did his advice entail? I suppose that Mordechai was seeking the peace of the city when he warned the king against the rebellious chamberlains, Bigthan and Teresh (Esther 2:21–23). "Peace" here means the security of rulers, a meaning it has often had in exilic history. Ahasuerus is obviously a problematic case, since he acceded to

Haman as readily as he did, later on, to Esther, but kings and oligarchs have many times protected Jews against populist attacks; and official Jewish politics-in-exile has tended to be conservative, supporting established authority on the Jeremian principle that "in the peace thereof shall ye have peace." The exiles in Babylonia and Persia are likely, then, to have obeyed the king's law, at least insofar as social order was concerned.

But they also obeyed a law of their own, and this might well have led them, as the book of Daniel indicates, to refuse obedience to the king. Even in less extreme cases than Daniel's, however, and even in relatively friendly environments, the laws of Israel with regard to worship, marriage, diet, Sabbath observance, and much else, would tend to isolate the exilic community and leave it always vulnerable to accusations like Haman's. At the same time, the laws made for the survival of the exiles as a community and barred the way to assimilation, the common fate of transported peoples in the ancient world. Survival and vulnerability go together, and that intractable association determines the character of exilic politics.

"Seek the peace of the city" is a political maxim, but what it suggests is a very limited political agenda. It doesn't invite the exiles to seek the peace of a certain sort of city, one whose customs and standards might match those of a certain sort of people. No, any city will do, so long as the Hamans of this world are powerless within it and there are Mordechais and Esthers who can intercede for the Jews. What is likely to be best is an imperial and cosmopolitan city, ruled with authority. So far as Babylonia was concerned, the exiles had and could have no larger political ambitions. They hoped for a return to Jerusalem, but Jeremiah's purpose in writing his letter was to persuade them to do nothing more than hope. And once the return had been accomplished—with the help of Cyrus, no Davidic king—those exiles who declined to go back, preferring their Babylonian houses and gardens, had nothing at all to hope for except "peace." Insofar as they could, they obeyed the laws of the foreign kings who were, apparently, chosen by God to rule over them.

Were the number of those who stayed behind a surprise? Ezekiel's dramatic vision of exile as a grave filled with dry bones (37) hardly suggests the contentment that many exiles apparently felt. The mood articulated in the surviving (and identifiable) exilic writings is at once apprehensive and expectant: contentment is radically absent. Sometimes the expectation reaches to independence and a reunified kingdom, but as I have already suggested, the stress falls elsewhere. There is enough restorationist royalism to produce, over time, a full messianic doctrine. But the emphasis of Ezekiel and Second Isaiah, it seems to me, is on physical and spiritual return—to God's favor, to Jerusalem, to Zion—far more than on political restoration. And this emphasis is entirely compatible, as it turns out, with accommodation and quiet obedience. It even lends itself to vicarious fulfillment: joyfully seeing off the returning exiles rather than actually joining them.

Peace facilitated an inward turning among the exiles. We see it plainly in the individualizing tendency in Ezekiel 18. But it is also visible in the new patterns of self-definition and religious association that begin to take shape in Babylonia. These are not easy to make out, for explicit doctrinal arguments are rare in the biblical texts that date from this period. Indeed, much of the writing that went on in the exile was editorial and redactional in character, and the new associations were tentative and experimental, creations of circumstance rather than of programmatic intention. Still, it was in the Babylonian writings that the people of the book and the synagogue made, as it were, their first appearance.

So long as Israel was independent, its priests, prophets, and scribes produced books of all sorts—legal codes, court chronicles, oracles, poems, epic tales—without any apparent impulse to fix them in some final form or to create a sacred canon. I don't mean that the books were unimportant; a section of Deuteronomy may even have been intended as a kind of constitution for a reformed kingdom. But political life was in some sense sufficient unto itself, so that no textual foundation was necessary; and it was sufficiently diverse, so that agreement on a single set of texts was probably impossible. The canonization of certain texts begins in Babylonia, and it seems likely that final or near-final versions of the Pentateuch, the histories, and some of the prophetic books were produced there. All these books had been worked on before; now it was said that the work was finished, the texts authoritative, subject only to interpretation, no longer to revision. It is as if the book or the book of books substituted for the state, providing a firm basis for collective identity. Unable to crown a king, the exiles canonized a set of texts.

This process also gave rise to a new kind of leadership, scribal rather than priestly or prophetic. I don't want to exaggerate this point. Prophecy continued in the exile—reaching great heights of religious intensity and poetic power with Second Isaiah—and the recorded visions and oracles of Haggai and Zechariah are important sources for the early history of the return. Nor were the priests inactive in Babylonia, despite the cessation of sacrifice; the biblical texts suggest that they studied their genealogies, maintained their social position, and planned for the future. Ezekiel 40–48 is a prophecy describing a temple-state, and we can easily imagine the prophet in his house expounding its baroque details—products of the imagination in exile—to gatherings of his priestly relatives. But the most important work of the priests in Babylonia was scribal work.

Whatever the disagreements among scholars today about the precise extent of the scribal work, few doubt that it was extensive.[7] Many people must have been involved, but as I have said before with reference to the work of the first lawmakers, we know nothing about the conditions and character of the scribes' involvement—where they met, what disputes arose among them, how they managed to produce (more or less) definitive texts. At the end of the process, Ezra, whose priestly lineage is traced back to Zadok, Phinehas, and Aaron, carries the new book to Jerusalem. So we are told, at any rate, and the implication is clear that Ezra had a leading part in the making of the book. He is "Ezra the priest, the scribe, even a scribe of the words of the commandments of the Lord, and of his statutes to Israel" (Ezra 7:11). His titles aren't new; kings had scribes, and so did prophets. But Ezra is the first unattached scribe, not a royal official, not a prophetic disciple; we may think of him as God's first editor.[8]

Once there were edited and authorized texts, there must also have been textual readings and expositions. Deuteronomy had been read to the people in Josiah's time, but that apparently was an exceptional event. The first reading of Ezra's new book (or books) is described in Nehemiah: "So they read in the book in the law of God distinctly, and gave the sense, and caused [the people] to understand the reading" (8:8). Second Chronicles suggests that readings of this sort were already going on in the days of the monarchy, but its account presumably reflects a later time: "And they [the Levites] taught in Judah, and had the book of the law of the Lord with them, and went about throughout all the cities of Judah, and taught the people" (17:9). The teaching of the law became a regular feature of Jewish worship—and persists today in the same two activities: reading the book and explaining it. I would guess that the two together were first experimented with in Babylonia. Religious services among the exiles are mostly a mystery to us, but there are scattered references in the prophetic writings (and in the story of Esther and in the Daniel legends, though these date from a later time), which the historian Yehezkel Kaufmann sums up: "The people assembled to seek 'righteous ordinances,' to hear the law, to fast, and to pray."[9] Their "new forms of devotion" are not described in the priestly writings of the Pentateuch; they must have been regarded as temporary or provisional; but they became, in time, "the essential cult."[10] What is decisively new here is the participatory character of the service; it lacks entirely the vicarious quality of temple worship, where the priests act for the people, and the people have nothing to do but watch.

As the cult takes on this new (Kaufmann calls it "democratic") intensity, it comes increasingly to define the people of Israel—making them something less like a political nation and more like a religious community or congregation. This transformation, begun in exile, continues after the return, despite the rebuilding of the temple and the resumption of the sacrifices. Indeed, "community" and "congregation" are favorite priestly terms, and some of the priests were apparently ready to imagine the temple, following Second Isaiah rather than Ezekiel, as a "house of prayer" and even as a "house of prayer for all people" (Isaiah 56:7). The new self-understanding opens the way for proselytism and religious conversion, and it is in Babylonia that the first conversions are reported. Second Isaiah promises "the sons of the stranger, that join themselves to the Lord, to serve him, and to love the name of the Lord . . . every one that keepeth the sabbath . . . and taketh hold of my covenant," that they will have "a place and a name . . . in mine house and within my walls" (56:5-6). They will return to Jerusalem with all the other Israelites. In pre-exilic literature, there are accounts of people who attach themselves to Israel by marriage or by long-term residence and assimilation. But there are no "joiners" in Second Isaiah's sense; nor did any of the exilic writers describe a procedure for "joining" or provide a doctrinal defense of it. The whole question was obviously a source of anxiety and, after the return, of bitter dispute. There were no precedents in the ancient world for religious conversion. Its appearance here suggests the extent of the transformation brought about by the exile experience.[11]

Whatever happened in the exile years happened without authoritative political direction. The adaptation to powerlessness was spontaneous, the product of an unplanned series of individual and small group decisions. The relative success of this adaptation—for Israel survived in Babylonia and then in a much wider diaspora—raises what is perhaps the central question of Jewish political thought: Just how important is sovereignty, independence, and authoritative direction? How important is it to have, like the other nations, kings of one's own, who appoint judges and fight wars?

This question has been endlessly debated in subsequent Jewish history. A long series of rebellions and messianic movements has aimed at the restoration of independence and, usually, of kingship. But the tradition that begins in Babylonia of political passivity and accommodation has never lacked communal support. Indeed, it has its own heroism, as Simon Dubnow most famously argued. He imagines the "providence of history" speaking to the Israelites at the moment of their exile and saying, "State, territory, army, the external attributes of national power, are for you superfluous luxury. Go out into the world to prove that a people can continue to live without these attributes, solely and alone through strength of spirit."[12] Esther, as she is described in her book, might well be a model of that strength. On the other hand, Mordechai clearly isn't, and yet he also is essential to the survival of the exiled people. When the Yiddish writer I. L. Peretz, commenting on the book of Esther from a Zionist perspective, called Mordechai an informer and a pimp, he was hoping for a state that would make court Jews like him, like Esther too, unnecessary.[13]

Both sides in this argument can claim biblical precedent. The Bible is, in most of its books, the record of an independent nation—so David Ben-Gurion could invoke it to defend the Zionist project.[14] But it is also the record of a nation whose God did not leave much room for independent decision-making. In contrast to Greek philosophers, the biblical writers never attach great value to politics as a way of life. Though the Sinai covenant would seem to imply a collective commitment to establish a political community of a certain sort, it is possible to reinterpret the covenant as an individual commitment, accepted by each member of the community, to live in a certain way. The institutions that defined the "way" did not have to be state institutions. They could be synagogues, academies, courts, councils, and communities (*kehillot*), operating with only limited autonomy. All those came later; and only later did it become clear that Babylonia was the place where something radically new was first thought about, discussed, and (perhaps) tested.

EIGHT

The Priestly Kingdom

Among the many and varied promises that God makes to Israel, one of the earliest (in the biblical account as we have it) is the promise of Exodus 19:6: "And ye shall be unto me a kingdom of priests and a holy nation." Exactly what a "kingdom of priests" is, isn't entirely clear, but the words have often been given a radical meaning. God promises a social transformation and a novel politics: a kingdom without kings, a universal priesthood. Israel as it was in Exodus 19 had neither kings nor priests, but it was only three months out of Egypt, where both were much in evidence. So, if we read these words in their textual place, as words spoken in the wilderness, they seem to promise an anti-Egypt. But they may also promise an anti-Israel, if they date, as many scholars think, from the later years of the monarchy, or from the time in Babylonia, or from Second Temple Jerusalem. Given any of those dates, the promise would seem to be an Israelite version of Luther's "priesthood of all believers," aimed at the established hierarchy—except that birth or nationality rather than faith is the crucial criterion for the priesthood. Second (or

Third) Isaiah (66:21) breaks the national connection, permitting foreigners to serve as priests, but for the author of Exodus 19 it is only Israelites—but all of them!—who are included in the promise. The whole nation will be holy.

This promise is tested only a little later in the biblical narrative, when Korah organizes a rebellion against Moses' rule (Numbers 16). The account of the rebellion must be later than the Exodus promise, since it is Korah's central argument that the promise has already been fulfilled: "Ye take too much upon you," he tells Moses and Aaron, "seeing that all the congregation are holy, every one of them, and the Lord is among them: wherefore then lift ye up yourselves above the congregation of the Lord?" Most biblical scholars regard the Korah episode, whatever old traditions it is based on, as a polemical tale written in the course of the exilic or post-exilic controversy between Levitical and Zadokite (Aaronite) priests (see Ezekiel 44).[1] Indeed, Moses takes Korah to be claiming equality with Aaron not for all Israel but only for himself and his relatives: "the sons of Levi." But Korah, in our text, clearly makes a larger claim, and Moses, if he is prepared to deny Levitical holiness, must also be prepared to deny the holiness of all Israel ("every one of them"). How would his denial work? He might insist that the special consecration of the priests, whoever the priests are, is a permanent feature of Israel's religion: all Israel is holy, but some Israelites are more holy than others. Or he might point to the future tense of the verbs in Exodus 19: Israel *will be* a kingdom of priests and a holy nation, but only when it learns to live in accordance with the law.

So there are three positions. The first and perhaps the earliest is conventionally hierarchical, stressing the distinction between priests and laypeople (and perhaps also between high and low priests). The second suggests a kind of priestly utopianism according to which the hierarchy is legitimate but temporary; at some point in the future, priestliness will be universal, at least among the men of Israel. The role of the priests, we might say, paraphrasing Lenin on intellectuals, is to make the priestly specialization unnecessary.[2] The third position is radical and immediate: the people are already holy and the priestly hierarchy is already unnecessary. Moshe Weinfeld argues that the book of Deuteronomy (the work of royal scribes, he thinks, and not of temple priests) defends a modified version of this third position. The authors insist throughout, and usually in the present tense, on the holiness of Israel: "For thou art an holy people unto the Lord thy God: the Lord thy God hath chosen thee" (7:6).[3] Priests have a place in the Deuteronomic account of Israelite society and government, as we shall see, but it is a less important place than in the accounts of Leviticus or Ezekiel or Chronicles, and the emphasis on the responsibilities of the people is concomitantly greater.

But the Deuteronomists are reformers, not rebels like Korah. Against Moses' argument in Numbers 16, they describe a unified priesthood, making no distinction between Levites and Aaronites; against the argument of Leviticus, they downplay the cultic significance of the priesthood as a whole, even allowing a considerable role for ordinary Israelites within the sacrificial system. At the same time, sacrifice seems to be less central to religious life in their book than it is in the priestly writings. They never say, however, that all Israelites are priests, or that they all will be or should be priests. The "constitutional" chapters of Deuteronomy (17, 18) explicitly describe a set of social roles and arrange the description in what we can recognize, from the histories and the prophetic texts, as the standard biblical order: kings, priests, prophets. Even if Israel is (right now) a holy nation, the everyday acting out of its holiness requires a differentiated social structure of a certain sort, in which priests still play an important, though diminished, part.

Still, priestly utopianism, the hope for an undifferentiated holiness, survives in Israel. It is reasserted, for example, by Second (or Third) Isaiah, when the prophet, addressing the entire people, recalls the Exodus promise:

> But ye shall be named the Priests of the Lord: men shall call you
> the Ministers of our God. (61:6)

I will suggest later on that some version of the same utopianism lies behind the Pharisaic and rabbinic claim to displace the priests and take over the task of instructing the people in the rules of holiness. That, however, is a post-biblical development; the claim cannot be realized until after the destruction of the temple.

What, then, is the biblical regime of which the "kingdom of priests" is the utopia? A government in which priests play the leading role comes only at the end of biblical history, in the centuries that follow the return from Babylonia. Throughout most of the Bible, priests occupy the second or, sometimes in more elaborated accounts, the third rank in the political/religious system. The order of prophetic denunciation, for example, is standardly hierarchical—as when Jeremiah foretells the destruction of Jerusalem, David's city,

> because of all the evil of the children of Israel and of the children of Judah, which they have done to provoke me to anger, they their kings, their princes, their priests, and their prophets, and the men of Judah, and the inhabitants of Jerusalem. (32:32)

"Princes" here (*na'sim*) probably refers to royal officials or local notables; their precise political role, constantly alluded to, is nowhere defined. The prophets, as I have already argued, make no claim to rule; they admonish and advise but do not govern. Hence the standard hierarchy can be and often is collapsed into a dyarchy: the regime of kings and priests, where kings are dominant, though the priests are not without their pretensions. The second book of Chronicles provides a quick summary of the dyarchic principle when it has King Jehoshaphat of Judah, a contemporary of Ahab, tell his judges: "Behold, Amariah the chief priest is over you in all matters of the Lord; and Zebadiah the son of Ishmael, the ruler of the house of Judah, for all the king's matters" (19:11). His announcement suggests a doubled judicial system, with priests in charge only of ritual matters. The line in Deuteronomy 17 about priests and judges doesn't make a division of this sort, but it is certainly possible that priests had, under the monarchy, no role at all in "the king's matters." Still, the "matters of the Lord," where they were dominant, were very important.

In practice, the chief priest was appointed by the king: thus Solomon, immediately after his accession, banishes the priest Abiathar from Jerusalem (1 Kings 2:26–27) and puts Zadok in charge of the new temple; and Jeroboam, after establishing an independent kingdom in the north, chooses an entirely new priesthood: "And he made . . . priests of the lowest of the people, which were not of the sons of Levi" (2:31). But Jeroboam is said to have sinned by his choice, and Solomon probably escapes censure only because the Zadokite family that he confirmed in the high priesthood held its position until the Maccabean revolt and wrote all the genealogies. In principle, the office of high priest, at least in Judah, where the temple cult never lapsed, was hereditary. The king, if he chose, chose from among the descendants of Zadok—the direct descendants, if the biblical text is to be trusted.

Since the priests were independently established, they were capable of opposing the king—and they seem to have done so frequently, though not as frequently as the prophets and never for the same sorts of reasons. They were more likely to defend the ritual than the moral code, as in the case of King Uzziah:

> For he [Uzziah] transgressed against the Lord his God, and went into the temple . . . to burn incense upon the altar of incense. And Azariah the priest went in after him, and with him fourscore priests of the Lord, that were valiant men: And they withstood Uzziah the king, and said unto him, It appertaineth not unto thee, Uzziah, to burn incense unto the Lord, but to the

priests the sons of Aaron . . . : go out of the sanctuary; for thou hast trespassed. (2 Chronicles 26:16–18)

This story does not appear in the book of Kings; it is a distinctively priestly story. But even in Kings, priests seem to be involved in palace politics—more or less routinely, if the story of Jehoiada and Jehoash is typical. Jehoiada, the chief priest, was married to Jehosheba, sister of King Ahaziah of Judah. At Ahaziah's death, when his mother seized power, murdering her own grandchildren, the priest and the princess rescued one of their nephews, the infant Jehoash, hid him in the temple for six years, and then, with the help of the palace and temple guards, crowned him king. The accounts in both 2 Kings 11 and 2 Chronicles 23 describe the coronation ceremony and the accompanying covenant: "And Jehoiada made a covenant between the Lord and the king and the people, that they should be the Lord's people; between the king also and the people." Jehoash was seven years old when he was installed, and his uncle served as regent: "And Jehoash did that which was right in the sight of the Lord all his days wherein Jehoiada the priest instructed him" (2 Kings 12:2). But once grown up, Jehoash seems to have fought with his priestly mentor, taking over the management of temple funds and possibly even killing Jehoiada's son Zechariah—not remembering, say the Chroniclers, the kindness of the father (2 Chronicles 24:20–22). The story is told differently in Kings. But both sets of biblical writers seem to regard the high priest as the appropriate regent and mentor for young kings.

Dyarchy had its ups and downs, but it lasted as long as the Judean monarchy. At the end, Jeremiah is still confident of the permanence of both the royal and the priestly partners: David will never lack an heir to sit upon the throne, he says; "neither shall the priests the Levites want a man before me . . . to do sacrifice continually" (33:17–18). And the prophet Zechariah, dreaming of a royal restoration after the exile, describes two rulers, Zerubbabel of David's house and Joshua the Zadokite high priest, each one wearing a crown, "and the counsel of peace shall be between them both" (6:13). In the event, Zerubbabel disappears from the historical record and seems to have been excised from the prophetic vision, leaving behind an interestingly odd sentence, much discussed by biblical scholars: "Then take silver and gold and make crowns, and set them upon the head of Joshua . . . the high priest" (6:11). Two crowns, but only one head: Joshua was the first of the priestly rulers of Israel.[4]

The condition of priestly rule was the destruction of the monarchy by a foreign army. The priests don't make a revolution and seize power; they don't clear the way for themselves; they simply fill a vacuum. Only in Ezekiel's vision of a temple-state do they rule over the king, turning him into what Joachim Becker has called a "supernumerary of the hierocracy, subject to detailed regulation."[5] In the temple-state of history rather than of prophecy, there is no Israelite king. His place is taken by the Persian emperor, named the Lord's servant by Second Isaiah, and then by a local governor, who preferred to rule indirectly, if he could, leaving the day-to-day government to the high priest. So the priestly kingdom, when it finally appears, is a collaborationist regime, without sovereignty or military strength. Deprived of a king, the scope of Israel's politics was drastically reduced.

But the high priest was nonetheless a political potentate, presiding over institutions, directing routine governmental (chiefly judicial) activities, collecting tithes and sometimes other taxes. Gradually, the priest took on the appurtenances of royalty: headdress and crown, tunic and breastplate, anointing oil. His splendor, as it is approvingly described by Ben Sira at the beginning of the second century BCE, certainly exceeded his power, but he embodied as well as symbolized whatever power was left to Israel.[6] Monarchy, when it reappeared, was constructed out of the priestly office. The Hasmoneans were priests before they were kings, and although for them the addition of the second title must have represented an advance, many of their contemporaries had no doubt that being a priest was better—more central to the scheme of things. Thus the author of the post-biblical Book of Jubilees compares the Levites to the highest order of angels, who minister directly to God, fulfilling the promise made to Levi, the son of Jacob, that the "seed of thy sons will be for glory, and greatness, and holiness."[7] This is the credo of the temple-state; it takes no account of the fact that the high priest was an instrument of earthly and foreign kings. Moreover, he was appointed, or at least confirmed, by those same kings, unlike the Judges of pre-monarchic Israel, who were "raised up" by God alone. What, then, made the rule of the priests legitimate in the eyes of lay Israelites?

The legitimacy of any priesthood depends on its priestcraft. Priesthood is an office, not a calling, and everywhere in the ancient world it was a hereditary office. Prophets were called, raised up like the Judges; they came from a place or from a family, and they were given a message to deliver, specific to their time and place. Priests were born to their office, heirs to a highly specialized and, in principle, unchanging knowledge, and they were trained in ancient ritual practices. When challenged, prophets describe the moment of their calling; priests recite their genealogies. Israel's priests might also recall Moses' blessing for the sons of Levi, which constitutes, as it were, their birthright:

> They shall teach Jacob thy [God's] judgments, and Israel thy law: they shall put incense before thee, and whole burnt sacrifice upon thine altar.

This is from Deuteronomy (33:10), and it characteristically reverses the conventional priestly understanding of priestcraft, which, as the book of Leviticus suggests, puts sacrifice first and makes the sons of Levi the teachers, most importantly, of the ritual law and the rules of purity. Other people can teach and judge, but ritual is the priest's exclusive province. At the altar he is truly sovereign.

The priests of the priestly writings (leaving the Holiness Code, Leviticus 18–26, aside for the moment) are the bearers of a very strong version of religious materialism. This doctrine is largely alien to the modern mind, so readers of the Bible today are likely to skip Leviticus, and much of Exodus and Numbers too, or to search in these texts for what they almost certainly don't contain: the symbolism of spirituality. Priests here do not manipulate symbols. They cut up animals and sprinkle the blood on the altar, and they do this because blood *is* (not because blood represents) the life force: "For the life of the flesh is in the blood" (Leviticus 17:11). And they burn the fatty entrails because God likes the smell: it is an "offering made by fire of a sweet savor unto the Lord" (1:9). The blood and the fat were God's "bread," his food, as the priest-prophet Ezekiel still believed (see 44:7), and the sacrifices were effective because of the satisfaction they afforded. It seems to be the doctrine of the priestly writings, hard as it is for us to understand, that God's forgiveness was won by the priestly offering and not by the regret, contrition, or mortification of the sinner. Nor does the offering express the regret; it is what it is, and that means: "it is the blood that maketh an atonement for the soul" (17:11). A substitution is involved—the blood of the animal for the blood of the sinner (sacrificial atonement works only in cases where the death penalty doesn't apply). But this is blood for blood; the blood on the altar does not, again, symbolize the mental state of the sinner.

And it is the priest alone who sprinkles the blood. Indeed, it is only when the priest himself is the sinner that anyone in Israel make atonement on his own behalf. All others, from the "ruler" or "chief" (*nasi*) to "one of the common people," must seek out the priest, provide the appropriate animals, and wait for divine forgiveness: "and the priest shall make an atonement for him concerning his sin, and it shall be forgiven him" (4:26, 31). The case is the same when the "whole congregation of Israel" sins; the priest makes atonement "for them" (4:20), and they, too, are forgiven. Here, surely, is a firm foundation for priestly legitimacy.

But note how the firmness is a function of materialist faith. Turn the sacrifice into a mere votive offering, or make its principal purpose "to provide nutriment for the destitute elements of Israelite society" (as Weinfeld argues the Deuteronomists do), or describe it as the symbol of something else, like regret or repentance, which is not in the priest's control, and priestly legitimacy and the power it supports is radically diminished.[8]

Alternative views of sacrifice are common enough among the prophets, most of whom insist, as we have seen, that it is moral behavior and not ritual strictness, not the blood and fat of "thousands of rams" (Micah 6:7), that ensures the well-being of the people and their security in the land. But in the latter days of prophecy, when the temple was rebuilt and the high priest ruled, the materialism of Leviticus seems to have taken on a new life. We know the power of the doctrine when it becomes the basis not only for ritual observance but also for prophetic denunciation—just as we know the power of the priests when they are blamed, as kings were once blamed, for Israel's sinfulness and subsequent suffering. Consider, then, the following lines from Malachi, the last of the literary prophets, proclaiming, like the first, divine displeasure with Israel but directly addressing the "priests that despise my name":

> Ye offer polluted bread upon mine altar; and ye say, Wherein have we polluted thee? In that ye say, the Table of the Lord is contemptible. And if ye offer the blind for sacrifice, is it not evil? and if ye offer the lame and sick, is it not evil? offer it now unto thy governor; will he be pleased with thee or accept thy person? saith the Lord of hosts. (1:7–8)

The reference here is to the commandment that animals offered to God should be "without blemish." "Blind, or broken, or maimed . . . ye shall not . . . make an offering by fire of them" (Leviticus 22:22). Malachi has these words in mind as clearly as Amos has the Exodus code in mind when he warns the rich against keeping the pledges of the poor (2:8). But what a difference! Amos defends the moral order, and Malachi the ritual order.

It is not my purpose here to criticize Malachi but only to stress the importance of the ritual order in his worldview. Nor do I mean to suggest that the ritual order isn't austere and rigorous. Malachi is himself a critic of lazy and arrogant priests who do not attend to their duties. Nor do these priests, whatever their sins, lack a moral doctrine. In much of Leviticus, as Israel Knohl writes, the "concept of holiness . . . has a ritual character devoid of any moral content." But the Holiness Code of chapters 18–26 (which I shall assume, following Knohl, represents a revision of earlier priestly writings) incorporates a powerful and original moral instruction into the ritual code.[9] Israel's holiness, according to this text, requires both morality and observance—popular righteousness as well as priestly rites. "Love they neighbor as thyself" is, after all, an injunction from Leviticus.

But love and morality in the priestly writings as a whole seem to take second place to holiness more narrowly conceived, sustained by the sin offerings and by the endless rites of purification. God, as the priests understood him, is offended not only by maimed animals on his altars but also by impure human beings in his land. Hence the authors of Leviticus are radically attentive to the dangers of menstrual blood, leprous eruptions, and nightly emissions; also to the dangers of unclean food; also to the dangers of incest, homosexuality, bestiality, and other sexual "abominations." All these matters are delivered to priestly regulation: "to make a difference between the unclean and the clean" (Leviticus 11:47). So the priests, who have limited powers in the usual realms of politics, rule instead over the most intimate aspects of everyday life. They prescribe the sacrifices, make atonement for the sins of the people, teach the people the laws of purity, preside over the rites of purification and determine their success. And these are matters of the utmost importance, for unclean people defile the land, and when "the land is defiled," God tells

In God's Shadow

Moses, "I do visit the iniquity thereof upon it, and the land itself vomiteth out her inhabitants" (18:25).

Because the priests play this critical role, they must observe stricter purity laws than other Israelites; and the rules are strictest for the high priest, who, on the annual Day of Atonement, enters the holy of holies, where God (or God's "glory") dwells, and atones for all Israel. The religious hierarchy is fixed in terms of relative holiness and legal constraint. The nations that surround Israel are unconstrained unless their members enter the land, which literally won't bear defilement; Israelites themselves are subject to the full cleanliness code, which applies in still more rigorous form to the different ranks of priests. These degrees of holiness correspond also to a spatial hierarchy: foreign lands, the holy land, Jerusalem, Mount Zion, the temple, and the temple's inner sanctum. Even Moses, according to the priestly writings, could not enter the inner sanctum (Exodus: 40:35). Israel's greatest ruler (and its original prophet, according to the Deuteronomists) was, so far as holiness is concerned, an ordinary Israelite—or, given his Levitical ancestry, one of the lower priests. The crucial act of sovereignty in the priestly kingdom was the entrance of the high priest into the (literal) presence of God. Here he was alone and supreme.

I want to stress again, however, that this hierarchical doctrine was accompanied by an anti-hierarchical doctrine, which looked forward to the priesthood of all Israel. The Holiness Code, without denying the special role of the priests, proclaims the holiness of Israel as a whole, and this is true of Deuteronomy too, where there is some diminution of priestly importance. When the Pharisees, in the immediate post-biblical period, took it upon themselves to observe the rules of priestly purity in their own homes, they were acting out one strand of the biblical tradition. They claimed no role in the sacrificial system, however, and it seems clear, for all their endlessly detailed study of the clean and the unclean, or better, because they were so intensely interested in *study*, that they had forsaken the central doctrines of priestly materialism.

Committed to the whole of the biblical tradition, they (and their rabbinic successors) maintained a certain respect for priestly genealogy: they acknowledged a religious hierarchy in which they did not come first. But the effective hierarchy, in their view (and in practice, once the temple was destroyed and the sacrificial system abolished) was radically anti-genealogical. A passage in Tractate Horayoth of the Babylonian Talmud suggests the new ranking. When captives are ransomed, the rabbis say, the order of priority is scholar, king, high priest, prophet. In political translation, this means that the rabbis claimed for themselves the first responsibility assigned by Deuteronomy to the priests. They taught "Jacob God's judgments, and Israel God's law." They made themselves the masters of purification, of sacrifice, too, though this was now a purely theoretical mastery, and they were also the masters of a "law" that extended beyond traditional priestcraft. They called upon Israel to study this law: holiness came from study rather than from ritual practice, even when what was studied was the law of ritual practice. There was nothing like priestly mediation or familial privilege in the classroom. Scholars quoted other scholars, but each one stood before the law on equal terms.

During the Babylonian exile and the centuries after the return, the exact character of the priesthood was bitterly debated. I have not found an authoritative or entirely convincing account of these debates, the heroic efforts of many scholars notwithstanding.[10] Nor do I believe it possible with any assurance to assign different pieces of the biblical texts to writers from the rival parties. All such assignments are risky—not only because of the frequent obscurity of the texts but also because the parties changed over time, were themselves divided, and shared many commitments and beliefs. They were all, above all, committed to priestly politics; they disagreed about who the priests were or about the powers and privileges of the different priestly clans. The utopia of a universal (Israelite) priesthood belongs to this period; it finds a suitably homely and material expression in the prophet Zechariah, who foresees a day when

In God's Shadow

the "pots in the Lord's house shall be like the bowls before the altar. Yea, every pot in Jerusalem and in Judah shall be holiness unto the Lord of hosts" (14:20–21).[11] The rabbis, as I have just suggested, are the heirs of this utopianism, though for them it isn't sacrificial pots but legal arguments that are holy unto the Lord. The priests were more interested in the rank ordering of the men who handled the pots. Given the central importance of the temple ritual (and the value of the gifts and offerings that flowed into the holy precincts), the assignment of priestly tasks—cleaning and policing the temple courtyards, guarding the gates, inspecting animals, chanting the psalms, keeping records, offering sacrifices—was of interest in every sense of that loaded word. The people who worked or performed in the temple must have numbered in the thousands; with their families, in the tens of thousands. They seem to have spent a lot of their time inventing genealogies and rewriting Israel's history to enhance their own role or disparage that of their rivals. The political stakes were high but not, so far as I can see, the doctrinal or religious stakes.

Another issue was more critical in the development of Israel's religion: if Zadokites, Levites, or whoever, were the priests, who were the lay men and women for whom they sacrificed and made atonement? Imagine Israel as a holy nation and a kingdom of priests and the answer to this question is clear: all the other nations are lay nations who will make Jerusalem and the temple their religious center. This golden dream of the whole world centered on the temple and its cult is one of the versions, perhaps the dominant version, of biblical universalism. It is sometimes triumphalist in character, as in the passage I have already quoted from Second (or Third) Isaiah. "But ye shall be named the Priests of the Lord . . . ," which continues: "ye shall eat the riches of the Gentiles, and in their glory shall ye boast yourselves" (61:6). But it is better known in the more generous words of the first Isaiah:

> And many people shall go and say, Come ye, and let us go up to
> the mountain of the Lord, to the house of the God of Jacob; and

he will teach us of his ways, and we will walk in his paths: for out of Zion shall go forth the law, and the word of the Lord from Jerusalem. (2:3)

We call such predictions "prophetic," and so they are; but it is worth stressing that the "house of the God of Jacob" is the temple and that the "law" (*torah:* instruction) that will go forth from Zion is the law that the priests claimed they were assigned to teach. This universalism is also priestly in character; it is worked out chiefly in the period of the exile and the return, when the priests were politically dominant; and it reflects their interests—their immediate interests, even before the last days, for the "going up" of the nations need not wait upon the priesthood of all Israel. Zadokites and Levites, or some among them, already imagined themselves at the center of the universe, presiding not so much over a nation as over a community of faith, ready to admit the "sons of the stranger, that join themselves to the Lord":

> Even them will I bring to my holy mountain, and make them joyful in my house of prayer: their burnt offerings and their sacrifices shall be accepted upon mine altar; for mine house shall be called an house of prayer for all people. (Isaiah 56:6–7)

The most interesting controversies reflected in the texts written or revised in the post-exilic period deal with the relations of Israelites with strangers or foreigners. At issue were intermarriage, admission to the temple, religious syncretism, and proselytism; and since this was a time of priestly dominance, intellectually as well as politically, priests were engaged on different sides of all these matters. Ezra's reform program, with its insistence upon an exclusivist Judaism, is often identified as priestly, and, indeed, Ezra was a member of the leading priestly family. But his opponents were the priests of Jerusalem (or many of them), who seem to have had a different understanding of Judaism, denounced by Ezra, Nehemiah too, as assimilationist and even idolatrous. In fact, there were many possible positions, and a good number of actual positions, between exclusivism and assimilation. I see no reason to doubt the religious faithfulness of those priests who were prepared to tolerate intermarriage; who were eager to admit foreigners to the temple services and even to the priesthood ("And I will also take of them [foreigners] for priests and for Levites, saith the Lord" [Isaiah 66:21]); who made their peace with (some) alien religious practices; and who encouraged non-Israelites to "join themselves to the Lord."[12]

All these positions fit very neatly with the generally accommodationist character of the priesthood, most of whose members seem to have been content to acknowledge a foreign sovereign. Elias Bickerman writes of the Chronicler that the "tendency of his work is to recommend a kind of political quietism that should please the court of Susa."[13] It isn't accidental, I think, that the only biblical critique of imperial rule, in Nehemiah 9:36–37, is immediately followed by a covenant of "separation." Political nationalism and religious exclusivism go hand in hand, whereas accommodation provides the more likely partner for a universalist faith. Baruch Levine has recently argued, in his commentary on Leviticus, that two favorite priestly terms, *ha-edah* and *ha-kahal*, "the community" and "the congregation," refer to Israel as a religious rather than a national-political body; they suggest no particular genealogical, familial, or tribal connection, nor do they suggest a geographical location. Levine thinks that this terminology "reflects the life situation of the Judean populace in the early, post-exile period."[14] But, assuming that the terms are late (which is by no means certain), they might more naturally reflect the life situation of Jewry as a whole—dispersed throughout and beyond the Persian empire and engaged locally in social and economic life but still looking to Jerusalem for instruction, sacrifice, and atonement. The priests in turn look to Jews everywhere as their constituents, as members of their congregation. And though they are concerned with their own genealogies, they might well be less concerned with everyone else's; they, or some among them, might even hope for a congregation enlarged by marriage and conversion. Recall that Ezra's mission, according to the decree of the Persian king Artaxerzes, was directed to "all such as know the laws of thy God" (Ezra 7:25). Ezra himself gave these words a very narrow interpretation; but a more broadly conceived priestly mission would seem entirely appropriate in an imperial context.

Accommodation served the priests, and perhaps all Israel, very well. Though we know little about the centuries of priestly rule, they seem to have been a time of prosperity and growth. Certainly the "congregation" of the priests was much larger at the beginning of the second century BCE than it had been at the end of the sixth. But priestly accommodation failed as a policy when it was challenged by the aggressive hellenizing imperialism of the Syrians. And after the Hasmonean revolt, led by one of the lesser priestly families, nationalist ideology reshaped the older politics of the priesthood. The new politics was successful for a time and then brought its own disasters; it was replaced by the new accommodationism of the rabbis, most of whom accepted Roman rule just as the priests had accepted Persian rule, in exchange for a relatively free hand within the Jewish community. At least one priest, known to us by his Roman name, Josephus, would have sustained the old priestly policy. He was a traitor to the short-lived nation-state of the Zealots but at the same time one of the greatest defenders of the Jewish religion as it had been: centered on the temple cult over which the high priest presided. After the destruction of the temple, he defended the Pharisees.[15]

As Josephus suggests, the rabbis were the heirs of the priests, and the temple-state of the priests (like the exile in which it was first imagined) was a kind of prefiguring of rabbinic statelessness. Ruled by men who lacked most of the prerogatives of sovereignty, who had no army and little police power, whose functions were mostly ritualistic, whose "subjects" were uncertain and at least partly self-defined, who compromised with foreign masters, the temple-state has been neglected by biblical students and political historians. What did the priests themselves

In God's Shadow

think of this regime? We hardly know; they must have thought it legitimate, perhaps divine; it is, after all, the regime for which Josephus coined the word "theocracy." But diaspora Jews who dreamt of a return to the land of Israel commonly imagined themselves led by kings rather than priests. The defense of the priesthood by Ben Sira was excluded from the biblical canon; and Josephus's defense was suspect. What account we have in the Bible itself of priestly politics (as distinct from priestly ritual) is confused and confusing, an overwriting of old texts rather than an explicit argument. Nonetheless, the temple-state survived about as long as the monarchy had; it was the last of the biblical regimes, and probably not the worst.

NINE

_____

The Politics of Wisdom

olk wisdom is of indeterminate age, as old, presumably, as the folk; it reflects the common sense of everyday life. But school wisdom, literary wisdom, the collection, refinement, and ideological reconstruction of what the folk produce, comes at a specific point in cultural history. School wisdom develops along with political institutions whose participants require schooling. The earliest forms have the appearance of directly transmitted knowledge: an official writing for his son or, as in Proverbs 31, a queen mother for a young king. It seems likely, though, that mediating figures, teachers, sages, "wise men," were present almost from the beginning. Wisdom literature is the work of the sort of people whom we call intellectuals. I will stick to "wise men" (or "the wise") to match the usage of the biblical texts; when they hold office, they are "counselors."

There were also "wise women" in ancient Israel, two of whom are mentioned in Second Samuel (14:2; 20:16). Wisdom, like prophecy, is nonhereditary and therefore accessible to both sexes (in contrast to priesthood and kingship, both of which descend in the male line). But the phrase "wise woman" appears only once in the wisdom writings (Proverbs 14:1), and women are not expected to serve as royal counselors. Mothers, of course, teach their sons how to live. The first piece of motherly advice, reported in Proverbs 31:3, is "Give not thy strength unto women." Misogyny is a common feature of Proverbs, Ecclesiastes, and the immediately post-biblical Ben Sira; its dominant note is fear of female sexuality rather than contempt for womankind (though that may be present). Like other Israelites, the wise are supposed to marry; the ideal woman is a virtuous wife. "She openeth her mouth with wisdom" (Proverbs 31:26), but this wisdom has to do with domestic, not public, affairs. The virtuous wife is, perhaps surprisingly, active in commerce but never in politics (see 31:16, 18, 24). The texts that we have, even the queen mother's, were presumably written by men.[1]

Still, "wise man" is by no means always a complimentary term—here it resembles its modern equivalent. The first wise men to appear in the Bible serve Egypt's pharaoh (Genesis 41:8, Exodus 7:11), and the identification of wisdom with Egypt is common among the enemies of the wise. In fact, both folk wisdom and school wisdom are international in scope, and Egypt is undoubtedly one of the sources from which Israel's wise men drew; an important section of Proverbs (22:17–24:22) is thought by most scholars to be modeled on the late New Kingdom *Instruction of Amen-em-ope*.[2] Pithy proverbs and gnomic sayings crossed borders as easily as pots and coins, and in all these cases, local products are also likely to be imitations. Wisdom is the most cosmopolitan of biblical genres; the prophets were hostile to it for just that reason. Though it is given an Israelite location in Solomon's and Hezekiah's courts, there is no suggestion of an Israelite history, no moment when wisdom was delivered to the people, like law and prophecy. Only in the Wisdom of Ben Sira is a historical account provided. Ben Sira describes a personified Wisdom seeking a "resting place" among all the nations of the world—until God himself intervenes:

Then the Creator of all things gave me a commandment, and the one who created me assigned a place for my tent. And he said, Make your dwelling in Jacob, and in Israel receive your inheritance. (24:8)[3]

But this nationalization of wisdom comes very late—and at a time when wisdom and *torah* have been effectively assimilated to one another. In the biblical texts, wisdom is recognized as a common possession of Israel and the nations. Wise men, from Pharaoh's officials to Job and his "comforters," are commonly non-Israelites, and though competitive claims are made—"And Solomon's wisdom excelled . . . all the wisdom of Egypt" (1 Kings 4:30)—these claims gain force only by admitting the strength of the competition. Similarly, when the Deuteronomist writes of Israel's revealed law,

> *This* is your wisdom and your understanding in the sight of the nations, which shall hear all these statutes, and say, Surely this great nation is a wise and understanding people (4:6),

he is assuming an international setting within which wisdom is appreciated and pursued.

Israel's wisdom is its law: this is the eventual position of the wise, and it makes their wisdom available, as the law is, to all Israel and not only to the social and political elite. But their original position was very different. A more restricted kind of wisdom can be found in the book of Proverbs, much of which probably dates from the centuries before the exile. The persistent identification of wisdom with Solomon's court may or may not be accurate, but it isn't mere sycophancy. Worldly wit, one of the crucial forms of wisdom, is naturally at home in the court of kings. Why not, then, in the court of Israel's most powerful king? Royal power requires from the courtiers who hope to share it or benefit from it the very qualities that school wisdom seeks to cultivate: prudence, self-control, and eloquence ("sweetness of the lips" in Proverbs 16:21). Though the collections of sayings were probably used in the classroom, wisdom itself was used at court, and we can find in the book of Proverbs a sophisticated and close-up view of life with the king, almost the only view that the Bible provides after the account of David's domestic troubles. This is, usefully, a view from below—though not very far below: it is written from the perspective of the aspiring courtier (or the aspiring teacher of the aspiring courtier). The elders of Israel sought a king so that they might be ruled "like all the nations," and the king's courtiers sought wisdom so that they might advance in office like all the courtiers.

Nothing surprising or original can be found in what we might think of as the royal proverbs—those whose source or target is the court. Their teaching addresses a universal question: how to make a career in the service of the king. A small number of proverbs, grouped largely in chapters 28 and 29, seem to describe a negative experience of kingship, but their style and the nature of the advice they offer is characteristic of the book as a whole. The focus is on an individual learning to find his way in a dangerous environment. As an earlier proverb says,

> The fear of a king is as the roaring of a lion: whoso provoketh
> him to anger sinneth against his own soul (20:2)

—which probably means, puts his life at risk. Proverbs 28:28 simply draws a conclusion from this about how the wise behave in bad times:

> When the wicked rise [to power], men hide themselves.

They don't defy the king either in private or in public; that's not the way of wisdom.

Wise men give advice to the king: How else could they display their wisdom, how else advance at court? "The king's favor is toward a wise servant" (Proverbs 14:35). The classic example of such a wise servant, advanced by royal favor, is Joseph in Egypt. The Joseph story is read by many scholars as a wisdom novella.[4] Joseph himself attributes his dream interpretations to God, but his policy proposals seem to be the product

of his own wisdom and discretion (see Genesis 41:33).[5] They certainly
give Pharaoh every reason to favor him, for their result is a great en-
hancement of royal power: the virtual enserfment of the Egyptian people
(47:20–21). The biblical writers make no comment on Joseph's policies,
though neither the Deuteronomists nor the prophets would have been
likely to accept them had they been enacted on behalf of an Israelite
king. Nonetheless, Joseph is a man "discreet and wise," the most successful of biblical courtiers (until Mordechai and Esther).

The relation between wisdom and success is rarely so direct. The
courtier in Proverbs must be patient and ingratiating as well as wise:

> By long forbearing is a prince persuaded, and a soft tongue
> breaketh the bone. (25:15)

Again:

> The wrath of a king is as messengers of death: but a wise man
> will pacify it. (16:14)

The picture here is of an absolute or near-absolute ruler, who needs advice and seeks it and rewards it. But those who hope to be his advisors
must first be his courtiers—literally: they must court him. The courtship
may require material support (what we call bribes):

> A man's gift maketh room for him, and bringeth him before
> great men. (18:16)

But sweet words, choice words, spoken softly and at exactly the right
moment, are even more important. So the wise must claim, at any rate, else
they would have no role to play in the world of the rich and powerful.

The young pupils addressed in Proverbs seem, indeed, to be children of the rich and powerful; they have to be persuaded that wealth,
while it "maketh many friends" (19:4), nonetheless requires the discipline of wisdom. So far as politics is concerned, this discipline of wisdom
is above all a discipline of the tongue. The young are also warned to

In God's Shadow

avoid strong drink and sexual adventures, and I don't mean to underestimate the importance of such pious and conventional advice; the fear of "strange women" is strong in Proverbs, setting up the portrait of the ideal wife at the end of the book. But the most specifically political advice, and the paradigmatic example of self-control at court, has to do with speech. It, too, can take pious forms:

> Righteous lips are the delight of kings; and they love him that speaketh right. (16:13)

It is more often, however, expressed in secular and prudential terms:

> Whoso keepeth [*shomer:* guards] his mouth and his tongue keepeth his soul from troubles. (21:23)

Or in terms that combine piety and prudence:

> The lips of the righteous know what is acceptable: but the mouth of the wicked speaketh frowardness. (10:32)

There is much else in Proverbs that suggests the character of the king's court, none of it specific to Israel, though it is presumably Israel's kings with whom the pupils of the wise are being taught to deal. What we can learn here is how much like everyone else's these courtiers are: there is no hint anywhere in Proverbs of prophets like Nathan or Elijah who rebuke and admonish kings. What the wise recommend is softness, flattery, fear, caution, and calculation. When you dine with the king, watch your manners (23:1); don't carry tales; learn the art of concealment (11:13). In bad times, take cover (28:12, 28); in better times, control your ambition, move slowly, and don't give yourself airs:

> Put not forth thyself in the presence of the king, and stand not in the place of great men: For better it is that it be said unto thee, Come up hither; than that thou shouldest be put lower in the presence of the prince whom thine eyes have seen. (25:6–7)

And most important of all:

> My son, fear thou the Lord and the king: and meddle not with
> them that are given to change. (24:21)

Nothing is said of the identity of these would-be "changers" (*shonim:*
reformers? rebels?). Except for this line, the only opponents of the wise
mentioned in Proverbs are the wicked. The opposite of wisdom is folly,
but active opposition comes from wickedness. Given the worldview of
the classical wisdom writers, these two are bound to overlap. But the
overlap can't be complete, for the wicked (always unnamed) seem mostly
to be rival courtiers who, since they are often successful, must also have
soft and clever tongues: wisdom of their own. We have no reason, however, to think that any of the wise men are committed to political or social change. More likely, it is Israel's prophets with whom the wise are
taught not to meddle.

Certainly, the prophets were uncomfortable with wisdom. In their
books, the king's counselors, explicitly recognized as wise, are frequently
denounced—because of the pragmatic advice they give and because
they give it in their own name and not in God's name: "Woe unto them
that are wise in their own eyes, and prudent in their own sight" (Isaiah
5:21). "They have rejected the word of the Lord; and what wisdom is in
them?" (Jeremiah 8:9). Whatever wisdom is in them is foreign, most
likely Egyptian; their counsel is identified with the specific policy of
seeking an Egyptian military alliance: "Woe to them that go down to
Egypt for help" (Isaiah 31:1). The wisdom writers permit themselves no
such local references. Their expressions of hostility are generalized and,
unlike those of the prophets, almost never focus on the king. The standard focus is familiar from every other experience of monarchic politics:
it's not the king who is wicked but only his (other) advisors.

> Take away the wicked from before the king, and his throne shall
> be established in righteousness. (25:5)

The few exceptions to this politic argument are similarly general; if they once referred to a specific king or royal policy, the reference is concealed (in accordance with the teaching of the wise):

> As a roaring lion and a raging bear; so is a wicked ruler over the poor people. (28:15)

Wisdom reflects and supports established institutions. The wise men of Proverbs believe in monarchy, accept the political and social hierarchy, endorse the rules of respectability. They are not above flattery:

> A divine sentence is in the lips of the king: his mouth transgresseth not in judgment. (16:10)

Nor do they lack confidence about their own place in the scheme of things:

> Where no counsel is, the people fall: but in the multitude of counselors there is safety. (11:14)

Against the prophetic demand that the king listen only to the word of God, the wise live comfortably in a world shaped by their own words:

> Every purpose is established by counsel: and with good advice make war. (20:18)

Their own good advice is worldly and strategic, aimed at accommodating differences, reaching a compromise, negotiating alliances, and, only as a last resort, making war. The wise are wholly engaged in the world as it is.

The worldliness of the wise should not be taken to mean that they were impious or immoral; in their own fashion they were teachers of righteousness. The world as it is has its own idealism. The privileged classes justify themselves to themselves, and one of the functions of the wise is to provide the terms of this justification. A far greater portion of the book of Proverbs is devoted to ethical admonition than to prudential advice. In fact, however, it is the central doctrine of classical wisdom that ethical admonition *is* prudential advice. No distinction is drawn between politic and pious wisdom. The wise man will respect the established moral and political order (as Joseph does when he spurns Potiphar's wife), and his respect will (eventually) be rewarded. God runs the world in such a way that those who do good also do well. Conversely, those who are already doing well can be reasonably sure of their own (past) goodness. The complacency is fairly amazing, though not uncommon in the long history of power and privilege. In the wisdom texts, complacency is so radical that it is almost impossible to parody; the standard example is from Psalms:

> I have been young, and now am old; yet have I not seen the righteous forsaken, nor his seed begging bread. (37:25)

Proverbs is full of similar assurances (see, for example, 10:3), and they are provided for the people as a whole as well as for the individual—though without any noticeable interest in the relation between the two. When the wise say,

> Righteousness exalteth a nation: but sin is a reproach to any people [or, in an alternative reading: sin impoverishes the people] (14:34),

they make no effort to specify the references: whose sin? which people? These questions, so central to the prophetic writings, are never asked in the wisdom literature, so the problems of collective punishment and individual responsibility are never raised. A strong though naive understanding of individual responsibility is fundamental to wisdom—required, perhaps, by the school setting. But this understanding is entirely unproblematic. It is also entirely ahistorical, and these two negative qualities may well be connected. The fate of nations and families, the punishment of one generation for the sins of another, the hope or fear of days to come—none of this can be imaginatively brought to mind without history. It is a striking feature of Job's indictment of God's justice that he never says a word about the death of his children, the loss of posterity. He is narrowly focused, as we shall see, on his own righteousness and his own suffering. When complacency collapses, wisdom is reduced to personal anger, despair, and cynicism (and together with these, or because of them, to a kind of philosophy); the prophets, by contrast, take refuge in eschatology.

Job's righteousness is the righteousness of Proverbs. He has lived in accordance with the moral sayings of the wise, and he claims, as it were, his material entitlements. If we believe that virtue is its own reward, or that it had better be its own reward since there is no other, we will view this claim as the sign of a low morality. But the level of performance required by the wise isn't low; nor should we assume that doctrinal complacency necessarily leads to personal slackness. Those who pride themselves on actually living up to the ethical requirements of Proverbs would be recognizable, even to the prophets, as good people. I want to stress this point: the ethics of the wisdom literature is a high ethics, even if it lacks the critical tone, the passionate engagement, and the historical specificity of other biblical writings.

The wise characteristically "turn away" from evil rather than confront it directly (just as the prudent courtier "hides" from the wicked):

> Enter not into the path of the wicked, and go not in the way of
> evil men. Avoid it, pass not by it, turn from it and pass away.
> (Proverbs 4:14–15)

Job is a man who "fears the Lord and *departs from evil*" in accordance with the advice of Proverbs 3:7; the italicized phrase is repeated five times in Proverbs and in a number of the Psalms; it is used only once elsewhere in the Bible (in Isaiah). The characteristic injunction of Deuteronomy, by contrast, is: "*put away* the evil from Israel"—a collective imperative requiring action rather than avoidance. The action required, in all nine passages where the phrase appears, is the killing of the evildoers. Proverbs is more benign: angry kings may threaten death; wise men appease them.

Proverbs and Deuteronomy are the two great instructional books of the Bible. They seem to come out of the same stratum of urban scribes and officials, but they are profoundly dissimilar—as if they were written, Proverbs before, Deuteronomy during or after, an extraordinary religious revival. Many of the injunctions are the same, though they appear as the advice of the wise in the first book and the commandments of the Lord in the second. The language and tone are different, befitting advice and command respectively, but more important, the arguments are different too. In Deuteronomy, God's commands are located within a historical narrative, accepted by the people in the form of a covenant, and justified by reference to the experience of Egyptian bondage. In Proverbs, there is no reference either to Egypt or to Sinai, no hint of a covenant. The rule of life, as it appears in (what are probably) the pre-exilic parts of the book, is sought out through human wisdom, and it is defended by reference to the God of creation, not the God of history:

> He that oppresseth the poor reproacheth his Maker. (14:31; 17:5)

> The rich and the poor meet together: the Lord is the maker of them all. (22:2)

Job, in self-defense, makes the same point:

> If I did despise the cause of my manservant or of my maidservant, when they contended with me; What then shall I do when God riseth up? . . . Did not he that made me in the womb make him? (31:13–15)

Wisdom's ethic is more universalistic than Deuteronomy's, a fact driven home by an interesting linguistic reversal: in Deuteronomy, the most common object of moral conduct is "your brother"; in Proverbs, it

In God's Shadow

is "your neighbor" (or, often in the King James version, "your friend": the Hebrew is *re'echa*). The word "brother" and its cognates appears some fifty times in Deuteronomy; "neighbor," eighteen times. In Proverbs, "neighbor" appears thirty-three times, "brother" only eight.[6] And since Israel itself is not mentioned in Proverbs, brotherhood for the wise, when they refer to it, is always a familial, not a national, relationship. Perhaps for this reason, the social ethic of Proverbs lacks something of the intensity of Deuteronomy. The wise urge their students to have mercy on the poor (14:21), to give them bread (22:9), not to rob them (22:22), not to oppress them by seizing their fields (23:10) or taking usury from them (28:8), and so on. But there is nothing like the power of the Deuteronomic command:

> If there be among you a poor man of one of thy brethren within any of thy gates . . . thou shalt not harden thine heart, nor shut thine hand from thy poor brother: But thou shalt open thine hand wide unto him. (15:7–8)

Wise men don't lack good will toward the poor, but a wide open hand is not their way.

Similarly, when the wise say, "with good advice make war," they are setting themselves against Deuteronomy's holy warfare, urging an alternative political ethic. They mean: seek military alliances, fight only when it is prudent, make peace as soon as the fighting ends. Since God created neighbors as well as brothers, the war of extermination is ruled out. Ahab was probably following the advice of his counselors when he signed a peace treaty with the Syrians (and was denounced by one of Israel's prophets). Warfare is a secular, not a religious activity; therefore its violence is limited. This is an important position, represented in some of the legal codes and exemplified in the histories, but without doctrinal defense anywhere in the biblical books. It is not defended even in the wisdom writings, only implied. The wise don't challenge God's warriors any more than they challenge the king. Theirs is not an ethics of confrontation, and so the alternative they embody doesn't take any forceful form.[7]

Political and moral advice in Proverbs is directed to individuals, never to the people as a whole.[8] But since these individuals are expected to become judges and officials, even kings, there is no lack of concern with the people's fate. The students may be focused on their own careers, but these are public careers, and the well-being of the public is their supposed object. "The king by judgment establisheth the land" (29:4)—and not merely his own throne. But this connection between the wise and the people, mediated by the practice of officeholding, disappears from the later wisdom literature. "To Koheleth [Ecclesiastes]," writes Elias Bickerman, "the idea of public service is alien; the government for him is tyrannical, and there is no word . . . on man's duties to his fellow men."[9] In fact, the author of Ecclesiastes still seems to be writing for young men with political ambitions who hope to attend the king in his court. But Bickerman is right to suggest that the king appears now only under the aspect of power, never of justice; and no effort is made to relate the ambition of the young to the well-being of the nation.

> I counsel thee to keep the king's commandment . . . Be not hasty
> to go out of his sight: stand not in an evil thing; for he doeth
> whatsoever pleaseth him. Where the word of a king is, there is
> power: and who may say unto him, What doest thou? (8:2–4)

The line "stand not in an evil thing" translates four Hebrew words that are thought by most modern scholars to have a more radical meaning. The King James version quoted above is apologetic. What the author is probably advising is something like "don't hesitate to do the bad things the king suggests" or "don't persist in things the king thinks bad."[10] Both these alternatives fit nicely into the passage as a whole, and they point to what has been called the "crisis" of classical wisdom.[11] The wise no longer believe that morality and prudence require the same behavior. And insofar as their wisdom is worldly wisdom, rooted in a claim to understand the way things really are, they can no longer give moral counsel. They can't say to their students what would now be necessary: act rightly and put your life at risk. That is not the way of the wise. The real advice of Ecclesiastes is to give up political ambition and avoid the public arena. (The author isn't entirely comforting about private life either, but that is not my subject here.) If you must attend the king, then obey him without question. Don't try to counsel him or turn him away from evil. Don't imagine that your righteous lips will delight him and win you a place by his side.

The historical background of this radical shift is not easy to make out. What events do the crisis of classical wisdom reflect? Or is Ecclesiastes the work, as it well might be, of a single disillusioned sage? It isn't difficult to imagine the author as an intellectual provocateur, challenging the complacency of his colleagues, enjoying their outrage. Indeed, he was one of them, as the epilogue to his book tells us: "[He] sought out, and set in order, many proverbs" (12:9)—exactly like the "men of Hezekiah" in Proverbs 25:1. But the world of Ecclesiastes, and not only the temperament of its author, seems entirely different from that of Hezekiah's wise men. The usual account of the difference holds that Ecclesiastes is a post-exilic book; the intellectual crisis is the product of political defeat, the destruction of the land, the trauma of deportation, the loss of sovereignty. Of course, if the standard scholarly dating is right (fourth or early third century BCE), then all that lies rather far in the background. The author seems to be the member of a secure and prosperous upper (if not ruling) class; he doesn't read like someone devastated by political loss—nor, like Job, by personal loss. The injustice he sees around him can't have been new; nor is there any reason to think that it was worse (how could it be worse?) than the injustice described by the pre-exilic prophets.

Perhaps the difference has to do with the prolonged experience of foreign rule. It is hard to imagine the wise men of Proverbs summing up their political understanding of Israel's monarchy in the fashion of Ecclesiastes:

> I noted all that went on under the sun, while men . . . had authority over men to treat them unjustly. (8:9—NJPS)

These unappealing "men" are certainly not Israelite kings; the point is confirmed in the most important of the political statements in Ecclesiastes, where Judea is referred to as an imperial province (*medina:* the word is used chiefly in the books of Ezra, Nehemiah, and Esther):

> If you see in a province oppression of the poor and suppression of right and justice, don't wonder at the fact, for one high official [*shomer*] is protected by a higher one, and both of them by still higher ones. (5:7–8—NJPS)

This sentence seems to describe a hierarchy of corrupt officials, each one preying upon the next below, protected by the next above, with the people the ultimate victims. And it may be that what makes the oppression so unsurprising is that these are not Israelite officials. The absence of surprise is a token of resignation and powerlessness.

Still, the intellectual crisis is not explained—for there were surely Israelite wise men (as there were priests) who accommodated themselves to Persian imperialism. We can't understand resignation and despair merely by getting their dates right. The pre-exilic prophets were not resigned; and the post-exilic Ben Sira, living under a later imperialism, was not despairing. In fact, we are never going to know what public or private experience drove the author of Ecclesiastes to his view of human life as empty and vain. But if we look more closely at this view, we can perhaps see what opens wisdom to despair.

Ecclesiastes calls all human activity into question, but the book is focused on competitive activity: the pursuit of wealth and office. It was precisely here that classical wisdom had promised success. The value of success was mostly taken for granted: it was a sign of God's favor; it served the public good; it was itself delightful; and it enhanced the lives of one's posterity:

A good man leaveth an inheritance to his children's children. (Proverbs 13:22)

Although it contains no vision of the future, the literature of wisdom is consistently forward-looking. Its direction is represented by its form of address: "my son." The form is figurative: the wise speak to all the sons of Israel or, at least, of Israel's elite, as if they were the children of their teachers, the legitimate heirs of wisdom. Taken by itself, however, wisdom does nothing to strengthen the ties that it presupposes. The priestly writers look back to Aaron and the building of the tabernacle in order to look forward to a time when the temple will be seen as the world's center. The prophets look back to Moses and the covenant in order to look forward to the blessings and the curses. Wisdom provides no view of the past, so its hold on the future is fragile and problematic.[12]

The crisis of wisdom is the crisis of men who have nothing to think about but their own careers. They can still make money and survive at court. But, for whatever reason, they have lost faith in the meaningfulness of these activities. Their wealth will not benefit their children, and their political success has no larger value.

For there is a man whose labor is in wisdom, and in knowledge, and in equity; yet to a man that hath not labored therein shall he leave it for his portion. (Ecclesiastes 2:21)

So much for "my son." He would do better to make his own way than to inherit from me—or this is closer to the spirit of the text: I can take no pleasure in leaving my wealth (or my wisdom) to him. Nor can the wise serve the people:

I . . . considered all the oppressions that are done under the sun: and behold the tears of [the] oppressed, and they had no comforter; and on the side of their oppressors there was power; but they had no comforter. (4:1)

Wisdom is not a literature of comfort; it is a literature of success. But if success brings no benefit, what is its point? The advice of Ecclesiastes is to focus all one's energies on one's own life, on oneself, without thinking about the legacy, public or private, that one might leave to future generations:

There is nothing better than that a man should rejoice in his own works; for that is his portion: for who shall bring him to see what shall be after him? (3:22)

But this joy is forever shadowed by the foreknowledge of death, which brings everything to an end. Act now, says the author of Ecclesiastes, for the time is fast approaching when you will never act again.

Whatsoever thy hand findeth to do, do it with thy might; for there is no work, nor device, nor knowledge, nor wisdom, in the grave, whither thou goest. (9:10)

I can think of no passages in the writings of priests or prophets where death is so clearly pictured as an absolute end—not that either priests or prophets believe in an afterlife: rather, they believe in a genea-logical and a national future. They give substance and particularity to wisdom's "my son," though the standard form of their address is "my people." It is because of his sense of historical connection that Second Isaiah can play the part that wisdom avoids: "Comfort ye, comfort ye my people" (40:1).

The author of Ecclesiastes gives up on the people, not because he thinks they are wicked but because he is incapable of helping them—incapable even of helping his own children. He recognizes no causal link between his efforts and their well-being. Wholly missing from his book is any commitment to an ongoing project—as in these lines from later rabbinic wisdom:

In God's Shadow

It is not thy duty to finish the work, but thou art not at liberty to neglect it.[13]

Some such idea might well underlie the work of collecting proverbs and instructing the young, but it finds no clear articulation in the writings of the wise. That is why the crisis of wisdom, whatever events it reflects, is inherent in the wisdom literature from its beginnings.

Retreating into himself, the author of Ecclesiastes is simply following the advice of Proverbs: when the wicked take power, the wise take cover. It would be a mistake, however, to describe this response (as I have been doing) in wholly negative terms. From their cover, the wise still watch the world, and they see it perhaps more clearly than priests and prophets do. They certainly see it with a more practical eye—thus the lines in Ecclesiastes about the bureaucratic hierarchy, perhaps the only biblical example of structural analysis; the cool rejection of all the conventional pieties about righteousness and its reward; and the first explicit appreciation (in the biblical writings) of bourgeois private life:

> Live joyfully with the wife whom thou lovest all the days of [thy] life. (9:9)

There are no children in evidence, however, to connect husband and wife to the larger community and to the future. What Ecclesiastes appreciates is a private life without responsibility: a quiet, reflective, skeptical, occasionally tender hedonism, whose (male) protagonist achieves greatness only because he is so angry at the world from which he has withdrawn.

> I saw . . . the place of judgment, that wickedness was there; and the place of righteousness, that iniquity was there. (3:16)

Wisdom disillusioned drifts toward philosophy; proverbs are replaced by questions and arguments. The drift is clearest in Job, a book that explicitly denies what Proverbs and even Ecclesiastes take for granted: the accessibility of wisdom. Deuteronomy, appropriating the traditions of the wise, says of Israel's own wisdom that "it is not hidden from thee." It is not in heaven nor across the sea, but very near: "in thy mouth and in thy heart" (30:11–14). But Job asks, "Where shall wisdom be found?" and answers that "it is hid from the eyes of all [the] living" (28:12, 21). Wisdom is hidden for the same reason that the wise are hiding: because of the triumph of wickedness in the world, which is as inexplicable as it is frightening. It can't be accounted for on the classical assumption of a visible moral order and a reasonably prompt and predictable divine justice. And so wisdom becomes God's secret, and philosophy is the human effort to search it out. To be sure, the conclusion of the argument in Job is that it can't be searched out; the only wisdom available to humanity is the fear of God. But this conclusion has rarely seemed persuasive to readers of the rest of the book. Job's questions are only a beginning.

Why does he ask his questions and then insist on them with such vehemence? It's not the case that no answers were available. Faced with the suffering of Israel, biblical writers managed to work out a number of more or less plausible explanations. But Israel for them was already located within a historical order, and so their explanations could look both backward and forward. There was room for maneuver. Job, by contrast, thinks only of the suffering individual and only of the present time; he wants to know why *he* is suffering *right now*. Israel knew itself as a people who had often failed to live up to its covenantal obligations. Job, by contrast again, was certain of his own righteousness; in accordance with the doctrine of Proverbs, he had always "turned away" from evil. It is his self-assurance and his self-absorption and his present-mindedness that drive his questions. He is in this sense the perfect heir of classical wisdom: radically focused on himself.

Martin Buber claims that when we read Job, "we think less of the sufferings of an individual than of the exile of a people."[14] Surely most readers of the book will find this claim surprising. I can't see anything in

In God's Shadow

the text that invites Buber's move from individual to collective experience. Indeed, from the beginning to the end of biblical wisdom, no effort is made to address the history of Israel. We have no more reason to read the complaint of Job than we have to read the advice of Proverbs as if it had some (secret) historical reference. The apolitical character of later wisdom may have a historical cause—imperial conquest and exile—but there is no evidence that the author of Job made this cause his subject. The suffering of a righteous man is subject enough.

Job has no public career, no life at court, no royal reward for the eloquence of his tongue. He is instead God's courtier, made rebellious by disappointment. And God, like a good king, does reward him in the end (even if the end is unbelievable) because he has spoken "the thing which is right" (42:8). Moshe Greenberg has written of Job that "his unmerited suffering opens his eyes to the injustice rampant in society at large."[15] The clearest example of this recognition comes from chapter 24, where Job speaks of the oppressed with a degree of compassion unmatched in the wisdom literature, perhaps in the Bible as a whole. The prophets, whose eyes are equally open, are so quick with judgment and menace that they rarely give themselves the room that Job takes here to describe the experience of oppression and, more particularly, the experience of poverty and homelessness:

> The poor of the earth hide themselves together. Behold, as wild asses in the desert, go they forth to their work . . . the wilderness yieldeth food for them and for their children . . . They are wet with the showers of the mountains, and embrace the rock for want of a shelter. (24:4-5, 8)

But this sort of thing is rare even in Job, for it is his *own* unmerited suffering that is the chief subject of his speeches. And when these speeches, as Greenberg says, "assume the character of a 'covenant lawsuit' in reverse, man accusing God instead of God accusing man," it is only his own case that Job presses. His is not a class action suit:

Behold now, I have ordered my cause; I know that I shall be justified. (13:18)

Behold, I cry out of wrong, but I am not heard: I cry aloud, but there is no judgment. (19:7)

Job is in no sense a political or legal spokesman for the oppressed. But he is something like a representative man. With no national identity, covenantal allegiance, or familial bonds, he is innocent and vulnerable. Out of his very self-absorption, he makes himself archetypal. The great philosophical question posed by the book, Why does man suffer?, is in fact a naively generalized version of the question Why am I suffering? Job offers no vision of a better society where suffering might be alleviated (for some people, some of the time). He doesn't "meddle with them that are given to change." He has made, indeed, a great discovery: he knows that the world is not as the wise have described it (and still describe it, sitting in front of him), and he demands an accounting. But he knows this and asks this *as one of the wise.* His own search for understanding is still driven by the hope for personal success—in the form, now, of divine vindication. And he still believes, like the author of Proverbs and unlike the author of Ecclesiastes, that "righteous lips are the delight of kings." If only God would listen to him, he says in his final speech,

I would declare unto him the number of my steps; as a prince would I go near unto him. (31:37)

It turns out, of course, that God has been listening all along. Job is indeed brought near, persuaded to stop his radical questioning (though his questions are never answered), and restored to prosperity. The epilogue to Job, describing his restoration, represents the end of the crisis of classical wisdom. I don't mean to make any claims about the chronology of the various texts (many scholars would date Ecclesiastes after Job), only about the meaning of this one. No doubt, the end comes too easily, but that is what happens with crises sometimes, in the intellectual if not in the practical world. Job learns to fear God and to turn away from philosophy. Wisdom is decisively subordinated to piety, without any further inquiry into piety's prudential value. Soon that value will be guaranteed by the doctrine of the afterlife, but Job's latter end, blessed by God, already anticipates the well-being of the wise in the world-to-come.

What happens to the pupils of the wise in this world once the crisis is over? The seven sons and three daughters of Job's second family, who live happily ever after, resuming unproblematically the life of his first family, might answer this question; but they are not allowed to speak. In fact, I suppose, they (the sons, at least) went back to school, where they studied proverb collections very much like those in the biblical book of Proverbs and learned how to make their way in the world. But this world was no longer centered on the royal court. We can get some sense of what it was like by looking briefly at the work of Joshua Ben Sira, who ran what must have been one of the last of the wisdom schools, in the years before these were replaced by the rabbinic academies.[16]

Ben Sira's book of wisdom is post-biblical, but I think that it reveals what we might think of as the progress of biblical wisdom. The book is wonderfully complex, and I shall make no effort here to grapple with its complexity. It includes a political history of Israel in the form of a Hellenistic encomium: a hymn of praise for famous (or pious) men, in which priests and prophets fare better than kings, and the wise are not mentioned at all.[17] It provides a portrait, perhaps a self-portrait, of the scribe who devotes himself at one and the same time to the study of God's law and the "wisdom of the ancients," to prophecies and proverbs—as if these two, carefully distinguished in the biblical texts, were now a single subject. And it offers, as I suggested at the beginning of this chapter, a vision of wisdom nationalized: it is the first explicitly Jewish proverb collection. None of this is my concern here; rather, I want to focus on

Ben Sira's book as an attempted restoration of biblical wisdom. He copies, imitates, and repeats the arguments of Proverbs (other books too, but this one above all), though always incompletely, one-sidedly, with subtle changes, so that we can see in his work the tendency of wisdom across its crisis—not the radical break of Ecclesiastes and Job but the underlying drift.[18]

Ben Sira is focused almost exclusively on the private life of his pupils. When he speaks of counsel, he rarely has in mind the advice that a wise man gives to a king; he thinks instead of friends counseling one another. His sexual ethic is not designed to free the ambitious courtier from distraction and danger but to stabilize the family and ensure the authority of the husband. When he describes proper behavior at a banquet, it is a private dinner party, not the royal table, that occupies his attention. His "instruction concerning speech," as important here as in Proverbs, has to do with gossip, bragging, vulgarity, and swearing in the streets and houses of the city, not with the politic discourse required in the presence of the powerful. All this is not to say that Ben Sira has no interest in secular ambition; he claims to teach his pupils, in the classical style, "how to serve great men" (8:8). But his emphasis falls elsewhere. Insofar as he speaks of public life, his reference is to the local assembly rather than the king's court, and nothing that he says suggests that attendance in the assembly is crucial to the careers of his young men.

Nonetheless, Ben Sira is a restorationist, focused once again on those careers and confident of their value. Wisdom is accessible again; it is only necessary to

draw near to me, you who are untaught, and lodge in my school.
(51:23)

And for all his emphasis on studying *torah*, the wisdom that Ben Sira teaches is still, mostly, like the wisdom of Proverbs, founded on experience and observation. It is more like worldly advice than religious command. His book is full of biblical quotations and paraphrases, but he is

In God's Shadow

very much an independent author, advisor, teacher, adding to the stock of wisdom:

> Those who understand sayings become skilled themselves, and pour forth apt proverbs. (18:29)

Politics is largely lost in this restoration. Looking back, however, from the perspective that Ben Sira provides, we can question whether it was ever as central to the wisdom tradition as I have made it seem. Wisdom is an ethic and a policy for everyday life. When the conditions of that life carried the pupils of the wise into the king's court, wisdom taught the courtier arts; when conditions changed, wisdom taught a more general civility. In fact, the wise, in Israel at least, never made politics crucial to the idea of a good life. That is why it was so easily abandoned during the crisis—and never resumed in its aftermath. The wisdom literature never expresses any strong political purposiveness nor any commitment to the well-being of a particular group of people. And, what is perhaps more important, the special kind of courage that politics (sometimes) requires is entirely alien to the self-understanding of the wise. Here, again, Ben Sira is a restorationist:

> Do not seek from the Lord the highest office, nor the seat of honor from the king . . . Do not seek to become a judge, lest you be unable to remove iniquity . . . and thus put a blot on your integrity. (7:4, 6)

> Do not contend with a powerful man, lest you fall into his hands. (8:1)

> Keep far from a man who has the power to kill, and you will not be worried by the fear of death. (9:13)

Because wisdom is so profoundly prudential, one might well hope for rulers who consult the wise: they will be less likely to take risks in public policy and so to impose risks on their subjects. But the wise won't insist on being consulted. "A wise man is cautious in everything," says Ben Sira (18:27), and he is cautious first of all on his own behalf and only after that on the city's behalf. There is no reason to look to wisdom for anything more than prudential advice: how best to go about doing whatever the ruler wants to do. The larger political question—What ought to be done?—lies beyond wisdom's reach, beyond the ambition of the young men. The larger question is important, however, as even the wise can sometimes understand. "Where there is no vision, the people perish" (Proverbs 29:18)—this is one of the most insightful and exceptional of wisdom's sayings, for "vision" (*hazon*) is nowhere else in the Bible associated with wisdom, only with prophecy. The biblical writers here reproduce a historic dichotomy, common to many cultures: The prudent men who whisper in the ear of the king have nothing to say about the nation's destiny; their angry adversaries in the streets of the city are radically imprudent. Or, in biblical terms, the wise lack vision, and the prophets have only disdain for political wisdom.

TEN

Messianism

I want to define messianism in the broadest possible way, to include any doctrine of a future redemption, whether or not the agent of redemption is an individual messiah. Only one qualification is necessary: messianic futures are radically discontinuous with the present. Messianism isn't developed through a projection of current trends, even if the trends are "progressive" in character; nor is it a matter of modest improvement in current conditions, even if the conditions are awful. The local and temporary deliverances described in the book of Judges are not messianic. The deliverers themselves may be proto-messiahs, early examples of a figure fully developed only in royalist ideology; but they work on a small scale, and the fact that their accomplishments need to be repeated proves their anchorage in an untransformed present.

Even Moses is only a proto-messiah, though he appears in Exodus as the divinely appointed agent of a literal redemption. Indeed, it is the failure of this first redemption to live up to its promise that produces, centuries later, the more radical or extravagant or visionary doctrine of a second redemption, which we call messianic. The second redemption escapes the historicity and conditionality of the first; it is final, and it is certain. It doesn't seem, however, to be responsive in the same way to the suffering of the people, whose "groaning" in Egyptian bondage was the immediate cause of God's call to Moses (Exodus 2:23–25). The story is similar in Judges: "And when the children of Israel cried unto the Lord, the Lord raised up a deliverer" (3:9). Messianic deliverance, perhaps because it doesn't occur within a conventional historical narrative, has no such clear-cut occasion.

But if the messianic age is in some sense post-historical, the doctrine of the messianic age is certainly a historical artifact, a construction of future time that emerges out of earlier constructions. From the beginning, biblical writers are committed to a forward-looking, future-oriented view of history. They seem to know nothing about, or perhaps they are opposed to, the standard ancient conception of cyclical time, shaped by natural processes: birth, maturity, death, and rebirth. Even when they urge their readers to remember the past—the exodus from Egypt and the covenanting at Sinai—they are pointing back to events that point forward, events full of promise, that lie on a (relatively) straight line with Israel's present or with days yet to come.

The simple linearity of the exodus story, however, isn't repeated in later biblical books. Except for Ezekiel's forced march through the wilderness (20:33–38) and Second Isaiah's opposing vision of a quick and painless return from Babylon (49:9–13), the image of people marching doesn't recur. It has become one of the central symbols of leftist politics: think, for example, of the Italian anthem "Avanti Populo" or the Yiddish socialist newspaper *Forwarts*. The march, according to the Czech novelist Milan Kundera, is the deep cliché of the left, but it suggests an active and participatory politics that has no place in biblical messianism.[1] We hear an echo of it, perhaps, in Hosea's and Jeremiah's denunciations of popular backsliding, but neither of these prophets says anything to suggest that the opposite of backsliding is a forward movement toward some political goal. Jeremiah's new covenant (31:31–34), which inaugurates what is certainly, in the extended sense of the word, a messianic age, requires nothing of the people, not even their consent; it is a pure gift of God. It fulfills unconditionally what had once been promised on terms, as a reward for human effort.

The deliverances in Judges seem to have a cyclical or, at least, recurrent character: sin, oppression, redemption, sin again. But this cycle is not a natural one; the recurrence is not preordained but historically specific, and the stories contain no bar to the dream of a complete and final deliverance. I assume that there was resistance to this dream and to the dream-politics that followed from it; there must have been practical-minded Israelites who thought that small deliverances were good enough: a place that was better than Egypt, even if it wasn't a perfect place; a peace that lasted more than a few years, even if it was followed, as in Judges, by renewed war; a victory that was more or less decisive, even if it wasn't the final victory in the last battle against the assembled forces of evil. But I don't know of any incremental view of events of this sort, any hope that the sum of small deliverances would be large enough to fulfill the divine promise. Those writers who thought that the promise was yet unfulfilled waited for a more dramatic fulfillment. So the stories in Judges were never added up or shaped into a single narrative; instead, the model story was, much later, enlarged and given world-historical significance. Not in these days, not in the world of the everyday, but in those days, at the end of days, *afterwards*, a deliverer would come whose story would be the last political story we would ever have to tell.

The last story culminates in a radical newness: unlike the nature cycle, its end is not the same as its beginning. And yet the end is always foreshadowed by the beginning, for even the messianic (and, similarly, even the revolutionary) imagination needs precedents and examples. Royal messianism looks back to David, though its promise—in Psalm 72, for example—far exceeds anything that the historical David achieved. Theocratic messianism looks back to God and Israel in the wilderness and to the Sinai covenant, though the prophets of God's kingdom mis-remember the wilderness period and hope for a new, not simply a re-newed, covenant. In post-biblical eschatologies, the messianic age is commonly described in edenic terms: a return to paradise. But this last version of messianism reflects a syncretism of Jewish and Hellenistic understandings and a surrender of the historical specificity of biblical thought.

Messianism grows out of the historical writings. It isn't easy to explain how this happens; nothing quite like the biblical doctrine of future time appears in the literature of other ancient peoples. I assume that the doctrine is religiously driven, even when the future is described in explicitly political terms: the rule of a good king, the reign of justice, the triumph of Israel over its adversaries. What is involved here is not simply an act of political/psychological transference, as if all that the people desire but can't have in the present is simply shifted into the future. No doubt a shift of this sort serves to relieve political tensions here and now, but it is hard to believe that the prophets had any such purpose in mind. This is the vulgar and reductionist explanation of any future-oriented faith, whether of a nation in the days to come or of an individual in the afterlife: "pie in the sky when we die."

The better understanding of messianism is religious, even theological, though the biblical writers offer nothing like an explicit theology. If God is active in history, then history must have an end worthy of his interest. It can't end in military defeat, destruction, and despair for his chosen people. Similarly, if God permits the wicked to prosper and the righteous to suffer in this life, he must plan appropriate punishments and rewards in another time and place: the "world to come" is a post-biblical invention, but it is driven by the same logic that drives biblical messianism. An argument of this sort can make for complacency (and also for recklessness) in the face of political crises. Amos is taking aim at that complacency when he has God ask, "Are ye not as children of the Ethiopians unto me, O children of Israel?" (9:7). But then, one might say, history can't end in destruction and despair for the Ethiopians either. If God is just and nothing more, then no one, as Hamlet says, will escape whipping; but if he is faithful, compassionate, and loving, there must be something better in store for Israel—and perhaps for the other nations, too.

This hope is fed by disappointment and gets more and more extravagant with each feeding. But disappointment is not an independent variable in human history; it is a function of expectation, which is to say, of hope itself. That is why the prophets could be disappointed even before the political disasters of 721 and 587: prophetic hopes were set very high. It isn't clear whether disappointment led them beyond the angry demand that Israel live right now in accordance with the covenant and the fierce warnings of disasters to come if their call went unheeded. Many commentators regard anything more than this, any prophecy relating to a time after the divine punishment, as a later addition. But the pre-exilic prophets may have imagined what their books, as we have them, suggest: failure now, punishment soon, and a new age of justice and peace afterward. The character of the new age is determined in the Bible by the hopes that the prophets have for Israel, qualified in two ways by their disappointment: first, the new age is now entirely God's work and not the work of the people or their leaders; and second, the new age takes on a kind of completeness and perfection that it cannot have had before it was set in the indefinite future, in God's time.

No single, authoritative picture of the messianic future emerges in the Bible; instead, many different pictures reflect different understandings of covenantal politics and different imaginings of peace (among nations, or individual men and women, or all God's creatures) and social justice (with kings and priests or without them). For our purposes, the crucial difference is between two versions of the future that follow directly from the arguments over monarchy. In their original form, these arguments have nothing to do with messianism. The kingdom of God as it appears in the books of Judges and Samuel is not a dream of days to come but an immediate reality. When God tells Samuel that the assembled people, demanding a king, "have not rejected thee, but they have rejected me, that I should not reign over them" (1 Samuel 8:7), he means to say that he *has been* reigning. And there is plainly nothing messianic about his human successors, even in the eyes of the people, who have, as I argued in Chapter 4, a thoroughly pragmatic understanding of kingship. In later years, however, both sides in this dispute, monarchists and theocrats, restate their claims in messianic terms.

I shall describe these restatements one by one, but I should say first that the two sides in the argument are historical constructions. They don't appear in the biblical texts as distinct political parties; nor are the individual protagonists sufficiently single-minded to be identified as partisans. In many of the prophetic books monarchic and theocratic views can be found in adjacent verses or chapters. Either the prophets themselves or the editors of their books must have regarded the two as somehow compatible—and, indeed, each of them can be stated in such a way as to leave room for the other. Nonetheless, they represent significantly different political/religious tendencies, and whatever differences they suggest in the days to come, they must also have made for more concrete differences in these days, in the Bible's here and now.

The first view, from which messianism in the narrow sense—the doctrine of a personal messiah—presumably derives, looks to an ideal Davidic king who will fulfill the highest promises of the high theory of monarchy. Such a king was first hoped for when Davidic kings actually sat in Jerusalem but had not yet fulfilled the promise—and were not likely to do so. Psalm 72, which was probably written for a coronation ceremony, expresses this hope in an ideological way—that is, as if the new king will in fact be the king described by the Psalmist. It is easy to see how this sort of thing, too often repeated, might lose its immediate legitimizing power and become instead a critical vision or a fantasy of transformation. We may think of Psalm 72 as proto-messianic: it makes the appropriate promises but conveys no sense of their radicalism. The new king, it says,

> shall judge the poor . . . he shall save the children of the needy, and shall break in pieces the oppressor.

This is the promise of justice. The king will also bring material prosperity:

> He shall come down like rain upon the mown grass: as showers that water the earth.

And finally he will bring security and triumph:

> Yea, all kings shall fall down before him: all nations shall serve him.

The only messianic promise missing here is the promise of peace, and that is often missing from the literature of monarchic messianism. What are kings for, after all, if not to fight wars? And yet the most extravagant picture of a universe at peace is provided by Isaiah in a prophecy that begins:

> And there shall come forth a rod out of the stem of Jesse, and a Branch shall grow out of his roots: And the spirit of the Lord shall rest upon him. (11:1–2)

These lines describe a Davidic king—some commentators think that the prophet is celebrating the birth of a royal heir—and Isaiah goes on to describe the reign of this king as a time when

> the wolf also shall dwell with the lamb, and the leopard shall lie down with the kid . . . And the suckling child shall play on the hole of the asp . . . They shall not hurt nor destroy in all my holy mountain: for the earth shall be full of the knowledge of the Lord, as the waters cover the sea. (11:6–9)

It may be that the last verses refer to a literal transformation of the natural world; or they may be allegorically intended, meaning only—miracle enough!—that Israel, represented by the lamb, the kid, and the child, will live in peace with its neighbors. If the lines are allegorical, then they are immediately contradicted by verses 14 and 15, which promise military victories over the historical enemies of the southern kingdom. But the later verses may come from another, more conventional prophecy. In any case, Isaiah's Davidic "branch" is a true messiah, who brings a new day, radically different from all previous days. After 587, promises of a Davidic king are also promises of political restoration; were they merely restorationist, looking to the return of kings like those denounced by Jeremiah, there would be no reason to call them messianic.[2] But the promises are no more realistic than was Isaiah's "birthday" prophecy (if that's what it was).

In fact, restoration now becomes the central motif of monarchic messianism: the king will return, the people will be brought back, the division between north and south will be healed, the temple will be rebuilt, the royal covenant will be renewed, and justice, prosperity, triumph, and peace will be everlasting. In these restorationist prophecies—Ezekiel 37:21-28 is an early example—the king-messiah is not himself the agent of return; God is the only agent: "And I will make them one nation in the land upon the mountains of Israel; and one king shall be king to them all" (22).

This king is "my servant David . . . their prince for ever" (25), but all he does is rule over the restored nation. There is no suggestion that he will do anything to bring about the restoration; there is no explicit invitation to political action. I can't say how someone like Zerubbabel read such texts; they may have seemed to him to justify an attempt to seize power in Jerusalem; he may even have read them as a guarantee of success. What they say, however, is that God alone will bring deliverance. *God alone* is the norm for biblical messianism. "The messiah of the Old Testament," writes a recent Christian commentator, implicitly comparing the Old to the New, "is never seen as a savior . . . He is only the preserver and defender of a redemption already manifest."[3] I would suggest only a modest qualification: since kingship is the carrier of political awareness in the Bible, we would expect kings and would-be kings claiming the messianic title to look for some way of vindicating their claim. The parade of claimants, however, is post-biblical.

The second view of the messianic future suggests a restoration not of David's but of God's kingship—redemption without any human king at all, as either agent or first beneficiary. Israel itself, the collective people, is the first beneficiary, and then, in many expressions of this second messianism, Israel becomes the agent of a wider redemption: "a light to the Gentiles" (Isaiah 49:6). This is not the light of enlightened domination but of priestly teaching and prophetic words.

> And many people shall go and say, Come ye and let us go up to the mountain of the Lord, to the house of the God of Jacob; and he will teach us of his ways, and we will walk in his paths: for out of Zion shall go forth the law and the word of the Lord from Jerusalem. (2:3)

The two most famous images of peace in the Bible—this one, which leads to the much-quoted line "they shall beat their swords into plowshares" (2:4), and the one I cited above, "the wolf also shall dwell with the lamb" (11:6)—occur, respectively, in a passage describing God's rule and in a passage describing the rule of a Davidic king. But the idea of a universal redemption, delivered through Israel and manifest in worship of God and obedience to his law, seems to be consistently non-monarchic. It may also be anti-monarchic—that is, it may reflect opposition in priestly and prophetic circles to the hope for a royalist restoration.

The priestly utopia that I discussed in Chapter 8 is clearly anti-monarchic: at least, there is no room for a king in a kingdom of priests. When Second (or Third) Isaiah tells the Israelites that they "shall be named the Priests of the Lord . . . the Ministers of our God" (61:6), he is imagining a global or at least a multinational congregation of lay men and women, attentive and obedient (and paying tithes) but not in any political sense subordinate to Israel. Politics itself has been superseded in this version of the messianic future. The prophet Joel makes a similar argument in a passage that recalls Moses' hope for a time when he will not be the sole speaker of the divine word:

> Would that all the Lord's people were prophets, and that the Lord would put his spirit upon them. (Numbers 11:29)

Joel seems, indeed, to look beyond a mere nation of prophets:

> And it shall come to pass afterward that I will pour out my spirit upon all flesh. (2:28)

But the rest of the passage suggests that those last words have a particular rather than a universal reference: not only "your sons and your daughters shall prophesy" but also "your old men" and "your young men." The repeated pronoun is important. Prophecy is more egalitarian than priestliness, but it is limited here to Israelites. Anyone, however, can hear and heed the prophetic teaching:

> And it shall come to pass that whosoever shall call on the name of the Lord shall be delivered. (Joel 2:32)

Where the word and the name are supreme in this way, there is no need for, and perhaps, again, no room for a king.

Most examples of messianism without a king are post-exilic, even when they occur in the books of pre-exilic prophets. That, at least, is the standard view among recent commentators, and I shall not dispute it. Without doubt, the prophets did not see the world as ordinary men and women do; nonetheless, it makes sense that the king should disappear from their visions at roughly the same time as he disappears from our sight. The most striking exception to this rule may serve to confirm it. Jeremiah describes the new covenant of the "coming day" in what must have been the very last days of the southern monarchy. Having given up on the last kings—recognizing, as it were, their lastness—he looks back not to the royal but to the national covenant, and then forward not to renewal but to transformation:

> Behold the days come, saith the Lord, that I will make a new covenant with the house of Israel and with the house of Judah: not according to the covenant that I made with their fathers in the day that I took them . . . out of the land of Egypt; which my covenant they brake . . . But this shall be the covenant . . . I will put my law in their inward parts, and write it in their hearts. (31:31–33)

When the law is addressed to the ears of the people, they can listen or not, choose the blessing or the curse; but when it is inscribed on their hearts, obedience is spontaneous and certain. As with any internalized morality, God's law no longer requires external pedagogic or political agents. In Jeremiah's vision, even priests and prophets seem to be unnecessary:

> And they shall teach no more every man his neighbour, and every man his brother, saying, Know the Lord: for they shall all know me, from the least of them unto the greatest of them. (31:34)

I quoted this same verse when discussing the end of hereditary and collective responsibility, for that end comes, according to Jeremiah, in the days to come, when politics itself has been transcended. I take "teach" in 31:34 to mean authoritative (priestly or Levitical) instruction and so to stand for authority in general. The prophet's lines also recall the earlier authoritative and brutally coercive work of the Levites, after the incident of the golden calf, when they were ordered by Moses to purge the idol-worshippers (Exodus 32:27). In the messianic age of the new covenant, neither coercion nor instruction will be necessary; nor do the hierarchical agents of coercion and instruction figure in Jeremiah's vision. "They shall all know me" suggests a radical egalitarianism, the realization at last of Korah's premature version of the same thing:

> All the congregation are holy, every one of them, and the Lord is among them: wherefore then lift ye up yourselves above the congregation of the Lord? (Numbers 16:3)

In the days to come, no one will lift himself up, or everyone will.

The happy time to come does not come easily, as if it were the telos of a progressive history to be approached, like the promised land, one step at a time. The messianic age lies on the other side of a temporal chasm, called by the prophets the "day of the Lord." The idea of such a day seems to have been a feature of popular religion throughout the monarchic period, and perhaps also of official religion, always imagined, however, as a day of triumph for Israel. Presumably, there were prophetic visions and even announcements of this coming triumph, though none of them are preserved by the editors of our Bible. What is preserved instead is Amos's harsh denial of the people's expectation:

> Woe unto you that desire the day of the Lord! to what end is it
> for you? the day of the Lord is darkness and not light. (5:18)

From Amos forward, the prophetic argument is entirely consistent; the day that is coming is the day of the Lord's vengeance, wrath, and destruction. A greater part of the prophetic texts is devoted to this day than to the days that come after. "Jewish messianism," writes Gershom Scholem, "is in its origins and by its nature . . . a theory of catastrophe."[4]

The day of the Lord is a day of judgment, but it isn't *the* day of judgment as it appears in later apocalyptic literature. There it is associated with the resurrection of the dead, when individuals are judged one by one and awarded or denied a place in the world to come. All such ideas are post-biblical, belonging to a later chapter in religious history. In the Bible, God judges and punishes nations, first Israel, using the others as his rod, and then the others, either for their own sins or for what they have done to Israel. The punishments are described in great detail and often with a relish that modern readers are likely to find disturbing. There are many places in the prophetic books where the prophet seems unbalanced, out of control, lost to his own anger at "them that are at ease in Zion" (Amos 6:1)—and in Nineveh, Babylon, Tyre, and many other places. All of them are doomed, and the doom seems collective, men, women, and children consumed by God's wrath (but Nineveh is spared). The descriptions of catastrophe are so overwhelming that it isn't all that consoling to know that the day of the Lord will not, in fact, be the last day, that it somehow begins (the transition itself never explained) a new, messianic, age. It is easy to sympathize with the rabbi who said that he hoped for the coming of the messiah, but not in his lifetime.

Descriptions of the day of the Lord vary a great deal, mostly in the imagery of awfulness. I am hesitant to discover any historical development in the different versions, though such discoveries are common in the critical literature, which is mostly aimed at explaining the full-fledged apocalypticism of the post-biblical period. Many passages in the prophetic books are impossible to date with any assurance, so they can readily be arranged in whatever chronological order is necessary to reach the appropriate ending. The logical order is suggested by Scholem, who writes as though it were also the actual order. "The national antithesis between Israel and the heathens," he claims, "is broadened into a cosmic antithesis in which the realms of the holy and of sin, of purity and impurity, of life and death, of light and darkness, God and the anti-divine powers, stand opposed."[5] In the Bible itself, only the national antithesis is clearly represented, though a few passages, which may or may not be late, suggest a final transnational battle between the forces of good and the forces of evil, allegorically portrayed:

> In that day the Lord with his sore and great and strong sword
> shall punish leviathan the piercing serpent, even leviathan that
> crooked serpent. (Isaiah 27:1)

Leviathan here may represent Egypt or Assyria or some other of Israel's actual enemies, or it may anticipate the beast of later apocalypses. On this second reading, what begins as a prophetic effort to interpret political history ends with a day of the Lord that is wholly mythical.

Arguing against this reading, however, is the standard prophetic view, early and late as far as I can see, of what follows upon that terrible day. Whether Israel is ruled by a king-messiah or directly by God, whether the people are priests or prophets or still the subjects of godly instruction, it is usually made clear that Israel and the nations coexist after the day of the Lord as they do before it. Nothing in the biblical texts suggests a transcendence of national identity: there is no Jewish version of a universal church triumphant.[6] In Ezekiel 36, which promises a new covenant with Israel, and in Ezekiel 37, which promises a restored monarchy, other nations watch and learn from the spectacle of divine deliverance:

> Then the nations that are left round about you shall know that I
> the Lord build the ruined places, and plant that that was deso-
> late. (36:36)

Isaiah's vision of a world at peace under God's government rests on the same assumption that this is still, after all the judgments and the wars, a multinational world:

> And he shall judge among the nations, and shall rebuke many
> people: and they shall beat their swords into plowshares, and
> their spears into pruninghooks: nation shall not lift up sword
> against nation, neither shall they learn war anymore. (2:4)

Maybe all that is left is a remnant of each nation; in any case, more than one remnant is left. The prophetic vision of the days to come is

In God's Shadow

often genuinely universalist, but it is the knowledge and therefore the dominion of God that is universalized, not the people of Israel. Humanity remains divided, though the division is no longer deadly. Given this picture, I am inclined to argue that the days to come are not, after all, the last days, the end of history suggested by post-biblical apocalypticism. If God can still be described as judging and rebuking the nations, then something like ordinary life is still being lived, human beings are still making choices, the common life is still going well or badly. The messianic age is indeed discontinuous with what preceded it, radically new, but still humanly recognizable—which is why the prophets can both see it and talk about it in public. "From the beginning," says Isaiah's God, "I have not spoken in secret" (48:16). Apocalyptic endings, by contrast, are literally secret; knowledge of their character is esoteric, revealed in a language that is, like the language of Daniel and the Christian book of Revelation, virtually impenetrable. The end of history can be the subject only of mystical and gnostic appropriation. Isaiah's vision, utopian and sometimes fantastic though it is, still invites, and has sometimes received, rational elaboration.

What is the political import of biblical messianism? Since God is the only actor in the prophetic visions, there would seem to be nothing for human agents to do. The prophets call for repentance and covenantal faithfulness to avert the day of divine wrath. But if there is no day of wrath, the days that are said to come after it presumably won't come. If Israel does well by itself, then God won't do better for the remnant that survives his judgment—a curious argument and for that reason, I suppose, not clearly articulated. It seems to be a matter of conviction among all the prophets that Israel won't do well by itself; God's work will be necessary. So what can pious men and women do but wait? Messianism seems to point, as Scholem says, to "a life lived in deferment," in which nothing substantial or significant can be accomplished.[7] In this sense, the prophetic visions undermine every form of political ambition; they make for quietude, resignation, and passivity. And so they serve a function often assigned to religion by hostile critics: they confirm the power of the powers that be.

This account of the effects of prophecy might seem inconsistent with my earlier argument about its subversiveness. If the prophets challenged kings and priests but offered no practical alternatives, kings and priests need not have been entirely unhappy about the challenge. No doubt, they did not want to hear, or want the people to hear, what the prophets had to say. But the prophets, speaking about the days to come, were not calling for a revolutionary politics or a new regime. Prophetic messianism was really not political at all. It is more like consolation than incitement: after the condemnation of Israel-as-it-was and the horrific oracles of doom, a few words of hope. There was nothing to do, in any case.

And yet so many people, over the years, have been incited by those words of hope. Post-biblical history is marked by a long series of messianic eruptions, political movements in the strict sense, aimed at forcing God's hand and hastening the arrival of his "day." Messianism undoubtedly produces a kind of politics, even if we find no trace of this politics in the Bible itself. Perhaps the more accurate criticism of the prophetic visions is twofold: they not only made (some) people passive but encouraged (other) people to rely recklessly upon a divine promise that has never yet been fulfilled. Political activists possessed by a messianic faith are cut loose from all the normal constraints on political action. They don't have to calculate their chances, cultivate popular support, prepare for a long march, build alternative institutions. It may well be, as Scholem also says, that an incitement to act is "inherent in [the prophetic] projection of what is best in man upon his future."[8] What the prophets failed to teach, however, is that this future is radically uncertain, and that success or failure, the blessing or the curse, as the Deuteronomists sensibly argued, lies entirely in human hands.

In God's Shadow

ELEVEN

Where Were the Elders?

How authority was actually exercised in ancient Israel, how politics worked or how it was imagined to work at the local as well as the national level—figuring these things out from the biblical texts isn't easy. Who did what to whom? The prophets provide a rhetorically powerful answer—and I am sure a true answer—to this classic political question: powerful men grind the faces of the poor. But that is what (some) powerful men always do. We want to know more: Who were the powerful men? How was their power understood by the biblical writers? How was power supposed to be used or not used? Were the poor justified in resisting? Who, besides the prophets, spoke for them? These questions can't be answered from the biblical texts in the way they can be answered from Greek and Roman texts, or from medieval European texts, or from the vast modern literature. Legal and administrative records have not survived, and the literature that has survived, while it contains many narratives of political action, is rarely focused on the big political questions: What is the best regime? How should political decisions be made? What are the obligations of citizens/subjects? I have said this before, but it bears repeating: politics, secular, everyday politics, the management of our common affairs, is not recognized by the biblical writers as a centrally important or humanly fulfilling activity.

For this reason, most of the political actors in the biblical histories remain shadowy figures. We know something about Israel's kings. As in many other cultures, the king's court and his family are subjects of great interest, though this is closer to what is today called human interest than to political interest. The extended story of the struggle to succeed David is certainly a political story, but none of the biblical writers ever comment on it or try to draw theoretical or practical conclusions from it. David's lament for Absalom is the only commentary we have on the most memorable of biblical rebellions. For the rest, we know very little about the status and work of those royal officials for whose support David and his son were presumably competing, who are variously referred to as princes, rulers, chiefs, governors, and masters of the palace, and we don't know much more about the king's judges and scribes—shadows all. But the most interesting shadows are the elders.

Elders of different sorts are mentioned some 140 times in the Bible, and in only a small number of these cases is the reference nonpolitical, to old men or women generally. Mostly, the elders are a group with a role to play, whose presence is required for some purpose. They are "elders of"—elders of Israel, Judah, and Jerusalem; of the people, the land, the city, and the priests. The phrase suggests a representative office and a sphere of responsibility. Elders were present at some of the crucial events in the history of Israel: they played a leading part in the Sinai covenanting and some less defined part in the great covenant renewals described in the books of Joshua and Second Kings (but not in Nehemiah). They seem to have ruled Israel after Joshua's death—not nationally, as God's representatives (the Judges played that part), but locally, for everyday purposes. They formed the delegation that came to Samuel to demand a king, which is perhaps the key political moment in biblical history.

In God's Shadow

They covenanted with David and anointed him king over Israel. They joined the procession that carried the ark to Solomon's temple. And, according to Ezekiel, writing about the very last days of the monarchy, "seventy men [the same number as at Sinai], ancients of the house of Israel" (Ezekiel 8:11), joined in idolatrous worship in that very temple. But who exactly were these men? And what did they do, what were they supposed to do, in between their textual appearances?

In fact, we hardly know what the elders did when they appear; we are told of their presence, only rarely of their actions or opinions. Insofar as they speak (in front of Samuel, for example, or at the "trial" of Jeremiah), it is always with one voice; we never hear elders arguing with one another or even talking to one another. The very first appearance of the elders—in this case, "the elders of Israel"—is a paradigmatic example of how they are treated by the biblical writers. In Exodus 3:16–18, Moses is commanded by God to gather the elders, tell them of the coming deliverance, and go with them to confront Pharaoh. So the elders are duly gathered, but when Moses gets to the palace, they seem to have disappeared: "And afterward, Moses and Aaron went in, and told Pharaoh . . ." A rabbinic commentator asks, "Where were the elders?" and goes on to suggest that they had gone along with Moses and Aaron at first but had then "stealthily slipped away, one by one" (Exodus Rabba 5:14). Slaves still, they were afraid to challenge their master. It is a nice, and possibly insightful, story about the psychological effects of slavery. But the narrator may simply have taken the presence of the elders for granted; they are not mentioned because they have nothing to do or say. They are silent witnesses, standing in for the people as a whole.

Stand-in seems to be a part they frequently played, most clearly at the covenant renewals (though some part of "the people" were also present on those occasions). But they could not have played this part unless they also had some more substantive responsibilities. I shall not try to say what those responsibilities were; that is a task for historians of ancient Israel.[1] I only want to know what the biblical writers tell us, and don't tell us, about these officials, if that is what they were. I shall respect the reticence of the writers, but not so much as to forgo the chance to question and explain it. Assume for now that the elders were significant actors in Israel's politics; otherwise, they would not appear so frequently in the texts. Why, then, are we told so little about them? Who were the elders? Where were they?

The name "elders" implies that they were the leaders of kin groups, patriarchs (the Hebrew noun is always masculine), who regularly acted together (the noun is always plural). Individual elders may have exercised authority over their own families or clans; in all the settings noticed by the biblical writers, "the elders" form a group. They come and go together, are consulted together (when they are consulted), are witnesses together, speak, as I have already noted, with a single voice. Only rarely, however, do we get a glimpse of an assembly of elders—and these cases have mostly to do with war, when the elders (in Chronicles, they are called "chiefs of the fathers" or "heads of the children") are presented as leading the tribal muster and counseling the king about military matters. It is possible that in pre-monarchic Israel, the tribal confederation was represented by some sort of occasional assembly—thus an obscure (and disputed) passage in the Blessing of Moses:

> And [God] was king in Jeshurun, when the heads of the people
> and the tribes of Israel were gathered together. (Deuteronomy
> 33:5)

But in none of the biblical texts is there anything like an institutionalized assembly, meeting regularly, with members chosen in such and such a way. No doubt, there were meetings of elders, but not of such a kind (or not dealing with subjects of such a kind) as to attract the interest of our authors. The standard biblical reference is not to the assembly, or congregation, or council *of* elders. The preposition always comes after the noun: elders *of* . . . ; the elders are always part of some larger whole, though their relation to the whole and to its other parts is radically unclear. Attempts to place the elders within a larger constitutional structure invariably misrepresent the openness of that reiterated preposition.

Consider, for example, "the elders of the city," who are most frequently mentioned in Deuteronomy, where they are assigned certain adjudicative responsibilities having to do with both criminal and civil (family) law.[2] They act alongside judges and priests, but with their own specific tasks and not, except in our construction, as members of a legal or administrative hierarchy. Nothing is said about how "the elders of the city" are chosen from among all the elders in the city. The book of Ruth provides the only account of elders actually performing one of the tasks assigned in Deuteronomy—acting as witnesses to a refusal (or, here, an acceptance) of levirate obligations. The witnesses are chosen, seemingly at random, by Boaz, the surviving brother, who intends to meet the obligations:

> And he took ten men of the elders of the city, and said, Sit ye down here [in the gate]. And they sat down. (4:2)

Any group of ten will apparently do; this is not a regular session of city elders.

It must have been a more determinate group of "elders of Gilead" who carried on the negotiations with Jephthah in Judges 11. Unlike Boaz, he didn't pick the men he dealt with; they approached him, and the promises they made implied a representative role for themselves. Their agreement with Jephthah is subsequently ratified by a larger group:

> Then Jephthah went with the elders of Gilead, and the people made him head and captain over them. (11:11)

We can imagine here an executive committee of elders and a popular assembly of male heads of families or of male warriors ("the people"). The elders have negotiating powers; the people have the power of ratification. Baruch Halpern has argued that this is the standard constitutional pattern in ancient Israel, but there are too few examples of, and too many exceptions to, this putative pattern: the argument is plausible but radically uncertain.[3] In any case, we are given no information as to how the executive committee was chosen or who its members were. The really important question is why the biblical writers had so little interest in the "constitution."

Halpern's pattern isn't visible in what must be the critical case: the acceptance of David as king by the northern tribes:

> So all the elders of Israel came to the king to Hebron; and king David made a league with them in Hebron before the Lord: and they anointed David king over Israel. (2 Samuel 5:3)

The people aren't mentioned here. On the other hand, the elders aren't mentioned in the account of the formal appointment of Solomon as David's successor, which is the work of courtier priests and prophets together with the palace guard; the people appear at the last minute not to confirm but merely to acclaim the new king:

> And they blew the trumpet; and all the people said, God save king Solomon. (1 Kings 1:39)

Where were the elders?

Once the monarchy was established, the role of the elders at the national level seems to have been largely, if not entirely, advisory and ceremonial. But their appearances in First and Second Kings are too infrequent to say even that with certainty. The elders famously oppose the tyrannical pretensions of Solomon's son Rehoboam, advising him to lighten the burden on his subjects and providing him with a very good prudential reason for doing so: "If thou wilt be a servant unto this people this day . . . and speak good words to them, then they will be thy servants for ever" (1 Kings 12:7). But this advice is summarily rejected. The elders have little authority when they speak and no recognized right to speak: they are advisors only when kings ask for their advice.

It is useful here to compare two narratives of Ahab's wars with Aram (Syria), in First Kings 20 and 22. In chapter 20, Ben-hadad, the king of Aram, demanded a heavy tribute from Israel, and Ahab "called all the elders of the land" to advise him on how to respond.

> And all the elders and all the people said unto him, Hearken not unto him, nor consent. (20:8)

Where the people came from is unclear, since only the elders had been called. Perhaps the people were only there by virtue of representation; their opinion is included in that of the elders. Or perhaps the call was a military call-up, and the advice was given by the officers and endorsed by the soldiers. All that the author of Kings wants us to know, however, is that Ahab did not act without consulting (some of) his subjects—and, in this case, following their counsel. Having done that, he fought a successful war. Three years later, in chapter 22, Ahab was ready to fight again, this time in alliance with Jehoshaphat of Judah. At Jehoshaphat's request, the two kings sought out the prophets to "inquire" of the Lord. They got conflicting responses from Ahab's four hundred court prophets and from the solitary Micaiah, son of Imlah, and then they decided for themselves.

Where were the elders? Did elders and prophets compete for the king's attention? How did the king decide whether to seek advice from the representatives of the people (if that's what the elders were) or from the prophets of the Lord? Certainly, no constitutional requirements emerge from these two narratives. What does emerge, again, is the radical disinterest of the narrator in the constitution.

Were the elders genuine representatives (or only witnesses, as in Ruth)? Even on ceremonial occasions, it is not apparent that they stood in place of some larger group. Consider the first two verses of Second Kings 23, which begin the account of Josiah's covenant renewal:

> And the king sent, and they gathered unto him all the elders of Judah and of Jerusalem. And the king went up into the house of

the Lord, and all the men of Judah and all the inhabitants of Jerusalem with him, and the priests, and the prophets, and all the people both small and great.

Why were the elders summoned first? Josiah apparently had nothing to ask of them, nothing for them to do. And where were the elders when everyone else went up to the temple? Second Chronicles (34:29–30) gives the same account of Josiah's covenanting, except that the prophets disappear and are replaced by the Levites. What the relation of the elders was to any of these groups remains obscure. When everyone was present, whom did the elders represent? If they had no representative role, why aren't they included in the historian's list of people who "went up"?

It is a popular and attractive idea, suggested, for example, by Yehezkel Kaufmann, that the elders carry forward into the monarchic period the "primitive democracy" of Israel's early history.[4] They are a democratic constraint on the king's power, as the priests are an aristocratic constraint. If the priests are more important in palace politics (Zadok and Solomon, Jehoiada and Jehoash), the elders are more important locally. They are close to the people; they rule in the city gates; and on national occasions, they represent all those men and women who stay home in Israel's villages and small towns. The picture in Second Kings 6:32 of the elders of Dothan sitting with Elisha, the plebian folk-prophet, fits reasonably well with this theory. So does the simplicity and informality conveyed by the story of Ruth—though Boaz was a wealthy man and the easiness of his relationship with the elders might well point to something other than democracy. Indeed, the theory of a democratic eldership is fanciful.

We have no historical account of Israel's "primitive democracy." "Elders of . . ." make fairly regular appearances in all the biblical writings, beginning with the story of bondage in Egypt. Moses' effort (following the advice of Jethro) to replace them with appointed "rulers of thousands, and rulers of hundreds, rulers of fifties, and rulers of tens"

In God's Shadow

(Exodus 18:19–25) seems to have failed. Later on, the king's mercenaries had rulers of this sort, but the people as a whole are never again said to be organized in accordance with Jethro's advice. Even the Deutero-nomic restatement of Exodus 18 makes a subtle but significant conces-sion to elderly and kin-group authority. The earlier account says, "And Moses chose able men out of all Israel," implying a meritocratic selec-tion, whereas in Deuteronomy, Moses says, "So I took the chiefs of your tribes, wise men, and known" (1:15), implying the acceptance of tradi-tional authority. Why should we imagine these tribal chiefs as demo-cratic leaders? Perhaps they are called wise because they are chiefs. Per-haps they are chiefs because their families are rich and powerful. Even then, they might command the respect of ordinary Israelites. And they might well represent the interests not only of their own families but also of their clans or tribes. But this is far from a democratic regime.

That the elders hardly ever figure in prophetic denunciations of the powers that be is, perhaps, a small sign that they did play a represen-tative and popular role in the minds of the biblical writers. Kings, priests, prophets, and judges are all condemned; the elders are rarely even mentioned. It may be, again, that the prophets did not think them im-portant: they didn't share the power of the powers that be. Or, Isaiah's one attack may tell the whole story:

> The Lord will enter into judgment with the ancients of his peo-
> ple, and the princes thereof: for ye have eaten up the vineyard;
> the spoil of the poor is in your houses. (3:14)

Once again, we know so little about the elders that we can construct the real world of the Bible in any way we wish. But primitive democracy is an especially hard construction given that the texts contain nothing that remotely resembles a doctrinal defense or even a nostalgic account of popular government. Certainly, the idea that *vox populi, vox dei*—"the voice of the people is the voice of God"—is unknown to the biblical writers. In the Bible, the voice of God is the voice of God. He speaks to

Moses and the prophets and, through them, to the people. The people are consistently pictured as standing, often willfully, at a distance. In accordance with this picture, we might say that the elders most faithfully represent the people when they repudiate God's rule and ask for a king. God does indeed tell Samuel to "Hearken unto the voice of the people in all that they say unto thee" (1 Samuel 8:7), and Samuel does what he is told, though he later criticizes the people for their "wicked" request (12:17). But it would be hard to find another time when the people are similarly heeded—in truth, they have very little to say in the rest of the biblical histories and no institutional occasions to speak up. Curiously, Samuel doesn't call the elders wicked, even though they are more forcefully present here than in any of their other textual appearances. They are representatives of some sort, but they are never recognized as the political force that democracy, even primitive democracy, requires.

We might nevertheless read many of the references to Israel's elders as if they reflect a certain modest democratic idea: that, on secular matters at least, the people or their representatives should be consulted and perhaps even obeyed. (God does, after all, give the people a king against his better judgment.) But that "should" is never explicitly stated, never given doctrinal articulation; the biblical writers never seem embarrassed or dismayed when they describe political decisions made in the absence of the elders and the people alike. And these include some of the most consequential decisions of Israel's (specifically, Judah's) kings: Hezekiah's rejection of the Assyrian demand for surrender and Zedekiah's rebellion against Babylonian rule. In both cases, prophets were consulted, and elders were not. (Where were the elders?) And the two kings, though one of them follows prophetic advice and the other doesn't, stand alike under the doctrinal demand that God's prophets *should* be heeded. The advice of the elders, sometimes solicited and sometimes not, carries no such authority.

It seems likely that the elders became newly important in the years of the exile and after—revived, it may be, by the collapse of the monarchy. The elders of Judah who sit in Ezekiel's house and listen to his prophecies (8:1) recall the elders who sat with Elisha: no similar alliance is attested for any of the prophets between these two. And it is the elders again who are said to have been strengthened by the prophesying of Haggai and Zechariah and enabled to complete the second temple (Ezra 6:14). The elders are prominent in the book of Ezra, though they don't appear at all in Nehemiah, whose author refers instead to "nobles" and "rulers" (these may be the same people—elders all—or maybe not). It makes sense that the disappearance of the king's household would make the other households, and their male heads, more visible. But the government of the Israelites returning from exile is hardly democratic. The texts seem to emphasize the autocratic character of Nehemiah's rule (Morton Smith plausibly compares Nehemiah to his contemporaries, the Greek tyrants).[5] This time the elders are *there*, at least in the Ezra text, but who they were and what powers they exercised are not revealed.

The minds and hearts of the biblical writers were not engaged by the elders. The office and the officeholders were treated casually, partly, I am sure, because readers were expected to have firsthand knowledge about them. But I think that there is another reason for this neglect, which has to do with the secular and non-covenantal character of the elders. Seventy elders of Israel did participate in some sort of covenantal meal on Mount Sinai, along with Moses and Aaron: "They saw God and did eat and drink" (Exodus 24:11). But the elders don't derive their authority from the Sinai revelation; they were already present in Egypt, despite their nonappearance at the meeting with Pharaoh; they marked the houses of the Israelites with blood in Exodus 12; they broke bread with Jethro, according to Exodus 18, just before his extraordinary proposal to choose "rulers of thousands," and so on—as if the elders weren't standing right there! The eldership is the only one of Israel's offices that has no biblical founding. It is not established by covenant, like the monarchy and the priesthood; its members are not called, like the prophets; nor is there a divine command that they be appointed, as with judges. Whether or not eldership is a democratic office, it is certainly a "primitive" office, that is, an early and ancient one. Even in Deuteronomy, where elders are assigned specific tasks in the legal system, their existence is simply assumed.

Though they are present at the covenantings, their activities, when we are told what it is they do, are consistently secular. They negotiate on questions of security with judges like Gideon and Jephthah. They act as low-level judicial officers in matters of criminal and civil law. They give "counsel" on matters of policy (contrasted by Ezekiel with the "vision" of the prophets and the "law" of the priests, both of which are divine in origin [7:26]). They ask Samuel for a king so they can be like the other nations. They sometimes consult with Ahab about war and peace. They recall a crucial precedent at the "trial" of Jeremiah (but play no further part in the proceedings). None of this is unimportant, but it is reported without comment; no effort is made in any of the biblical texts to describe the work of the elders in general terms or to fix their place in the political (or legal) hierarchy.

Even more interesting than this omission is the nonappearance of the elders in the messianic visions. They have no place at all, it seems, in the days to come. "Your old men shall dream dreams," Joel says (2:28), but though he uses the Hebrew word that is commonly translated as "elders," it is clear that he is referring to all the old men and not to some set of officeholders. The sole reference to elders in the visions of the prophets occurs in Isaiah 24:23, describing a future time:

> when the Lord of hosts shall reign in mount Zion, and in Jeru-
> salem, and before his elders gloriously.

But these are God's elders, not Israel's—Isaiah is probably referring to a group that appears occasionally in other prophetic writings: "the elders of the priests." Priests certainly have a place in the messianic age, and so do prophets, though there are suggestions that both these specialized roles will be abolished: all Israel will offer sacrifices and prophesy. "Would

God that all the Lord's people were prophets!" says Moses (Numbers 11:29). Kings have a central place, at least in some of the visionary futures. Judges, too, make an occasional appearance, since justice must be done, even in the messianic age; in Isaiah 2, God is judge of the nations; in Ezekiel's visions, the priests seem to double as judges. But where are the elders? Will their specialized tasks, whatever they are, be shared among all the people? We will all grow old, but will we all be elders in the days to come?

I suspect that the elders have no place in the messianic age because they have no specifically religious meaning or function. Anciently established and familiar to the people, they could not be expunged from the historical record. The elders, moreover, may have been useful participants in (or witnesses to) the covenantings. Perhaps we are told that they were there in order to strengthen our sense that we were also there and are bound vicariously by their presence. But they have no further or future purpose, and all their secular functions were simply of no interest, beside the point. In a divine politics and a theological history, elders, without charisma or calling or divine appointment, were entirely superfluous. On any of the biblical accounts of holiness, they derived from a time before Israel became a holy nation. Whatever their actual role in Israel's politics, they were not part of the main story.

The main story could have been told differently—and, I suspect, sometimes was. First Maccabees, written only a little too late to be considered for canonization, suggests the possibility, and long passages surviving in the Bible record the secular history of Israel as it must have been understood by some group of Israelite writers. The founding of the monarchy and the story of the Davidic succession, to which I have already referred, are prime examples, and it is worth noting the prominence of the elders in these examples—confronting Samuel, counseling Absalom, and negotiating David's return to Jerusalem. Chronicles doesn't mention the demand of the elders for a king, and it reduces the succession narrative to a single line (1 Chronicles 23:1): "When David was old and full of days, he made Solomon his son king over Israel." This is sacred history without any politics at all, without rebellion, without negotiation—and without the elders.

The book of Judges brings the two possible histories, religious and secular, into sharp focus. According to the narrative frame, God "raises up" each successive judge-deliverer. Why, then, does Jephthah have to negotiate the terms of his employment with the elders of Gilead? The Gideon story is closer to our expectations about how divine deliverance should work: "The spirit of the Lord came upon Gideon, and he blew a trumpet ... And he sent messengers," and all the people gathered around him (Judges 6:34–35). Jephthah, by contrast, is called to a job interview—not with God but with the tribal elders. The Israelites had already assembled on their own and were waiting only for a military commander; the elders functioned as a search committee (10:17–18). Clearly, the Jephthah story was originally written outside the deliverance frame. It suggests the possibility of a different kind of history, in which politics as human contrivance would play a larger part—and so would actors like the elders. Israel might have had a complete rather than a fragmentary and intermittent history of this kind, except that the crucial historians or the last editors, who assembled the available materials and discarded whatever didn't suit their purposes, were theologically committed. Had a secular political history been written, or had it been fully preserved, we would probably know far more than we do about Israel's constitutional arrangements, the limits on royal authority, the rival power centers, the nature of political conflict, the relations of local and national officials. We would probably know exactly who the elders were, what they did, and where they were.

TWELVE

Politics in the Shadow

The religion of ancient Israel, as it is reflected in the biblical texts, anticipates certain features of democratic culture (the term is obviously anachronistic): equality and lay participation figure importantly in its doctrine and perhaps also in its practice. The democracy, such as it was, was a democracy under God, and God, as the Israelites conceived him, did not have the character, the style, or the demeanor of a democratic leader. Omnipotence was, after unity, his most important attribute. In the Bible, God is repeatedly described with the metaphors of monarchy; he is a king who will reign forever. But he is not described as a feudal king, connected to his subjects through complex hierarchical mediations; all Israelites are equally his subjects. Nor, though his power is absolute, does he rule absolutely; he has chosen to bind Israel to himself with a covenant and to shape the conduct of its people through laws. This choice of Israel's God presumably reflects Israelite conceptions of freedom and free will. I won't speculate as to the social origins of these conceptions; they appear full grown in the biblical texts.

Divine sovereignty and human freedom are the determining ideas of the religious culture. Together they account for its almost-democratic character and also, as we shall see, for its failure to give that democracy any political form.

Israel's almost-democracy has three features, which have to do with covenant, law, and prophecy. First of all, God's covenant requires everyone's adherence; individuals are not bound by God's will, but only by their own agreement. And "everyone" here seems to be understood literally, to include socially subordinate and politically powerless groups. The actual agreement is collective; like the elders (and unlike the prophets), the people speak with one voice, very much as they do in later "general will" theories of democracy. We may doubt, in all such cases, ancient and modern, whether the wishes of the poor and the weak are actually included in the general will. In the biblical texts, poor people, women, and even strangers, are at least ceremonially included and are recognized as moral agents, whatever the actual extent of their agency. As Delbert Hillers writes, "There is a fundamental equality of status so far as Yahweh is concerned."[1]

Second, God's law, in principle delivered to everyone and accepted by everyone, seems in fact to have been both widely known and remarkably open to interpretation and revision. To be sure, there wasn't anything like a democratic procedure for making law, no political working-out of this religious openness. In my discussion of the three legal codes, I called lawmaking in ancient Israel a "secret" activity; I meant that it was unacknowledged, interpretive rather than legislative, but not that it was esoteric or mysterious: it was off the record, not, had we been there to see it, out of sight. A relatively large number of people, given the social circumstances, must have been involved. But the kings of Israel and Judah were not involved either in making or interpreting the law. They were subject to it, just as, in principle, every Israelite and every "stranger in the gates" was subject; subjection was not qualified in any way by rank, though priests had additional rights and obligations.

Third, the prophets, who were, along with priests, judges, scribes, and elders, the interpreters of divine law, spoke in public places to ordinary men and women, who listened to and presumably understood what they were saying (we have far greater difficulty with the language of the prophetic books). Though sometimes persecuted, these religious demagogues, as Weber called them, seem to have had considerable leeway in what they could say. The prophets about whom we are given biographical information came from low as well as high social strata (we know nothing about Ahab's four hundred, but their very number and also their servility suggest lowly origins), and some of them denounced the most powerful men in Israelite society—and denounced everyone else, too. Their public and uninhibited criticism is an important signifier of religious democracy—at least in this sense: that the people to whom the prophet addressed his denunciations and warnings, though they were not yet citizens, were recognized as responsible members of the covenantal community.

Only the priesthood, restricted in its membership and authoritarian in its practices, stands outside and against Israel's almost-democracy. Priests are hierarchical figures, and not only in relation to laypeople; they tend to arrange themselves in ranks and orders and to cultivate the insignia of status. Like any aristocracy, their likely vice is arrogance. Yet even the priests, or some of them, sustained a vision of days to come, when all Israelites would share their prerogatives. Nor did they ever achieve unchallenged religious dominance in the biblical here and now; they coexisted with prophets, judges, scribes—and also with ordinary men and women, as Deuteronomy suggests: "for thou art an holy people" (7:6). By and large, except for some aspects of priestcraft, the ritual and legal requirements of Israelite religion seem to have been widely known and were probably not all that difficult to meet. Even the moral requirements that the prophets added to or substituted for the ritual law, which were much harder to meet, demanded no special knowledge: "He hath shewed thee, O man, what is good" (Micah 6:8).

But this religious culture had no clear political correlative—except, perhaps, in the time when "every man did that which was right in his own eyes" (Judges 21:25). This was a bad time in the eyes of the author or final editor of Judges. "Everyman" is not an admired figure in the Bible; of populist sentiment there is very little; nor is any regime described that incorporates the democratic features of Israel's religion: covenantal inclusiveness, legal interpretivism, and prophetic freedom. Biblical writers seem to have had little interest in designing ideal regimes. The messianic kingdom is radically underdescribed. "Nowhere," writes Nicholas Wolterstorff, do the biblical writers "attempt anything approaching principles for the social structure of the messianic age."[2] At the local level, in Israel's clans and villages, in ordinary and everyday life, the religious culture may have worked politically, spontaneously producing its own counterpart (the primitive democracy of the elders, perhaps): we just don't know. There was no counterpart, however, at the national level—except perhaps in the Deuteronomic description of a king who studies and obeys God's law, but this king makes no further appearance in the biblical texts.

The reason for this largely missing politics probably lies in the religious culture itself, in the powerful idea of divine sovereignty. In a sense, every political regime was potentially in competition with the rule of God. There can't be fully sovereign states, or a worked-out theory of popular (or any other) sovereignty, so long as God is an active sovereign. The people consent, but they do not rule. Only when God is conceived to withdraw, to stand at some distance from the world of nations, to give up his political interventions, is there room for human politics.

The high theory of monarchy is the closest the Bible comes to an account of an ideal political regime—and it is the very opposite of a democratic regime. The king imitates divine sovereignty and claims God's unconditional support, but he clearly hopes to govern on his own. Solomon's wisdom, though described as a divine gift, extends to secular understanding: statecraft as well as *torah*. The alliance with Hiram of Tyre, a Canaanite king, reflects the independence of the monarchy at its height, as do Solomon's many marriages with alien and idol-worshipping women. Saul had been punished for lesser offenses against religious law; Solomon is only admonished—not in person by a judge like Samuel or a prophet like Nathan but after the fact, in the history books. We can sense considerable self-confidence behind the mythic appropriations of the royal psalms. Power and piety are permanently united—so the court prophets and the temple singers say—in the person of the king.[3]

But in the eyes of some, perhaps many, Israelites, this very union challenged as well as imitated God's sovereignty: monarchy represented a rejection of divine rule, as God told Samuel and Samuel told the elders. And this rejection doesn't go unanswered. When God is called a king, the independence of his royal subjects is denied. When God is called a man of war, the need for royal warriors is called into question. The prophets conclude that human kings should not be guided by human counselors; they should not attempt to develop policies of their own or make political decisions. Their wisdom is ineffective or nonexistent. Nor would it be any help to consult the people or their representatives. Kings should "inquire of the Lord"—that is, consult the prophets and rely exclusively on divine protection. They need to learn that God's "is the hand that is stretched out upon all the nations." They have little else to learn.

Political prudence and mysteries of state are alike alien to the biblical worldview (the wisdom literature is only a partial exception to this general rule, for biblical wisdom focuses more on private than on public life). No doubt, kings sought secular as well as religious counsel and struggled to make a place for themselves among the nations. But the idea that any political leader could, on his own, shape the destiny of Israel is not to be found in the prophets or the histories. Israel's destiny was firmly in God's hands, as it had always been, ever since God himself overthrew the Egyptians: "the horse and his rider hath he thrown into the sea" (Exodus 15:1).

All political regimes, monarchy included, are effectively relativized by this religious argument. Whether the prophets were hostile to monarchy itself or only critical of particular kings is a question much debated by scholars, but it is a secondary question. What is more important is that all the prophets deny the independent value of monarchy, the consequentiality of kings as kings themselves must have conceived it. No other regime, however, is any more valuable, no other rulers any more consequential. When kings obey God, things go well for Israel; when they disobey, things go badly. Worldly rulers, the powers that be, whatever their social or political character, are more likely to disobey than to obey, but disobedience is a function of human recalcitrance and stiff-neckedness, not of institutional imperfection.

It appears, then, that the Bible has no political teaching, not, at least, in the sense in which it can be said to have religious and moral teachings. Disagreements about religion and morality are reflected in the text, but we can also make out a large area of agreement; some general propositions are endorsed by all the biblical writers. In politics, there is only a negative teaching; the one proposition that most of the writers would probably endorse is that the relation of rulers and ruled matters little compared to the relation of God and Israel. Insofar as political questions are engaged at all, as in the case of the monarchy, disagreement is the norm. Perhaps because the engagement is distanced and largely nondoctrinal, little effort is made (except by the king's ideologists) to conceal or resolve the differences. The Bible contains an explicit history of political change—from judges to kings to priests—even as it explicitly repudiates the idea of change in religion and morality. Its writers invite, though they do not practice, a comparative politics; they neither invite nor practice a comparative religion. Each successive political regime has its defenders; no alternative religion is ever defended or, for that matter, seriously described. Even if someone wanted to be a political (as distinct from a religious) fundamentalist, it would be difficult to fix on the fundamentals.

Seekers of a fundamentalist politics are left mostly with questions. Which of the regimes described in the histories is the authentic biblical regime—the kingship of God? the kingship of (Davidic) kings? the priestly kingdom? the mixed government of kings, judges, priests, and prophets suggested by Deuteronomy 16–18? How are the three law codes to be reconciled—and by whom? Are priests, or prophets, or judges, or scribes the authoritative interpreters of God's law? What is the role of the elders? What place does Israel occupy among the nations? Should Israel's foreign policy be governed by the principle of self-defense or the principle of territorial expansion or the principle of appeasement and accommodation—or should Israel have no foreign policy at all? Is Israel best conceived as a political nation or as a community of faith?

If we were to focus on a particular moment in biblical history, we might be able to answer some of these questions. But the answers would be circumstantial in the strict sense, for what the Bible records is a series of adjustments to changing circumstances. The establishment of the monarchy is only the most obvious case—an inventive or imitative response to practical necessities, for which Deuteronomy provided, retrospectively, divine permission. Priestly rule is similarly responsive, not to local war but to imperial conquest; it received its retrospective defense in what turned out to be non-canonical, post-biblical writings (like the Wisdom of Ben Sira). But these retrospections serve only to make clear the absence of any political a priori, any regime that is presumptively the best. Israelite religion, like every other religion, can be pressed into the service of many different regimes, but there is a sense—I suspect, a deep sense—in which it is politically indifferent.[4]

This indifference might simply leave politics free, open to prudential and pragmatic determination. Indeed, pious men and women have a biblical license to consider institutional alternatives without reference to religious doctrine. Who makes decisions and how decisions are made:

these are questions in which the biblical writers take no sustained or critical interest. The central concerns of political philosophy as the Greeks understood it—ruling and being ruled, the best regime, the meaning of citizenship, the deliberative process, civic virtue, political obligation— were never central in Israelite thought. We can maybe tease out perspectives and positions relevant to these concerns, but we can't find arguments.

Political indifference, however, does not extend to the content of the decisions that were made. Both the legal and the prophetic texts have a great deal to say about what political leaders, whoever they are, ought to do. Policy is not free. Leaving royalist ideology aside, and speaking still in the Greek mode, we can say that God, as he was conceived in ancient Israel, did not decree a politics, but he certainly did decree an ethics.

Curiously, God's ethical decrees do not appear to govern international relations. The first chapters of Amos, which suggest a universal code, a kind of international law, set no precedent for later prophecy. And the moral issues that Amos raises figure hardly at all in the historical writings. It seems that God's engagement with the nations preempts any human engagement—or, at least, any reflective human engagement. Kings were engaged, but unreflectively; and prophets were engaged, but only as the carriers of God's word. Insofar as a prophetic doctrine emerges from the texts, it is a doctrine enjoining an entirely passive reliance on God. As the prophets understand him, God's word doesn't enjoin an ethics of self-defense, or a policy of international cooperation and benevolence, or anything like a religious crusade. The Deuteronomic holy war has, so far as I can tell, no retrospective support among the literary prophets. Verses taken out of context might inspire a foreign policy of this or that (of almost any) sort. A God engaged in history is a dangerous God, for it is always possible to read his intentions and try to help him out, usually by killing his enemies. In principle, God doesn't need help—the prophets are absolutely clear about this—but in practice, more often than not, his enemies seem to have the upper hand, or he moves with such slowness that we fear never to see their final defeat. God's engagement makes for human impatience. Prophetic passivity is in tension with this impatience, but they are two sides of the same coin. The cast of mind needed to confront a world from which God is disengaged, a world where politics is ambiguous and contingent, is wholly different.

But if God rules international society, he doesn't seem to rule the inner life of Israel. Here individuals rather than nations relate to one another, and individuals are free to choose—which also means free to create a good or a bad society. Here there are policies to pursue, laws to obey, court decisions to deliver. Here there is room for ambiguity and contingency. God is at least temporarily disengaged, or he is engaged only after the fact, judging rather than determining what happens. It seems to be the biblical understanding, until Job, that God punishes bad individuals and bad societies and rewards good ones, here and now, without necessarily waiting for the day of the Lord. He allows both individuals and societies days of their own in which they can go bad or do good, and he threatens punishment before he delivers it (as in the case of Nineveh) to give them time to repent. The world is God's stage, where he displays his power and accomplishes his purposes. But domestic society belongs, for a time at least, to humankind.

The biblical texts don't always plumb the depths of this belonging, but they do sometimes manage to suggest that human beings, choosing between good and bad, blessing and curse, are likely to make mixed choices. The reality of moral life—so long as God is waiting in the wings and there is room for moral life—will be complex. And then politics, too, will be complex, for the individual relationships in which biblical writers take an interest include the fraught associations and conflicts of the powerful and the weak, the rich and the poor—and also, throughout biblical history, of monotheists and polytheists, of men and women with and without covenantal commitment.

Each of these relationships hangs on individual choice, and though the choices are mostly presented in stock terms, and the choosers as stock figures, we do sometimes find mixed judgments and complicated stories, which we are likely to think more realistic. Consider the account in Second Kings of the reign of Amaziah of Judah—which deals, as the histories commonly do, only with his religious policy:

> And he did that which was right in the sight of the Lord, yet not like David his father . . . The high places were not taken away: as yet the people did sacrifice and burn incense on the high places. (14:3–4)

Amaziah is, despite this relatively favorable judgment, an unsuccessful king; he provokes a war with the northern kingdom, loses it, watches helplessly as the army of Israel tears down the walls of Jerusalem and loots the temple, and is subsequently deposed by his own subjects. Now consider the reign of Jeroboam (the second) in the north, described in the same chapter. He "did that which was evil in the sight of the Lord," and yet he is a triumphant soldier who finds Israel oppressed by its neighbors and delivers it from oppression. His victories are at first attributed to himself (14:25) and then to God, who is said to have "saved [Israel] by the hand of Jeroboam" (14:27). I cannot make out what was in the mind of the historian who wrote the two stories; in any case, his perspective is not a simple one. These kings are operating in a world where good and bad don't come in neat packages.

Prophetic diatribe, by contrast, is a simplifying discourse. Nations, cities, and social classes are collectively condemned—as in the case of Jeremiah, who cannot find one righteous person in the whole of Jerusalem (5:1). But prophecy, too, has its complexities, most clearly, again, when it is focused on the internal life of Israel and on its political and religious leaders. I have already referred to the scholarly debate about the attitude of the prophets toward the monarchy. It seems likely to me that some of the prophets were hostile to the institution, but that is not to say that they denied the authority of the kings of their own time or ceased to demand justice and covenantal faithfulness from them. Their attitude toward the priesthood was probably similar. Those prophets who denounced the sacrifices intended to replace the people's belief in their efficacy with a new belief: that only moral conduct would make Israel the holy nation it was meant to be. And yet no prophet urged the abolition of the sacrificial system or denied the legitimacy of the priests. Similarly again, the savage denunciations of the rich did not derive from some kind of primitive communism: prophecy was never at odds with property rights. Rather, the prophets had a complex and measured view of the social obligations entailed by the idea of justice. Though they made wholesale judgments, they had, as it were, a retail program, and it is possible to imagine a society that went some way, though not all the way, toward meeting this program. About such a society we might say what the prophets themselves never said about actual Israelites:

> And they did that which was right in the sight of the Lord, yet not all that was commanded by Moses their teacher.

If anything in biblical politics is fundamental, it is this retail program, the social ethic of a covenantal community: do justice, protect the weak, feed the poor, free the (Israelite) slave, love the (resident) stranger. Mesopotamian kings claimed to be committed to a similar ethic. What seems to distinguish biblical Israel is the collective character of its commitment.[5] The covenant, if it is serious, ought to give rise to obligations shared by all Israelites and to a pervasive fellow feeling. Much of Israel's law can be read as an effort to express this feeling—literally, to enact it. That is the point of the slavery laws, the ban on usury, the laws about corners of fields and gleanings (Leviticus 19:9), the regulation of pledges (pawns) and wage payments, and the reiterated injunction to care for the stranger, the fatherless, and the widow. These injunctions are set against the background of Egyptian bondage. Israelites are commanded again and again to remember that they were slaves and strangers in Egypt. Since all of them know what it feels like to be oppressed, they ought not to oppress one another. Strangers "in thy midst" are included in the communal ethic; foreigners and foreign nations definitely are not.

Violations of the covenant have their beginning in the refusal of fellow feeling where fellow feeling is due. The prophets rarely denounce particular violations without indicating their source. Wealth and power are odious because of the complacency and moral indifference they commonly breed; the refusal of covenantal law follows from the complacency and indifference, not from wealth and power directly. It remains possible to imagine goodness in high places. Even Amos's rich Israelites, with their summer houses and winter houses and their beds of ivory, who "drink wine in bowls and anoint themselves with the chief ointments," might pass moral muster,

but they are not grieved for the affliction of Joseph. (6:6)

We are responsible for our fellows—all of us for all of us: this is the social ethic of the biblical writers. It invites a book that might sit alongside this one: a moral philosopher reads the Hebrew Bible.

The social ethic can be understood as a political program, as I have several times suggested in these chapters. We might even think of it as the biblical version of a prudential politics—for remembering Egyptian slavery and doing justice at home are, along with faith in God, all that is necessary for the preservation of Israel's existence in its land. A good domestic policy is the best foreign policy. But the social ethic of the prophets is never actually presented as a political program. Nor did it lead to constitutional proposals (beyond the minimalist account of kings, priests, prophets, and judges in Deuteronomy) or to policy deliberations. It may be that the enduring radicalism of the Hebrew Bible owes something to these absences: generations of oppressed men and women, reading the biblical texts, could freely imagine what a good society would look like and what practical measures were necessary to get there. But they also could, like some of the prophets, attack the existing order without any concrete or practical alternative in mind, the vehemence of the attack masking their actual passivity vis-à-vis the social hierarchy or the fantasy-ridden character of their politics.

The belief in God's sovereignty and in his historical engagement works to turn radical aspiration into messianism: it leaves too little room, even in domestic society, for everyday political action. The prophets know what ought to be done, but they have little faith in the capacity of men and women, unaided, to do it. The secret source of messianic politics is a deep pessimism about the self-government of the covenantal community. I can't say whether this pessimism was justified. I would guess that it had less to do with the actual state of the community than with a reluctance to think about that community in political terms—in terms, that is, of disagreement, negotiation, and compromise; of partial measures and incremental progress; of one thing after another. Israel was more often the subject of absolute judgment than of conditional assessment and counsel. Absolutism is at once the great strength and the great weakness of the prophets.

Given the biblical alternatives, the only way to avoid prophetic absolutism is to focus on the laws. A policy focus on practical reason, debate in the assembly, popular decision-making—what we might think of as the Greek alternative—was never considered. The author of the First Book of Maccabees, a post-biblical text, enviously describes Roman politics:

> Not one of them has put on a crown or worn purple as a mark of
> pride, but they have built for themselves a senate chamber, and
> every day three hundred and twenty senators constantly delib-
> erate concerning the people, to govern them well. (8:15)

I quoted part of this passage before, to make the point that no biblical writer ever said anything like it. Obedience to God's law doesn't require deliberation or arguments or votes; it only requires a moral choice. But this is also, in practice, a human choice, conditioned by human frailty, always tentative and uncertain, never completely consummated. The prophets had no time for frailty. Though they always assume the force of the legal codes, their standard demand is not for itemized obedience but for overall commitment, expressed in the idea of *hesed*, "covenantal faithfulness." They seem to think that the people as a whole or their leaders as a whole are either wholly faithful or not. (In some biblical texts, plausibly identified as late, we find descriptions of a "remnant" of the people who will be faithful in the end.) What is excluded or unmentioned by the prophets is the possibility suggested by the historian's account of King Amaziah: that some of the people and some of their leaders are faithful to some extent some of the time.

By contrast, this kind of ambiguity belongs to the very nature of the laws: they are sometimes obeyed and sometimes not. If they were never obeyed, we would hesitate to call them laws; if they were always obeyed, we might doubt their necessity. Laws are more or less effective constraints on conduct. Thinking about them leads us to hope for the best possible elaboration of a legal system, subject to the requirement of more rather than less effectiveness.

The hope of such a legal system largely determined the development of post-biblical Judaism. The scribes and sages, and later the rabbis, aimed to avoid the pathologies of ethical absolutism and political messianism. Their course undoubtedly had dangers of its own, summed up by the word "legalism," which signifies the narrow-mindedness of the law. They, too, avoided politics (or, we might say, politics avoided them: they were denied the opportunities of sovereignty), but they turned legal discussion into a kind of practical deliberation. And they took full responsibility for the outcome of their discussions. As against the prophets, who waited for the day of the Lord, they affirmed the principle on which politics necessarily rests: "it is not in heaven."

NOTES

Preface

1. Michael Walzer, *Exodus and Revolution* (New York: Basic Books, 1985).

2. See Allan Silver's commentary on the critical biblical texts in Michael Walzer, Menachem Lorberbaum, Noam J. Zohar, and Yair Lorberbaum, eds., *The Jewish Political Tradition*, vol. 1: *Authority* (New Haven: Yale University Press, 2000).

3. See Eric Nelson, *The Hebrew Commonwealth: Jewish Sources and the Transformation of European Political Thought* (Cambridge: Harvard University Press, 2010). For an ingenious construction, very much in the spirit of the seventeenth-century Hebraists that Nelson writes about, see Yoram Hazony, "Does the Bible Have a Political Teaching?" *Hebraic Political Studies* 1, no. 2 (Winter 2006): 137–161.

4. On the meaning of canonization, see Moshe Halbertal, *People of the Book: Canon, Meaning, and Authority* (Cambridge: Harvard University Press, 1997).

5. But it is fun to speculate: see Richard Elliott Friedman, *Who Wrote the Bible?* (New York: Summit Books, 1987).

6. Michael Fishbane, *Biblical Interpretation in Ancient Israel* (Oxford: Clarendon Press, 1985).

7. *Tanakh: The Holy Scriptures* (Philadelphia: Jewish Publication Society, 1985).

8. *The Five Books of Moses*, trans. Robert Alter (New York: W. W. Norton, 2004).

ONE

The Covenants

1. The familial covenant with Abraham is the model for the covenant with David and his descendants, which I will take up in Chapter 3. See Delbert R. Hillers, *Covenant: The History of a Biblical Idea* (Baltimore: Johns Hopkins University Press, 1969), chap. 5.

2. On covenantal equality, see Hillers, *Covenant*, 78–89.

3. *Tanakh: The Holy Scriptures* (Philadelphia: Jewish Publication Society, 1985), henceforth cited in the text as NJPS. The Babylonian Talmud (BT) and other post-biblical Jewish works are also cited in the text unless fuller citations, to books that include commentaries, for example, are necessary.

4. The tension is helpfully explored in Daniel J. Elazar, ed., *Kinship and Consent: The Jewish Political Tradition and Its Contemporary Uses* (Piscataway, NJ: Transaction, 1997).

5. I have written about the Sinai covenant and consent theory in *Exodus and Revolution* (New York: Basic Books, 1985), chap. 3.

6. BT Shabbat 88a: see Michael Walzer, Menachem Lorberbaum, Noam J. Zohar, and Yair Lorberbaum, eds., *The Jewish Political Tradition*, vol. 1: *Authority* (New Haven: Yale University Press, 2000), 28–29, and the commentary by Michael J. Sandel, 30–31.

7. Hillers, *Covenant*, chap. 3; George E. Mendenhall, *Law and Covenant in Israel and the Ancient Near East* (Pittsburgh: Biblical Colloquium, 1955); John Bright, *Covenant and Promise: The Prophetic Understanding of the Future in Pre-Exilic Israel* (Philadelphia: Westminster Press, 1976), chap. 1; Moshe Weinfeld, *Deuteronomy and the Deuteronomic School* (Oxford: Clarendon Press, 1972), part I, chap. 2.

8. Daniel J. Elazar constructs a full-scale biblical political doctrine on the basis of the covenantal model, but it is very much a construction, not a finding. The covenant is there, in the texts; the doctrine, it seems to me, isn't. See Elazar, *Covenant and Polity in Biblical Israel: Biblical Foundations and Jewish Expressions* (New Brunswick, NJ: Transaction, 1995).

9. Hillers, *Covenant*, 76–77.

10. Needless to say, not all biblical women consent to their marriages; the marriage contract (*ketubah*) is a post-biblical invention. But there is the model of Rebecca, who is asked, "Wilt thou go with this man? And she said, I will

go" (Genesis 24:58). When the prophets imagine God as Israel's husband, they seem also to be imagining a consenting bride. On marriage in the Bible, see Carol Meyers, *Discovering Eve: Ancient Israelite Women in Context* (New York: Oxford University Press, 1988), 182–187.

11. Joshua A. Berman, in *Created Equal: How the Bible Broke with Ancient Political Thought* (Oxford: Oxford University Press, 2008), makes a strong case for the importance of this covenantal collective. But it is an exaggeration to say that Deuteronomy's "thou" "constitutes a fraternal and egalitarian citizenry that is the foremost political body in the polity" (60). One would expect the foremost political body to act politically, but there is no sign that the Deuteronomists, or any other biblical writers, ever imagined political action of that sort.

12. BT Sotah 37a–b: see Walzer et al., *Jewish Political Tradition*, 1:34–35.

13. I made this argument years ago in *Interpretation and Social Criticism* (Cambridge: Harvard University Press, 1987), chap. 3.

14. See Jacob M. Myers, introduction to *Ezra. Nehemiah* (Anchor Bible), ed. and trans. Myers (Garden City, NY: Doubleday, 1963).

15. Albert O. Hirschman, *Exit, Voice, and Loyalty: Responses to Decline in Firms, Organizations, and States* (Cambridge: Harvard University Press, 1970).

TWO

The Legal Codes

1. Louis Ginsberg, *The Legends of the Jews*, trans. Henrietta Szold (Philadelphia: Jewish Publication Society, 1910), 3:242.

2. Michael Fishbane, *Biblical Interpretation in Ancient Israel* (Oxford: Clarendon Press, 1985).

3. Joseph Blenkinsopp, in *Wisdom and Law in the Old Testament: The Ordering of Life in Israel and Early Judaism* (Oxford: Oxford University Press, 1983), 94, argues that Deuteronomy represents the first effort to create a "canonical" text—that is, a text that becomes the sole basis of continuing commentary and interpretation.

4. Some disagreements may have been written out of the text and therefore are unknown to us. But many remain.

5. Fishbane, *Biblical Interpretation in Ancient Israel*, 272.

6. For an argument about the three codes and their probable historical settings, see Blenkinsopp, *Wisdom and Law*, chaps. 4 and 5.

7. Moshe Weinfeld, *Deuteronomy and the Deuteronomic School* (Oxford: Clarendon Press, 1972), 179–189.

8. The lack of principles of inclusion and order does not deter attempts to find or invent ordering principles that will account for the text as we have it; see, for example, Calum M. Carmichael, *The Laws of Deuteronomy* (Ithaca, NY: Cornell University Press, 1974).

9. The text reads as if the author has a comparison or a set of comparisons in mind, but it is impossible to say what other nations he is thinking of. For a modern comparison, arguing to a similar conclusion, see Léon Epsztein, *Social Justice in the Ancient Near East and the People of the Bible*, trans. John Bowden (London: SCM Press, 1986).

10. I follow here the argument of Moshe Greenberg, "Some Postulates of Biblical Criminal Law," in *Essential Papers on Israel and the Ancient Near East*, ed. Frederick Greenspahn (New York: New York University Press, 1991), 333–352.

11. See W. W. Davies, *The Codes of Hammurabi and Moses* (New York: Methodist Book Concern, 1905).

12. Martin Noth, *The Laws in the Pentateuch* (London: SCM Press, 1984), 14.

13. But the daughters' victory is later compromised. See Numbers 36 and the discussion in Fishbane, *Biblical Interpretation in Ancient Israel*, 98–99 and 104–105.

14. Jewish commentators commonly assume that the fugitive is a foreigner; see, for example, Ramban (Nachmanides), *Commentary on the Torah: Deuteronomy*, trans. C. B. Chavel (New York: Shilo, 1976), 287–288.

15. David Weiss Halivni, *Midrash, Mishnah, and Gamara: The Jewish Predilection for Justified Law* (Cambridge: Harvard University Press, 1986).

16. H. W. F. Saggs, *Civilization before Greece and Rome* (New Haven: Yale University Press, 1989), 167.

17. Geoffrey Hartman, "The Struggle for the Text," in *Midrash and Literature*, ed. Geoffrey Hartman and Sanford Budick (New Haven: Yale University Press, 1988), 13.

THREE

Conquest and Holy War

1. W. D. Davies, *The Territorial Dimension of Judaism* (Berkeley: University of California Press, 1992), 15–16. See also Dan Jacobson, *The Story of Stories: The Chosen People and Its God* (New York: Harper and Row, 1982), 37.

2. See Regina M. Schwartz, *The Curse of Cain: The Violent Legacy of Monotheism* (Chicago: University of Chicago Press, 1997), chap. 2.

3. James B. Pritchard, ed., *The Ancient Near East: An Anthology of Texts and Pictures* (Princeton: Princeton University Press, 1958), 209–210.

4. I single out this feature from among a number of features commonly ascribed to the holy war doctrine because it is of special interest to political theory—and of general interest to all those readers capable of imagining themselves among the consecrated. For a full account of the doctrine and an effort to fix its historical setting, see Gerhard von Rad, *Holy War in Ancient Israel*, trans. Marva J. Dawn (1951; repr., Grand Rapids, MI: William B. Eerdmans, 1991); and Susan Niditch, *War in the Hebrew Bible: A Study in the Ethics of Violence* (New York: Oxford University Press, 1993), chaps. 1 and 2.

5. Max Weber, *Ancient Judaism* (1921), trans. Hans H. Gerth and Don Martindale (Glencoe, IL: Free Press, 1952), 93.

6. Weber, *Ancient Judaism*, 302.

7. Michael Fishbane, *Biblical Interpretation in Ancient Israel* (Oxford: Clarendon Press, 1985), 199–200.

8. See Michael Walzer, "War and Peace in the Jewish Tradition," in *The Ethics of War and Peace: Religious and Secular Perspectives*, ed. Terry Nardin (Princeton: Princeton University Press, 1996), 95–114.

9. Fishbane, *Biblical Interpretation in Ancient Israel*, 207.

10. Oliver O'Donovan, *The Desire of the Nations: Rediscovering the Roots of Political Theology* (Cambridge: Cambridge University Press, 1996), 55.

11. Moshe Weinfeld, *Deuteronomy and the Deuteronomic School* (Oxford: Clarendon Press, 1972), 167.

12. Weber, *Ancient Judaism*, 112.

13. Weinfeld, *Deuteronomy and the Deuteronomic School*, 211–212.

14. Jean-Jacques Rousseau, *L'état de guerre and projet de paix perpetuelle*, ed. Shirley G. Patterson (New York, G. P. Putnam and Sons, 1920), 25.

15. Jean-Jacques Rousseau, "Considerations on the Government of Poland," in *Political Writings*, ed. Frederick Watkins (Edinburgh: Thomas Nelson, 1953), 176.

16. Martin Buber, *Kingship of God*, trans. Richard Scheimann (Atlantic Highlands, NJ: Humanities Press, 1990), 80.

FOUR

The Rule of Kings

1. Delbert R. Hillers, in *Covenant: The History of a Biblical Idea* (Baltimore: Johns Hopkins University Press, 1969), esp. chap. 5, stresses the similarity of patriarchs and kings, whose covenants with God are familial in character—unlike the Sinai covenant between God and the people of Israel.

2. Martin Noth, *The Laws in the Pentateuch and Other Studies*, trans. D. R. Ap-Thomas (London: SCM Press, 1984), 28–29.

3. Max Weber, *Ancient Judaism*, trans. Hans H. Gerth and Don Martindale (Glencoe, IL: Free Press, 1952), 90.

4. *Midrash Rabbah: Deuteronomy*, Shoftim 5:8, in *The Jewish Political Tradition*, vol. 1: *Authority*, ed. Michael Walzer, Menachem Lorberbaum, Noam J. Zohar, and Yair Lorberbaum (New Haven: Yale University Press, 2000), 148. See also Allan Silver's commentary on First Samuel 8, pp. 122–126.

5. Mishnah Sanhedrin, chap. 2, in Walzer et al., *Jewish Political Tradition*, 1:136–137, and see my commentary, 139–141.

6. Ramban (Nachmanides), *Commentary on the Torah: Deuteronomy*, trans. Charles B. Chavel (New York: Shilo, 1976), 210.

7. Bernard M. Levinson, *Deuteronomy and the Hermeneutics of Legal Innovation* (New York: Oxford University Press, 1997). Chapter 4 provides a full discussion of Deuteronomic judicial procedures.

8. Henri Frankfort, *Kingship and the Gods: A Study of Near Eastern Religion as the Integration of Society and Nature* (Chicago: University of Chicago Press, 1948), 341–342.

9. Frankfort, *Kingship and the Gods*, 339.

10. See Martin Buber, *Kingship of God*, trans. Richard Scheimann (Atlantic Highlands, NJ: Humanities Press, 1990).

11. Frank Moore Cross, *Canaanite Myth and Hebrew Epic: Essays in the History of the Religion of Israel* (Cambridge: Harvard University Press, 1973), 243.

12. My account follows Hillers, *Covenant*, chaps. 4 and 5.

13. This is not set as a poem in the King James Bible, but it is set here as a poem because it really is one. See Hillers's reading of this psalm, in Hillers, *Covenant*, 113–118; for a very different, christological reading, see Aubrey R. Johnson, *Sacral Kingship in Ancient Israel* (Cardiff: University of Wales Press, 1967),

25–28, 110–113; and for a general account of royal psalmody, see John H. Eaton, *Kingship and the Psalms*, 2nd ed. (Sheffield, England: JSOT Press, 1986).

14. For another view of this passage, see J. P. M. Walsh, *The Mighty from Their Thrones: Power in the Biblical Tradition* (Philadelphia: Fortress Press, 1987), 104–105. Walsh argues that Ahab was trying "to make Israel an expansionist, imperialistic nation-state, and so he incurred the judgment of Yahweh, pronounced by the prophet." This is a liberationist reading, though I hope not a characteristic one, preferring genocide to international trade.

15. The Gerondi text quoted here and below is reprinted in Walzer et al., *Jewish Political Tradition*, 1:156–161; see also the commentary by Menachem Lorberbaum, 161–165.

FIVE
Prophets and Their Audience

1. Stuart Hampshire, *Innocence and Experience* (Cambridge: Harvard University Press, 1989), 51–52.

2. I quote the translation of 1611 (revised in 1894 and 1957), in *The Apocrypha* (Revised Standard Version), ed. Bruce M. Metzger (New York: Oxford University Press, 1965), 240.

3. See the discussion of these texts in Job Y. Jindo, *Biblical Metaphor Reconsidered: A Cognitive Approach to Poetic Prophecy in Jeremiah 1 24*, Harvard Semitic Monographs 64 (Winona Lake, IN: Eisenbrauns, 2010), 75–82.

4. "The biblical prophet is a poet par excellence; his creative use of metaphor is the hallmark of his prophetic calling." Jindo, *Biblical Metaphor Reconsidered*, 266.

5. "No two prophets convey their messages in the same way" (BT Sanhedrin 89a), in Michael Walzer, Menachem Lorberbaum, Noam J. Zohar, and Yair Lorberbaum, eds., *The Jewish Political Tradition*, vol. 1: *Authority* (New Haven: Yale University Press, 2000), 224. See also the commentary by Suzanne Last Stone, 231–235.

6. Max Weber, *Ancient Judaism*, trans. Hans H. Gerth and Don Martindale (Glencoe, IL: Free Press, 1952), 278.

7. Robert P. Carroll, in *From Chaos to Covenant: Prophecy in the Book of*

Jeremiah (New York: Crossroad, 1991), 91–95, provides an account of the "trial" and attempts to explain the difficulties of the text.

8. On Jeremiah and the Josianic reformation, see Joseph Blenkinsopp, *A History of Prophecy in Israel* (London: SPCK, 1984), 161–162.

SIX
Prophecy and International Politics

1. Max Weber, *Ancient Judaism*, trans. Hans H. Gerth and Don Martindale (Glencoe, IL: Free Press, 1952), 275.

2. Weber, *Ancient Judaism*, 267.

3. Weber, *Ancient Judaism*, 274.

4. Gerhard von Rad, *The Message of the Prophets*, trans. D. M. G. Stalker (New York: Harper and Row, n.d.), 150–151.

5. Norman Gottwald, *All the Kingdoms of the Earth: Israelite Prophecy and International Relations in the Ancient Near East* (Minneapolis: Fortress, 1964), 199 ff.

6. Oliver O'Donovan, *The Desire of the Nations: Rediscovering the Roots of Political Theology* (Cambridge: Cambridge University Press, 1996), 71.

7. Joseph Blenkinsopp, *A History of Prophecy in Israel* (London: SPCK, 1984), 114; Norman Gottwald, *The Hebrew Bible: A Socio-Literary Introduction* (Philadelphia: Fortress, 1985), 379.

8. Weber, *Ancient Judaism*, 319.

9. "Return" here means repentance; the Hebrew word can also be translated as "stillness," as in NJPS.

10. Martin Buber, *The Prophetic Faith* (New York: Macmillan, 1949), 135.

11. Buber, *Prophetic Faith*, 137.

12. Gottwald, *All the Kingdoms*, 137.

13. See also Ezekiel's wholesale condemnation of alliance politics: "Thou hast committed fornication with the Egyptians . . . Thou hast played the whore also with the Assyrians . . . Thou hast moreover multiplied thy fornication . . . unto Chaldea" (16:26–29). Ezekiel's ideas about foreign policy are discussed in Andrew Mein, *Ezekiel and the Ethics of Exile* (Oxford: Oxford University Press, 2001), 84–94.

14. Moshe Halbertal and Avishai Margalit, *Idolatry*, trans. Naomi Goldblum (Cambridge: Harvard University Press, 1992), 234–235.

SEVEN
Exile

1. *Ezekiel 1–20* (Anchor Bible), trans. Moshe Greenberg (Garden City, NY: Doubleday, 1983), 343, 341. See also the interestingly ambivalent discussion of this text in Andrew Mein, *Ezekiel and the Ethics of Exile* (Oxford: Oxford University Press, 2001), esp. 187–188.

2. Greenberg, in *Ezekiel 1–20*, 342.

3. Robert Alter, *The Art of Biblical Narrative* (New York: Harper and Row, 1981), 34. For the arguments, see *Esther* (Anchor Bible), trans. Carey A. Moore (Garden City, NY: Doubleday, 1971), xxxiv–xlvi.

4. André LaCocque, in *The Feminine Unconventional: Four Subversive Figures in Israel's Tradition* (Minneapolis: Fortress Press, 1990), 77, describes the massacre at the end of the book of Esther as "wishful thinking on the part of perennial victims." But wishful thinking has consequences: see Elliott Horowitz, *Reckless Rites: Purim and the Legacy of Jewish Violence* (Princeton: Princeton University Press, 2006).

5. See Barry Dov Walfish, *Esther in Medieval Garb: Jewish Interpretation of the Book of Esther in the Middle Ages* (Albany: State University of New York Press, 1993), 122–123.

6. See, for example, *The Five Megilloth*, ed. A. Cohen (London: Soncino Press, 1952), 211–212.

7. For an argument that scribal work was very extensive, see Karl Van Der Toorn, *Scribal Culture and the Making of the Hebrew Bible* (Cambridge: Harvard University Press, 2007).

8. David Weiss Halivni discusses the role of Ezra in *Revelation Restored: Divine Writ and Critical Responses* (Boulder, CO: Westview Press, 1997).

9. Yehezkel Kaufmann, *History of the Religion of Israel*, vol. 4: *The Babylonian Captivity and Deutero-Isaiah*, trans. C. W. Efroymson (New York: Union of American Hebrew Congregations, 1970), 173.

10. Kaufmann, *History of the Religion of Israel*, 4:44–45.

11. On proselytism, see Elias Bickerman, *From Ezra to the Last of the Maccabees: Foundations of Postbiblical Judaism* (New York: Schocken, 1982), 18–20.

12. Simon Dubnow, *Nationalism and History*, ed. Koppel S. Pinson (New York: Atheneum, 1970), 262, quoted in Daniel L. Smith, *The Religion of the Landless: The Social Context of the Babylonian Exile* (Bloomington, IN: Meyer-Stone Books, 1989), 207–208.

13. I found this text (with the help of friends) in a Hebrew edition: *Kol Kitvei Y. L. Peretz*, vol. 5: *Mishal Ve'Dimyon*, book II, trans. Shimshon Meltzer (Tel Aviv: Dvir Press, 1949), 188.

14. See David Ben-Gurion, *Ben-Gurion Looks at the Bible*, trans. Jonathan Kolatch (Middle Village, NY: Jonathan David, 1972).

EIGHT

The Priestly Kingdom

1. Morton Smith, *Palestinian Parties and Politics That Shaped the Old Testament* (London: SCM Press, 1987), 128.

2. Vladimir Il'ich Lenin, *What the "Friends of the People" Are* (Moscow: Progress Publishers, 1951), 286.

3. Moshe Weinfeld, *Deuteronomy and the Deuteronomic School* (Oxford: Clarendon Press, 1972), 226–228.

4. See *Haggai, Zechariah 1–8* (Anchor Bible), trans. Carol L. Meyers and Eric M. Meyers (Garden City, NY: Doubleday, 1987), 337–373, for a review of the literature and an extraordinarily elaborate and convoluted effort to argue that the second crown is meant for a future "eschatological enthronement of a Davidic king."

5. Joachim Becker, *Messianic Expectation in the Old Testament*, trans. David E. Green (Philadelphia: Fortress Press, 1980), 62.

6. See Burton L. Mack, *Wisdom and the Hebrew Epic: Ben Sira's Hymn in Praise of the Fathers* (Chicago: University of Chicago Press, 1985), 84–87.

7. Book of Jubilees, 30:14 and 31:14; see the discussion of these passages in C. T. R. Hayward, *The Jewish Temple: A Non-Biblical Sourcebook* (London: Routledge, 1996), 85–88.

8. Weinfeld, *Deuteronomy and the Deuteronomic School*, 212–213.

9. Israel Knohl, *The Sanctuary of Silence: The Priestly Torah and the Holiness School* (Minneapolis: Fortress Press, 1995), 151. For the historical argument, see chap. 5.

10. Smith, *Palestinian Parties and Politics*, esp. chap. 7.

11. Compare Ezekiel 24:3–10 on the defiled pots of a corrupt priesthood.

12. Elias Bickerman, *From Ezra to the Last of the Maccabees: Foundations of Postbiblical Judaism* (New York: Shocken Books, 1982), 18–20.

13. Bickerman, *From Ezra*, 30.

14. Baruch A. Levine, *The JPS Torah Commentary: Leviticus* (Philadelphia: Jewish Publication Society, 1989), xxxiii; on the use of the words *kahal* and *edah*, which have "no genealogical, familial, or tribal connotation," see xxxi.

15. For Josephus's idealized description of the priestly regime, see especially *Contra Apion*, II:104–107 and 184–189.

NINE
The Politics of Wisdom

1. The gender bias of Proverbs is so evident that it hardly needs comment. Still, a feminist critique is helpful: see Dianne Bergant, *Israel's Wisdom Literature: A Liberation-Critical Reading* (Minneapolis: Fortress Press, 1997), chap. 4.

2. Stuart Weeks, *Early Israelite Wisdom* (Oxford: Oxford University Press, 1994), chap. 1 and appendix.

3. *The Apocrypha of the Old Testament* (Revised Standard Version), ed. Bruce M. Metzger (New York: Oxford University Press, 1963), 159. All my quotations from Ben Sira are from this translation.

4. But Stuart Weeks, in *Early Israelite Wisdom*, chap. 6, reviews the literature and argues against any connection between the Joseph novella and the wisdom schools.

5. Joseph Blenkinsopp, in *Wisdom and Law in the Old Testament: The Ordering of Life in Israel and Early Judaism* (New York: Oxford University Press, 1983), 38, stresses the role of providence in the story. The wisdom of Proverbs is more secular; still, Joseph seems to act out some of its precepts.

6. I made a similar comparison between Deuteronomy and Leviticus in Chapter 3. It is probably true that both the wise men and the priestly writers are more universalistic than the Deuteronomists, which is worth thinking about. But the wise men and the priests are not similar in any other respects.

7. Susan Niditch notes the existence of a "pragmatic ethic of war as statecraft" in the Bible, which doesn't, however, find much expression. See Niditch, *War in the Hebrew Bible: A Study in the Ethics of Violence* (New York: Oxford University Press, 1993), 35–37.

8. Yehezkel Kaufmann, *The Religion of Israel: From Its Beginnings to the Babylonian Exile*, trans. and abridged by Moshe Greenberg (Chicago: University of Chicago Press, 1960), 328–329.

9. Elias Bickerman, *Four Strange Books of the Bible* (New York: Schocken, 1967), 152.

10. See Robert Gordis, *Koheleth—The Man and His World* (New York: Bloch, 1955), 172–173.

11. Burton L. Mack, *Wisdom and the Hebrew Epic: Ben Sira's Hymn in Praise of the Fathers* (Chicago: University of Chicago Press, 1983), 143 ff. See also Blenkinsopp, *Wisdom and Law*, 46–52.

12. James L. Kugel and Rowan A. Greer, *Early Biblical Interpretation* (Philadelphia: Westminster Press, 1986), 48.

13. Pirke Avot 2:21, in *The Living Talmud: The Wisdom of the Fathers and Its Classical Commentaries*, ed. Judah Goldin (Chicago: University of Chicago Press, 1957), 116.

14. Martin Buber, *The Prophetic Faith* (New York: Collier Books, 1949), 189.

15. Moshe Greenberg, *Studies in the Bible and Jewish Thought* (Philadelphia: Jewish Publication Society, 1995), 340.

16. For a scholarly discussion of what those schools might have been like and an evaluation of the evidence for their existence, see James L. Crenshaw, *Education in Ancient Israel: Across the Deadening Silence* (New York: Doubleday, 1998), chap. 3.

17. See Mack, *Wisdom and the Hebrew Epic.*

18. For an account of how Ben Sira revises the argument of Proverbs and other biblical texts, see Seth Schwartz, *Were the Jews a Mediterranean Society? Reciprocity and Solidarity in Ancient Judaism* (Princeton: Princeton University Press, 2010), chap. 3. Schwartz argues that Ben Sira provides a kind of sociology of dependency, patronage, and reciprocity—something never attempted by the biblical writers.

TEN

Messianism

1. Milan Kundera, *The Unbearable Lightness of Being*, trans. Michael Henry Heim (New York: Harper Perennial, 1987), 257, 261.

2. Joachim Becker calls this "restorative monarchism" and denies that it is in any way messianic. See Becker, *Messianic Expectation in the Old Testament*, trans. David E. Green (Philadelphia: Fortress Press, 1980), chaps. 7–9.

3. Hartmut Gese, "Prophecy and Psalms in the Persian Period," in *The Cambridge History of Judaism*, vol. 1: *The Persian Period*, ed. W. D. Davies

and Louis Finkelstein (Cambridge: Cambridge University Press, 1984), 183. See also Andrew Mein, *Ezekiel and the Ethics of Exile* (Oxford: Oxford University Press, 2001), 249: "The royal figure does not act to help YHWH restore Israel to the land; his rule appears more like one of the beneficial results of YHWH's action."

4. Gershom Scholem, *The Messianic Idea in Judaism*, trans. Michael A. Meyer and Hillel Halkin (New York: Schocken Books, 1971), 7.

5. Scholem, *Messianic Idea in Judaism*, 6.

6. Joseph Klausner makes this point very clearly in *The Messianic Idea in Israel: From Its Beginning to the Completion of the Mishnah*, trans. W. F. Stinespring (New York: Macmillan, 1955), 70.

7. Scholem, *Messianic Idea in Judaism*, 35.

8. Scholem, *Messianic Idea in Judaism*, 15.

ELEVEN
Where Were the Elders?

1. Hanoch Reviv has written an excellent historian's book about the elders: *The Elders in Ancient Israel: A Study of a Biblical Institution*, trans. Lucy Plitmann (Jerusalem: Magnes Press, 1989).

2. Bernard M. Levinson argues that the authority of the elders is actually reduced by the Deuteronomists, but this is not evident to the uneducated reader. See Levinson, *Deuteronomy and the Hermeneutics of Legal Innovation* (New York: Oxford University Press, 1997), 124–127.

3. Baruch Halpern, *The Constitution of the Monarchy in Israel* (Chico, CA: Scholars Press, 1981), 198–206.

4. Yehezkel Kaufmann, *The Religion of Israel: From Its Beginnings to the Babylonian Exile*, trans. and abridged by Moshe Greenberg (Chicago: University of Chicago Press, 1960), 256, 262.

5. Morton Smith, *Palestinian Parties and Politics That Shaped the Old Testament* (London: SCM Press, 1987), 103–104.

TWELVE
Politics in the Shadow

1. Delbert R. Hillers, *Covenant: The History of a Biblical Idea* (Baltimore: Johns Hopkins University Press, 1969), 78.

2. Nicholas Wolterstorff, *Justice: Rights and Wrongs* (Princeton: Princeton University Press, 2008), 68.

3. See Frank Moore Cross, *Canaanite Myth and Hebrew Epic: Essays in the History of the Religion of Israel* (Cambridge: Harvard University Press, 1973), esp. part. 4.

4. For a radically different view, see Daniel J. Elazar, *Covenant and Polity in Biblical Israel* (New Brunswick, NJ: Transaction, 1995).

5. See Joshua A. Berman, *Created Equal: How the Bible Broke with Ancient Political Thought* (Oxford: Oxford University Press, 2008); and also, for a more cautious comparison of Israel and its neighbors, Moshe Weinfeld, *Social Justice in Ancient Israel and in the Ancient Near East* (Jerusalem: Magnes Press, 1995).

INDEX

Given the omnipresence of God in this book, it made no sense to include an entry for him in the index. Biblical books and personages (Exodus, Moses) are indexed only when they are discussed, not when they are mentioned. Except for Jerusalem, place-names are not included. Authors cited in the notes are indexed the first time their books appear in the notes for each chapter and whenever the notes include commentary.

Abraham, covenant with, 1–3, 62–63; at Sodom, 29, 112

Absalom, 51, 186

Achan, 37

Ahab, 68, 155, 191, 219*n*14; and Naboth, 23, 67, 78

Ahasuerus, 119–120

Ahaz, 101–102

Ahikam, son of Shaphan, 85

Alter, Robert, xvii, 116, 213*n*8, 221*n*3

Amaziah, 83, 208, 212

Amos, 13, 75, 135–136, 172, 180; at Beth-el, 83–84; and rules of war, 40–41, 94, 206; and social justice, 81, 107

Anarchy, 59–60

Antipolitics, xiii, 67–68, 88, 125, 183–184, 203; and foreign policy, 96–106

Assyrians, 102–105, 110; cruelty of, 90; as "rod" of God, 93, 97–98

Athaliah, 51, 76

Babylonians, 109–110; as "servant" of God, 93

Becker, Joachim, 132, 176 (quoted), 222*n*5, 224*n*2

Ben-Gurion, David, 125, 222*n*14

Ben Sira, Joshua, 132, 143, 158, 224*n*18; Wisdom of, 145–146, 165–168

Bergant, Dianne, 223*n*1

Berman, Joshua A., 215*n*11, 226*n*5

Bickerman, Elias, 141, 156, 221*n*11, 222*n*12, 224*n*9

Blenkinsopp, Joseph, 102, 215*n*3, 219*n*8, 219*n*7 (chap. 6), 223*n*5, 224*n*11

Boaz, 189

Bright, John, 214*n*7

Buber, Martin, 49, 162–163, 217*n*16, 218*n*10, 220*n*10, 224*n*14; on "theopolitics," 103–104

Canaanites, 34; extermination of, 36–38; ideology of, 62–63; survival of, 38–40

Canonization, 122

Carmichael, Calum M., 216*n*8

Caroll, Robert P., 219*n*7

Chosen people, 3–4, 15, 172–173

Chronicles, 18, 129, 131, 197

Circumcision, 1–2

Citizenship, xii, 12, 32, 108, 206

Conquest of Canaan, 34; two versions of, 36–40

Conversion, 124, 140–142

Covenant: with Aaron, 4; with Abraham, 1, 62–63; covenant lawsuit, 94, 163–164; with David, 4, 62–64; new, 171, 178–179, 182; renewal of, 9–11, 191–192; Sinai, 1–2, 4–9, 62, 112, 125; voluntary, 5–11

Crenshaw, James L., 224*n*16

Cross, Frank Moore, 61–62, 218*n*11, 226*n*3

Cyrus, 110, 120; as God's "anointed," 93, 112

Dan, tribe of, 49

David, 75, 87, 171, 186, 190; covenant with, 62–64; family of, 51–52; succession to, 190, 197; and Uriah, 67. *See also* Kings, Davidic

Davies, W. D., 216*n*1

Davies, W. W., 216*n*11

Day of the Lord, 180–182, 207

Deliberation, 73–75, 86, 88, 212

Democracy, 25, 82, 192–194; religious, 199–202

Deuteronomic writers, 19, 57–58; and holy war, 36, 41–43, 46–49

Deuteronomy, 17, 189; compared with Leviticus, 47, 223*n*6; compared with Proverbs, 153–155; as a constitutional text, xiv, 57–58, 101, 128, 205; law of kings, 4, 56, 61–65

Dubnow, Simon, 125, 221*n*12

Eaton, John H., 218*n*13

Ecclesiastes (Koheleth), 156–161

Elazar, Daniel J., 214*n*4, 214*n*8, 226*n*4

Elders, 12, 32; as advisors, 190–192; and democracy, 192–194; mentions of, 186–187; secular character of, 196–198; as witnesses, 187

Elijah, 23, 78

Epsztein, Léon, 216*n*9

Equality, 23, 126–127, 180, 200

Esther, 116, 119, 125; book of, 117–120, 221*n*4

Exile, 116–118, 124–125; Babylonian, 109, 119, 125; politics of, 118–120; responsibility for, 111–116; scribal work in, 122–123

Ezekiel, 110–111, 121, 132, 220*n*13; on individual responsibility, 114–115; and the temple-state, 122

Ezra, 9–10, 122–123, 140

Fishbane, Michael, xvi, 17–18, 41, 43, 44, 213*n*6, 215*n*2, 216*n*13, 217*n*7

Frankfort, Henri, 58–59, 218*n*8

Friedman, Richard Elliot, 213*n*5

Gerondi, Nissim, 69–71, 219*n*15

Gese, Hartmut, 224*n*3

Gibeonites, 37–38, 43–44

Gideon, 54, 66

Ginsberg, Louis, 215n1

Gordis, Robert, 224n10

Gottwald, Norman, 95, 102, 104, 220n5, 220n7

Greeks, politics and political theory among, xii, 54, 125, 195, 206

Greenberg, Moshe, 21, 115–116, 163, 216n10, 221n1, 224n15

Halbertal, Moshe, 108, 213n4, 220n14

Halpern, Baruch, 189–190, 225n3

Haman, 117–120

Hampshire, Stuart, 72–73, 79, 219n1

Hartman, Geoffrey, 33, 216n17

Hayward, C. T. R., 222n7

Hazony, Yoram, 213n3

Hegel, G. W. F., 98

Herem, 36, 37, 39, 42–46. *See also* War: holy

Hezekiah, 102–105

Hierarchy: political, 81–82, 128–130, 158; religious, 126–127, 137–138, 201; social, 13, 76, 81, 138

Hillers, Delbert, 200, 214n1, 218n1, 218nn12–13, 225n1

Hirschman, Albert, 15, 215n15

Holiness, 46–47, 126–128; Code, 136–137

Holmes, Oliver Wendell, 22

Horowitz, Elliott, 221n4

Hosea, 59, 88

Intermarriage, 3, 43–45, 140–141

Isaiah, 81, 193; antipolitics of, 101–102; on the Assyrians, 97–98; Second, 121, 124, 160; on social justice, 106–107; vision of, 177, 182

Jacobson, Dan, 216n1

Jehoash, 131

Jehoiachin, 65

Jehoshaphat, 129, 191

Jephthah, 189, 198

Jeremiah, 24, 74, 80, 86, 88, 113–114; on the Babylonian invasion, 105–106; letter to the Babylonian exiles, 119–120; new covenant of, 171, 178–179; and the political hierarchy, 81–82; on social justice, 107; trial of, 84–85

Jeroboam, 56, 130

Jerusalem, 57, 139–140

Jethro, 192–193, 195

Jezebel, 23

Jindo, Job Y., 219nn3–4

Job, 116, 153–154, 161–165

Joel, 178

Johnson, Aubrey R., 218n13

Joseph, 117–118, 147–148, 223n5

Josephus, 142–143, 223n15

Joshua, 9, 53; book of, 36–37

Joshua (high priest), 131–132

Josiah, 13; reformation of, 85, 88, 191–192

Judges, 32, 52–53, 75; book of, 39–40, 52, 60, 92–93, 169–171, 198

Justice: absolute, 69–70; pursuit of, 106; social, 21–22, 81, 106–108, 209–210

Kaufmann, Yehezkel, 123, 192, 221n9, 223n8, 225n4

Kings, Davidic, 171–176; and the law, 23–25, 69–71, 200; oppose holy war, 36, 40, 46, 67–68, 96; and priests, 129–133; and prophets, 67, 76, 204, 208–209; as secular and instrumen-

Kings, Davidic (*continued*)
tal, 58–59, 70; as sons of God,
63–64; and wisdom, 88, 150–151
Kingship: of God, 53, 59–60, 171–172,
177; high theory of, 60–65, 71, 91, 111,
174, 202; low theory of, 91; necessary
for social order, 69–71; and normal
politics, 66–68; and self-reliance,
91–92, 100
Klausner, Joseph, 225n6
Knohl, Israel, 136, 222n9
Korah, 127, 180
Kugel, James L., 224n12
Kundera, Milan, 170, 224n1

LaCocque, André, 221n4
Lamentations, 110, 113
Law/laws: arguments about, 28–33;
criminal, 21; of king, 4, 56, 64–65;
against murder, 21; of purity, 47,
136–137; reasons for, 26–29; of Sab-
bath, 24; of seduced city, 44. *See also*
War: laws of
Legal codes, 16; compared, 21–22,
30–31; in Deuteronomy, 20–21; in
Exodus, 20; in Leviticus, 20
Lenin, V. I., 128, 222n2
Levine, Baruch A., 141, 223n14
Levinson, Bernard M., 218n7, 225n2
Lorberbaum, Menachem, 219n15

Maccabees, First Book of, 73, 197, 211
Mack, Burton L., 222n6, 224n11
Malachi, 135–136
Manasseh, 64, 111–112
Margalit, Avishai, 108, 220n14
Mein, Andrew, 220n13, 221n1, 224n3
Mendenhall, George E., 114n7

Mesha of Moab, 35, 40
Messianism, 65–66, 108, 211; political
import of, 183–184: royal, 171; theo-
cratic, 171–172, 177–180
Meyers, Carol L., 214n10, 222n4
Meyers, Eric M., 222n4
Micah, 116
Micaiah, 74, 77–78
Misogyny, 145, 149
Mixed multitude, 2–3
Monarchy. *See* Kingship
Mordechai, 119–120, 125
Moses, 7–8, 137, 169, 178, 192–193; as
first prophet, 74; and Korah, 127; at
Red Sea, 101–102
Myer, Jacob M., 215n14

Nahmanides, 57, 216n14, 218n6
Nathan, 61, 78
Nehemiah, 3, 117; as tyrant, 195
Nelson, Eric, 213n3
Niditch, Susan, 217n4, 223n7
Noth, Martin, 22, 52, 216n12, 218n2

O'Donovan, Oliver, 45, 99, 217n10,
220n6

Peretz, I. L., 125, 222n13
Pharisees, 137–138
Philistines, 53
Pluralism, legal, 6, 17–19, 31–33
Politics, xii, 69–70; and agency, 11,
99–101; autonomy of, xiii, 66, 71, 97;
exilic, 118–120; normal, 67–69, 71.
See also Antipolitics; Greeks, poli-
tics and political theory among;
Wisdom: politics of
Priestcraft, 133–137

Priests, 4, 12, 32, 201, 209; in Babylonia, 122; disputes among, 138, 140–141; kingdom of, 126–129, 137; and kings, 129–131; universalism of, 139–140

Pritchard, James B., 217*n*3

Prophecy, 67, 208–209; as social criticism, 13, 86–88; test of truth of, 77–78

Prophets, 12–13, 33, 209; absolutism of, 211; antipolitics of, 99–100, 108; and kings, 67–68, 76, 204, 208–209; and public space, 80–81, 87; visions of the future, 99; and wisdom, 150. *See also* Amos; Ezekiel; Isaiah; Jeremiah; Malachi; Zechariah

Proverbs, book of, 146–152; compared with Deuteronomy, 155

Psalms, royal, 63–64

Public space, 11, 80–81, 110–111

Punishment, capital, 21, 70

Rashi, 65

Rebecca, 214*n*10

Rehoboam, 55–56, 190

Responsibility: collective, 13, 112–113; individual, 114–116; political, 12–13, 82, 210–212

Reviv, Hanoch, 225*n*1

Rousseau, Jean-Jacques, 48, 217*nn*14–15

Ruth, 3; book of, 189

Sacrifices, 128, 134–136, 209

Saggs, H. W. F., 216*n*16

Samuel, 54–56, 59, 174, 186; first book of, 54

Sandel, Michael, 114*n*6

Saul, 36, 65, 67

Scholem, Gershom, 66, 180–181, 183–184, 225*n*4

Schwartz, Regina M., 217*n*2

Schwartz, Seth, 224*n*18

Sectarianism, 10, 14–15

Silver, Allan, xiv, 213*n*2, 218*n*4

Slavery, 25–26, 30–31, 86, 113

Smith, Daniel L., 221*n*12

Smith, Morton, 195, 222*n*1, 225*n*5

Solomon, 55, 57, 87, 190; wisdom of, 146; and his wives, 58, 64, 68, 203

Stone, Susan Last, 219*n*5

Temple, the, 61, 139; as a house of prayer, 124, 140

Temple-state, 122, 132–133, 142

Tribes, confederation of, 52–53

Universalism: prophetic, 94–95, 183; priestly, 139–140; and wisdom, 154–155, 223*n*6

Uzziah, 130–131

Van Der Toorn, Karl, 221*n*7

von Rad, Gerhard, 91, 217*n*4, 220*n*4

Walfish, Barry Dov, 221*n*5

Walsh, J. P. M., 219*n*14

War, 91–92, 96; holy, 35–36, 67–68, 155, 206, 217*n*4; laws of, 40–44; secular, 155, 223*n*7

Weber, Max, 24, 39, 41, 46, 53, 217*n*5, 218*n*3, 219*n*6, 220*n*1; on the prophets, 82, 89–90, 102, 201

Weeks, Stuart, 223*n*2, 223*n*4

Weinfeld, Moshe, 46, 128, 135, 214*n*7, 216*n*7, 217*n*11, 222*n*3, 226*n*5

Weiss Halivni, David, 27, 216*n*15, 221*n*8

Wisdom: crisis of, 156–158, 161, 164; and Egypt, 145, 150; in the king's court, 147–149; nationalization of, 146, 165; and philosophy, 161–162; politics of, 146–151, 156–157, 167–168; restoration of, 166–167

Wise, the, 144–146; and the priests, 223n6; and the prophets, 150

Wolterstorff, Nicholas, 202, 226n2

Women, 13, 31, 46–47, 76; captive, 42–43; fear of, 145; slave, 31; strange (foreign), 44–45, 58, 149; wise, 144

Zadokites, 130

Zechariah, xvii, 79, 131–132, 138–139

Zedekiah, 65, 194

Zelophehad, daughters of, 23–24

Zerubbabel, 65, 131–132